COOKING HEALTHY
ACROSS AMERICA

COOKING HEALTHY ACROSS AMERICA

A Healthy Exchanges® Cookbook

JoAnna M. Lund

with Barbara Alpert

G. P. PUTNAM'S SONS

New York

Before using the recipes and advice in this book, consult your physician or health-care provider to be sure they are appropriate for you. The information in this book is not intended to take the place of any medical advice. It reflects the author's experiences, studies, research, and opinions regarding a healthy lifestyle. All material included in this publication is believed to be accurate. The publisher assumes no responsibility for any health, welfare, or subsequent damage that might be incurred from use of these materials.

G. P. Putnam's Sons
Publishers Since 1838
a member of
Penguin Putnam Inc.
375 Hudson Street
New York, NY 10014

Published simultaneously in Canada

For more information about Healthy Exchanges products, contact:

Healthy Exchanges, Inc.
P.O. Box 124
DeWitt, Iowa 52742-0124
(319) 659-8234

Diabetic Exchanges calculated by Rose Hoenig, R.D., L.D.

ISBN 0-399-14595-8

Printed in the United States of America

1   3   5   7   9   10   8   6   4   2

This book is printed on acid-free paper. ∞

BOOK DESIGN BY AMANDA DEWEY

This book is dedicated in loving memory to my parents, Jerome and Agnes McAndrews, who both enjoyed the diversity of our great nation. My mother, as a young woman, moved from her small Iowa hometown to the "big cities" of Chicago and Los Angeles in pursuit of her dream of becoming a vocalist. My father, as a young man, followed the wheat harvest all over the USA and Canada. Both returned to Iowa, met, married, and began raising a family during the Great Depression. Due to family obligations, neither ever again traveled much. But, oh, how they traveled in their minds!

They shared their love of travel and adventure with my sisters and me. Every ride in our family car included a geography quiz as our father and mother tested our skills in identifying state capitals. Of course, that was a "pre–car radio" time of life, but I'm sure even if our automobile had been equipped with one, Daddy still would have made time for our geography lessons.

I found this beautiful poem in my mother's vast collection. It speaks both of their love of our country and their faith. May you enjoy Mom's words and my recipes as you make your own travels across our great land, whether in person or in your mind.

God's Five Favorite Colors

God truly loves beauty and color, for
    He uses both everywhere,
From the deep canyons in the mountains
    to the birds soaring in the air.
Behold the brilliancy of colors in the
    sunrise, sunset and rainbow, too,
Or, gaze upon the seas and oceans
    sparkling with shades of turquoise blue.
Admire the panoramic beauty in the desert
    and all throughout the West,
Then, ponder the glitter in the moonbeams
    when the day finally comes to rest.
God painted this Garden of Eden by blending
    shades of proper tone,
For, He is the master artist and the glorious
    palette are hues of His own.
God has five favorite colors, though, and
    for these He has a special plan,
When He breathes a soul into each Race
    and in His own image creates Man.

—Agnes Carrington McAndrews

ACKNOWLEDGMENTS

■ ■ ■

No matter where you live in this great nation—be it in a small rural town or a large metropolis—nothing speaks "home" louder than good old-fashioned comfort food! For helping me share my comforting and healthy recipes with all of you, I want to thank:

Cliff Lund—my Head of Transportation; my Official Taste Tester; my Business Partner; my Husband; and my Friend. Without him, I never could or would have gone forward with my love of sharing my "common folk" healthy recipes!

Becky and John Taylor (and Spencer), James and Pam Dierickx (and Zach, Josh, and Aaron), Tom and Angie Dierickx (and Cheyanne)—my Children and Grandchildren. All have moved away from home, but we still visit as often as possible. Whenever we travel to their homes, we make sure we enjoy the flavors of their area!

Mary Benischek, Regina Reyes, Loretta Rothbart, Dale Lund, Juanita Dithmart, Marge and Cleland Lund—my Family. They each willingly lend us a helping hand whenever we need something done, be it for Healthy Exchanges or otherwise. They never judge; they just help!

Shirley Morrow and Rita Ahlers—my Right Hands. They help me get my recipes ready for publication. Shirley types, then types and types again as Rita and I test them over and over to ensure that they are "just right!"

Rose Hoenig, R.D., L.D.—my Nutritional Advisor. Even though she's busy with her private practice, she always makes time to calculate my recipes. Best of all, Rose does it in Real World Language!

Barbara Alpert—my Writing Partner. She's traveled with me long enough now in Recipe Land to know just what I mean—even when my words don't always mean what they say. Barbara keeps our working relationship fun!

Angela Miller and Coleen O'Shea—my Agents. I'm so pleased that they asked me to join them at the table so I could create and write in my "Grandma Moses" style. They took this middle-aged grandma to places I never knew I could go!

John Duff—my Editor. He continues to believe in my Mainstream America recipes—made over in *The Healthy Exchanges Way*. John makes writing my books a pure joy!

God—my Creator. When I began my own personal journey toward good health, He blessed me with the ability to create and share my "common folk" healthy recipes with others, so they, too, could start their own journeys. Through Him all things are possible!

CONTENTS

■ ■ ■

THE RECIPES

A Nation of Abundance, a Land of Diversity

Ever since I first began sharing my Healthy Exchanges recipes, I've wanted to share my passion for the recipes of people from every corner of the nation. For although I rarely left Clinton County, Iowa, until I married my truck-drivin' husband, Cliff, I traveled far and wide around this country through the many cookbooks I read. And long before I ever had the chance to try any of those regional specialties from all over the United States, I tasted them in my mind.

Cooking Healthy Across America is a celebration of my love for America, the America of church and community cookbooks, the America where our strength is in our diversity, and where there is always room for one more at the table.

I've been blessed with the opportunity over the past few years to travel all over this great nation sharing the message of Healthy Exchanges with people from all walks of life and from every ethnic group that has helped make this country a magnificent melting pot. As we've roamed the highways and byways in our motor home, I've enjoyed the privilege of visiting with old and young, women and men and children, people whose ancestors came here more than a hundred years ago, and people who are recent immigrants themselves.

So I'd like to think of this book as my gift to the country that welcomed my own ancestors, the land that has given me such a wonderful life in its very heart.

WANDERLUST, AND THE WORLD FAR FROM HOME

I was born in a little tiny town called Lost Nation, Iowa, and lived there most of my growing-up years. Oh, we did go to some family reunions in eastern Iowa, and occasionally we would bring my great-aunts up to Wisconsin—take them up in the spring and bring them back in the fall. That was a big family outing for us. But for the most part, I stayed close to home.

When I was eighteen, I was working in my first job at a bank, and eventually I became eligible for a paid week's vacation. Six months prior to it, I started planning a trip to New York City for my parents, my younger sister, and me. I organized the whole thing, planning our itinerary from beginning to end, even booking the hotels. My father raved to his dying day about how his daughter drove him all the way from Lost Nation, Iowa, to a hotel in downtown New York City—and never once got lost and never once asked for directions.

The memory of that trip had to last me a long time. After that, I didn't go anywhere for years. I was married for the first time at twenty-one and became a farm wife. We couldn't afford that kind of vacation anymore. I never went away to college (which I didn't start until I was in my thirties and working), and I wasn't even sent anywhere on business by the insurance company I worked for until after I met and married Cliff.

So instead I traveled by reading cookbooks, especially regional cookbooks. I was determined to "see the USA," even if it was only in my mind, not a Chevrolet!

ON THE ROAD WITH CLIFF—
A TRUCKER'S WIFE

The first time I ever saw the Pacific Ocean was thanks to Cliff. We had been going together for about a year when he had to fly out to California for a friend's wedding. Two days later, he called me and said that it would be more fun if I were out there with him. So he told me to go to his mom's and get one of his signed checks, then go to the airport, buy a plane ticket, and come out for the weekend.

Just like that, right? A working mom with three children, and he wants me to drop everything and fly to California. Then my parents volunteered to watch my kids. Well, Mom said yes right away, but Dad said, "No daughter of mine is going out to California with a man she's not married to!" That seemed to be the end of it, but my mom called as soon as they got home and said, "Your father and I have had a long discussion, and he's changed his mind. He said that if you've got a chance to have a nice weekend, you should take it. So you go, and we're going to watch the kids."

That was that. I flew out and stayed with some of his friends. We had a really beautiful two days. The best part was when Cliff took me to the ocean. I'd seen the Atlantic when we went to Coney Island, but it was so cold and dreary and gray. But California was like a dream—beautiful blue water as far as your eye could see. And the food out there was just wonderful—everything fresh and delicious!

After we got married, I started doing my wifely duty by taking one week's vacation every year with Cliff in his truck. (We used to go somewhere else, too, because riding in the truck was no vacation for him. He always took each of my kids with him for at least two weeks in the summer, so they got to travel and see a lot of the country at a very early age.)

Early in our marriage, we left on what was supposed to be a short trip to Oklahoma City. But when we got there, there was nothing coming back our way. The only load that was available was going to Denver, so Cliff said, "You always wanted to see the mountains, didn't you?" So that's where we went.

Our fifth night out we spent in a truck stop in Atlantic, Iowa, a night I'll never forget until the day I die. I was trying to sleep on this piece of plywood. There was no air-conditioning, no radio, and we'd been riding all day long. By the time we got to Omaha, I would have gladly taken a bus home, and Cliff would have gladly put me on it! But we kept on going. It was still 100 degrees at 10 P.M., and every single security light was glaring in the windows. To add insult to injury, a truck loaded with cattle pulled in right next to us with their air-conditioned diesel motor running. Just imagine it—the diesel smell, the cattle manure smell, no darkness, no movement of air. It was just stifling, probably the closest thing to hell on earth I'd ever endured. When we got home to DeWitt the next day, I literally kissed my front door. We decided if we could make it through that trip, then the rest of our marriage was going to be pretty easy.

(A few years later, Cliff upgraded and bought a very nice Peterbuilt tractor-trailer that had a built-in sleeper and comfortable Air-Ride seats. It was like night and day going with him after that. We still had to pay for our showers in truck stops, and I had to learn to read with the bumps as he drove down the road. My eyes had to learn to go up and down as the bumps went up and down, so I didn't lose my place on the page.)

All those hours in the truck (and later, in the van or in our motor home) helped give rise to the idea for this book. When we travel, I'm usually doing one of three things: I'm either napping, visiting with Cliff, or reading. I began picking up regional cookbooks along the route and losing myself in them, traveling the country on the page as well as on the highway. I've always been interested in learning about family fare in all the different regions we drove through. I wanted to know what the people were eating everywhere we went. And these local cookbooks are a real reflection of the food *and* the culture of their communities. Of course, I can always count on Cliff's expertise in this area, too.

"Over the years, I've always eaten pretty well on the road," he says. "Some of the meals that stick in my memory? Driving through southern Missouri, I remember eating hamburger milk gravy and great biscuits. Italian food was always good, and I found lots of great Mexican all through the Southwest and in Los Angeles. I like roast beef and barbecue, though I don't order it that much when I'm traveling because you don't know what you're going to get. Usually, I'll settle for a hamburger steak because it's reliable. I had some great tenderloin in Malcolm, Iowa, though, and also in Kearney, Missouri, near Kansas City. That was the biggest, best tenderloin I ever ate! I love good bread, too, and enjoyed some really great sourdough bread in northern California near the redwood forests."

A COOKBOOK COLLECTION
FOR THE AGES

Today my library includes thousands of volumes ranging from church and community cookbooks and regional specialties to self-published books (like my original *Healthy Exchanges Cookbook*) and commercially produced recipe collections. These books have been an inspiration, giving me great insight into the way people eat and work in every corner of the country.

SO WHY IS JOANNA LUND
"COOKING HEALTHY
ACROSS AMERICA"?

I've found that every group that came here from somewhere else brought with them their recipes for their kind of comfort food, the dishes that would forever remind them of home. Over the years, all those ways of preparing meals have been woven into the tapestry of what we call American regional cooking. It has long been my goal—and one of my dearest dreams—to collect several hundred of those recipes, give them my best Healthy Exchanges makeover, and share them with my readers everywhere.

Each of the eight regions that make up this collection has touched my heart and inspired my tastebuds in dozens of ways, and each section contains my choice of recipes I feel represents the best of that place and the people who've settled there.

I've tried to focus on what we honor about each unique region: the cozy warmth of New England, where the Pilgrims shared that first great potluck meal; the bounty of the sea that is so much a part of life along the Eastern Seaboard; the old-fashioned hospitality that is served with every meal in the South; the fiery spirit that spices suppers across the Southwest; the freshness and creativity that flavor all the dishes of the West; the magnificent abundance that greeted pioneers at the end of the Oregon Trail in the Northwest; the down-home comfort of family that inspires every menu in the Heartland; and the time-tested traditions of the foods we love best in All-American Classics.

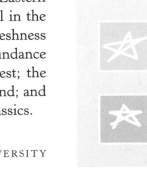

Whether you live in one of the nation's largest cities or, like me, in a lovely small town, I want you to experience the thrilling variety of foods and festivities of the entire country.

I want this collection to celebrate all that is good in America, to provide a greater appreciation of the country we live in, and to share what I've learned in my travels and research for this very special project. Along with the recipes I've included a smattering of geography and history, plus lots of fun facts and footnotes about food.

This is a true book of the heart for me, a valentine to a country I love very much. It's about pride, too—pride in who we are, where we come from, and where we're going as a nation. I hope that *Cooking Healthy Across America* delivers a very special kind of satisfaction: a world of recipes that fill the plate, fill the tummy, and fill the soul.

THE
RECIPES

HOW TO READ
A HEALTHY
EXCHANGES RECIPE

■ ■ ■

THE HEALTHY EXCHANGES
NUTRITIONAL ANALYSIS

Before using these recipes, you may wish to consult your physician or health-care provider to be sure they are appropriate for you. The information in this book is not intended to take the place of any medical advice. It reflects my experiences, studies, research, and opinions regarding healthy eating.

Each recipe includes nutritional information calculated in three ways:

Healthy Exchanges Weight Loss Choices™ or Exchanges (HE)
Calories; Fat, Protein, Carbohydrates, and Fiber in grams; Sodium and
   Calcium in milligrams
Diabetic Exchanges

In every Healthy Exchanges recipe, the diabetic exchanges have been calculated by a registered dietitian. All the other calculations were done by computer, using the Food Processor II software. When the ingredient listing gives more than one choice, the first ingredient listed is the one used in the recipe analysis. Due to inevitable variations in the ingredients you choose to use, the nutritional values should be considered approximate.

The annotation "(limited)" following Protein counts in some recipes indicates that consumption of whole eggs should be limited to four per week.

Please note the following symbols:

☆   This star means read the recipe's directions carefully for special instructions about **division** of ingredients.

❋   This symbol indicates **FREEZES WELL.**

NEW ENGLAND

. . .

The continent of North America was something of a surprise to the sailors who first sighted its Eastern shores. They thought they'd found a shortcut to the Far East and the Spice Islands. Instead, they'd discovered what the mapmakers hadn't imagined—the New World. A couple of centuries later, settlers went ashore on the craggy coast of what would be called "New" England. The rocky soil would make farming a challenge, but the waters off the coast were rich in shellfish and ocean fish. Those who made their homes in the region were subject to harsh weather and uncertain crops, but the demands of daily life in the Northeast gave birth to a special breed of men and women, survivors who would start the American Revolution when all the odds were stacked against them.

That passion for independence and a willingness to make the best of whatever they had created the "Yankee" character, and the region's recipes celebrate those hardscrabble virtues that would be echoed in the American pioneer spirit for years to come. Those hardy immigrants made it through that first difficult winter, with the help of friendly Indians who introduced them to native foods like corn, squash, and beans. (Corn was perhaps the most important of these because it could be dried and stored for months, providing a kind of insurance policy for times when other foods became scarce. Cornmeal, too, was used for many different dishes, and you'll find a sweet and delectable *Indian Pudding* in this section!)

The nearby wilderness provided meat for the pioneers' tables, and the ocean waters gave up an astonishing abundance of shellfish that the Indians taught them to steam-cook. The settlers harvested wild berries, tapped the maple trees for sap they could turn into sugar and syrup, and preserved meat through salting and drying in order to make it through the cold, hard winters. Sea captains who plied the West Indies introduced molasses into the region's recipes, while sailors returned from more distant voyages with rare spices, dried fruits, and exotic teas. (Yes, the very same teas that would one day inspire a "tea party" and ignite a rebellion!)

This is a region of recipes as nutritious as they are warming: hearty stews and thick soups, beans baked over a fire for hours and salted meat boiled until it becomes incredibly tender. It's also a part of the country where the changing of the seasons is a vital part of the life rhythm, where the climate and the length of the day influence what's on the menu.

New England is a region I've often read about but haven't gotten to see very much. I've always wanted to go to Maine, to sit in one of those wooden Adirondack chairs on a big wraparound porch overlooking the sea and drink icy cold apple cider. I'm sure I had that image in mind when I was creating and testing my recipe for a New England favorite called *Apple Betty*. Just one bite, and I feel as if I'm strolling through those beautiful Maine woods.

I was particularly inspired by the special flavors of the Cape Cod area, where millions of cranberries are harvested every year and sent in bags to stores all over America. There are other delicious berries in this region, which I've stirred into a wonderful dish called *Cape Cod Berry Grunt*. But this is cranberry country in a big way, and so I've included the best recipes I could find that shine a spotlight on this tart ruby jewel.

This section of recipes also includes some dishes that are still prepared in much the same way they were more than a hundred years ago. Well, okay, I've updated the cooking methods slightly, so you don't have to dig a hole in the ground and build a fire in order to prepare a true *New England Boiled Dinner*, and I've substituted your handy slow cooker instead of a great big black iron pot to make *"Almost" Boston Baked Beans.* And you won't have to go out and tap your own tree, then make your own maple syrup for my *Baked Maple-Glazed Carrots.*

I do think I have a lot of Yankee in me, in that I'm thrifty, hardworking, and a true believer in using up my leftovers in clever ways. That's why you'll always find a "hash" or two in my cookbooks, and two of my favorites are featured here. Even if you're not the biggest fan of beets, I hope you'll give *Red Flannel Hash* a try. It's tasty and filling, and it looks so great on the plate. I think the name is a lot of fun. When I was stirring up this recipe, I couldn't help envisioning myself as a busy New England cook frying this up for my husband— and there, in my mind's eye, I saw Cliff, dressing in bright red flannel underwear (no, not the kind with feet, but the kind with the flap in the back. . .). I admit it, I started laughing really hard, and Cliff could hear me from all the way downstairs in the basement!

NEW ENGLAND

Tomato, Chicken, and Mushroom
   Soup

New England Clam Chowder

Pilgrims' Corn Chowder

Sour Cream Slaw

New England Parsnip Slaw

Orange-Cranberry Relish

Classic Harvard Beets

Forefathers' Succotash

Nor'eastern Green Bean Casserole

Baked Maple-Glazed Carrots

Cauliflower with Mustard-Cheese
   Sauce

"Almost" Boston Baked Beans

Kedgeree

Rinktum-Ditty

Fish Cakes with Tartar Sauce

Fireside Chicken and Biscuits

Creamed Turkey over Savory
   Cornbread

Savory Meat Pie

Yankee Pot Roast

New England Boiled Dinner

Corned Beef Hash

Red Flannel Hash

Boston Brown Bread

Maple Fruit Compote

Indian Pudding

Apple Betty

Cape Cod Berry Grunt

Boston Cream Pie

Majestic Lemon Meringue Pie

Plymouth Rock Cranberry Pie

Maple Majestic Apple Pie

Sour Cream Raisin Pie

Thanksgiving Pumpkin Pie

Easy Gingerbread Cake

New England Nutmeg Sauce

Tart and Tasty Stuffing

Grape Lemonade

Tomato, Chicken, and Mushroom Soup

■ ❄ ■

I get lots of letters from readers who live in New England, and they're always asking me for more great-tasting soups to keep them warm through those chilly long winters. I hope this tomato-veggie blend is as comforting to them as my Iowa taste-testers found it. There were quite a few inches of snow on the ground out here when I first stirred it up!

Serves 6 (1½ cups)

4 cups (two 16-ounce cans) Healthy Request Chicken Broth
½ cup water
1½ cups (8 ounces) diced cooked chicken breast
¾ cup shredded carrots
½ cup (one 2.5-ounce jar) sliced mushrooms, drained

1¾ cups (one 14 ½-ounce can) stewed tomatoes, undrained
1 cup (one 8-ounce can) Hunt's Tomato Sauce
1 teaspoon Italian seasoning
1 cup (3 ounces) uncooked Minute Rice

In a large saucepan, combine chicken broth, water, chicken, and carrots. Bring mixture to a boil. Stir in mushrooms, undrained stewed tomatoes, tomato sauce, and Italian seasoning. Lower heat, cover, and simmer for 10 minutes. Add uncooked rice. Mix well to combine. Lower heat and simmer for 10 minutes, stirring occasionally.

HINT: If you don't have leftovers, purchase a chunk of cooked chicken breast from your local deli.

Each serving equals:
HE: 1⅔ Vegetable, 1⅓ Protein, ½ Bread, 5 Optional Calories

142 Calories, 2 gm Fat, 16 gm Protein, 15 gm Carbohydrate, 866 mg Sodium, 56 mg Calcium, 2 gm Fiber

DIABETIC: 1½ Vegetable, 1 Meat, 1 Starch

New England Clam Chowder

■ ❉ ■

There are few regional soups more celebrated than this one—but even confirmed Yankees don't always agree about what the classic recipe should include! Clams, of course, and milk, plus a bit of butter, onion, and traditionally, bits of salt pork, are the main ingredients, but as you travel the rocky coasts of this corner of the country, you'll taste versions that include potatoes, as I have. A chowder is a meal in itself, and this chowder delivers the flavor of New England in just one spoonful!

Serves 4 (1½ cups)

1 cup clam juice
2 cups (10 ounces) diced raw
    potatoes
1 cup finely chopped onion
2 (4.5-ounce drained weight)
    cans clams, undrained

⅛ teaspoon black pepper
1½ cups (one 12-fluid-ounce can)
    Carnation Evaporated Skim
    Milk
3 tablespoons all-purpose flour
¼ cup Hormel Bacon Bits

In a large saucepan, combine clam juice, potatoes, and onion. Bring mixture to a boil. Lower heat, cover, and simmer for 15 minutes or until potatoes are tender. Stir in undrained clams and black pepper. In a covered jar, combine evaporated skim milk and flour. Shake well to blend. Add milk mixture to clam mixture. Mix well to combine. Continue simmering until mixture thickens, stirring often. When serving, top each bowl with 1 tablespoon bacon bits.

Each serving equals:

HE: 2¼ Protein, ¾ Skim Milk, ¾ Bread, ½ Vegetable, ¼ Slider,
5 Optional Calories

230 Calories, 2 gm Fat, 13 gm Protein, 40 gm Carbohydrate, 722 mg Sodium,
308 mg Calcium, 2 gm Fiber

DIABETIC: 2 Meat, 1 Skim Milk, 1 Starch

Pilgrims' Corn Chowder

■ ❄ ■

Some say the Pilgrims would never have survived the bitter winters if not for the help of the Indians, and no one provided more urgent help than an English-speaking Indian called Squanto, who taught them to plant corn. Now a staple of the American diet, corn makes a hearty and delicious chowder that will keep anyone warm through and through!

Serves 6 (scant 1 cup)

¾ cup chopped onion
1 cup (5 ounces) diced raw potatoes
3 cups water ☆
2 cups frozen whole-kernel corn, thawed
1 cup Carnation Nonfat Dry Milk Powder

3 tablespoons Hormel Bacon Bits
7 small fat-free saltine crackers, made into crumbs
1½ teaspoons paprika

In a large saucepan sprayed with butter-flavored cooking spray, sauté onion for 5 minutes. Add potatoes and 1 cup water. Mix well to combine. Cook over medium heat for 10 minutes or until potatoes are tender. Stir in corn. In a medium bowl, combine remaining 2 cups water and dry milk powder. Add bacon bits and cracker crumbs. Mix well to combine. Stir milk mixture into corn mixture. Lower heat and simmer for 3 to 5 minutes or until mixture is heated through, stirring often. When serving, sprinkle ¼ teaspoon paprika over top of each bowl.

HINT: 1. Thaw corn by placing in a colander and rinsing under hot water for one minute.
2. A self-seal sandwich bag works great for crushing crackers.

Each serving equals:
HE: 1 Bread, ½ Skim Milk, ¼ Vegetable, 13 Optional Calories
153 Calories, 1 gm Fat, 8 gm Protein, 28 gm Carbohydrate, 229 mg Sodium, 149 mg Calcium, 2 gm Fiber
DIABETIC: 1½ Starch, ½ Skim Milk

Sour Cream Slaw

■ ■ ■

Each section of the country seems to have its own traditions when it comes to coleslaw. I found that New Englanders enjoyed a slaw with a sour-cream-based dressing, so I decided to give it a try. It's a little sweeter and creamier than what you may be used to, but the flavor is something special. *Serves 6 (½ cup)*

½ cup Land O Lakes no-fat sour cream
2 tablespoons white vinegar

Sugar substitute to equal 2 tablespoons sugar
3 cups shredded cabbage

In a large bowl, combine sour cream, vinegar, and sugar substitute. Add cabbage. Mix well to combine. Cover and refrigerate for at least 30 minutes. Gently stir again just before serving.

Each serving equals:

HE: 1 Vegetable, ¼ Slider, 2 Optional Calories

28 Calories, 0 gm Fat, 1 gm Protein, 6 gm Carbohydrate, 33 mg Sodium, 43 mg Calcium, 1 gm Fiber

DIABETIC: 1 Vegetable

New England Parsnip Slaw

■ ■ ■

It's a crunchy, tart, and tangy way to serve one of the most commonly available root vegetables, and it delivers a wallop of healthy fiber in every serving! If you've passed by the parsnips in your produce section because you weren't sure how to prepare them, take a tip from those original settlers, and shred, shred, shred!

Serves 4 (½ cup)

⅓ cup Land O Lakes no-fat sour cream

¼ cup Kraft fat-free mayonnaise

Sugar substitute to equal 2 teaspoons sugar

2 teaspoons lemon juice

⅛ teaspoon black pepper

1 tablespoon finely chopped onion

1 tablespoon chopped fresh parsley or 1 teaspoon dried parsley flakes

2 cups peeled and shredded parsnips

1 cup (2 small) cored, unpeeled, and chopped Red Delicious apples

In a medium bowl, combine sour cream, mayonnaise, sugar substitute, lemon juice, and black pepper. Stir in onion and parsley. Add parsnips and apples. Mix well to combine. Cover and refrigerate for at least 1 hour. Gently stir again just before serving.

Each serving equals:

HE: 1 Vegetable, ½ Fruit, ¼ Slider, 11 Optional Calories

88 Calories, 0 gm Fat, 2 gm Protein, 20 gm Carbohydrate, 34 mg Sodium, 54 mg Calcium, 4 gm Fiber

DIABETIC: 1 Vegetable, ½ Fruit, ½ Starch/Carbohydrate

Orange-Cranberry Relish

■ ■ ■

When we see those handy bags of cranberries appear for their short season in our supermarket produce sections, we don't always think about where they come from. Those marshy bogs where cranberries grow in gorgeous, rosy profusion along Cape Cod in Massachusetts must have a secret in their soggy depths. Otherwise, how would such tart and terrific fruit emerge from there each year without fail? The orange juice gives this relish an added sweetness that still has an edge.   *Serves 6 (⅓ cup)*

> *1 (4-serving) package JELL-O*　　*½ cup water*
> *　sugar-free cranberry gelatin*　*3 cups fresh or frozen cranberries*
> *½ cup unsweetened orange juice*

In a medium saucepan, combine dry gelatin, orange juice, and water. Stir in cranberries. Cook over medium heat for 8 to 10 minutes or until cranberries soften, stirring often. Place saucepan on a wire rack and let set for 10 to 15 minutes, stirring occasionally. Spoon mixture into a bowl and refrigerate for at least 30 minutes. Gently stir again just before serving.

Each serving equals:
HE: 2/3 Fruit, 7 Optional Calories
32 Calories, 0 gm Fat, 0 gm Protein, 8 gm Carbohydrate, 4 mg Sodium,
5 mg Calcium, 2 gm Fiber
DIABETIC: 1 Fruit

Classic Harvard Beets

■ ❄ ■

One of the oldest universities in the country, Harvard chose as its school color a rich crimson red. What better name to give this rosy-colored vegetable dish than that of the school whose education Americans believed would equal that provided by the great British universities of Cambridge and Oxford? When your dinner plate needs a fresh burst of color, beets are a terrific choice!

Serves 4 (scant ½ cup)

⅓ cup pourable Sugar Twin or
    Sprinkle Sweet
1 teaspoon cornstarch
2 cups (one 16-ounce can) diced
    beets, drained, and ¼ cup
    liquid reserved

¼ cup white vinegar
2 tablespoons reduced-calorie
    margarine

In a medium saucepan, combine Sugar Twin, cornstarch, reserved beet liquid, and vinegar. Cook over medium heat until mixture thickens and starts to boil, stirring often. Add beets. Mix well to combine. Lower heat and simmer for 10 to 12 minutes, stirring often. Just before serving, stir in margarine.

Each serving equals:
HE: 1 Vegetable, ¾ Fat, 10 Optional Calories

59 Calories, 3 gm Fat, 1 gm Protein, 7 gm Carbohydrate, 220 mg Sodium, 13 mg Calcium, 1 gm Fiber

DIABETIC: 1 Vegetable, 1 Fat

Forefathers' Succotash

■ ❋ ■

The word *succotash* is a variation on the Indian word for boiled corn. The early New Englanders added lima beans and seasonings to that "old reliable" and served this dish often. While it's especially tasty when prepared with fresh corn shaved off the cob, it's equally good when prepared with handy frozen corn and beans. *Serves 6 (scant 1 cup)*

2 tablespoons reduced-calorie
  margarine
3 cups frozen green lima beans,
  thawed
3 cups frozen whole-kernel corn,
  thawed

⅔ cup Carnation Nonfat Dry
  Milk Powder
½ cup water
1 tablespoon pourable Sugar
  Twin or Sprinkle Sweet
⅛ teaspoon black pepper

In a large saucepan, melt margarine. Stir in lima beans and corn. Cover and simmer for 6 to 8 minutes. In a small bowl, combine dry milk powder and water. Add milk mixture to vegetable mixture Mix well to combine. Stir in Sugar Twin and black pepper. Continue simmering, uncovered, for 5 to 6 minutes or until mixture is heated through.

HINT: Thaw lima beans and corn by placing in a colander and rinsing under
      hot water for one minute.

Each serving equals:
HE: 1 Bread, 1 Vegetable, ½ Fat, ⅓ Skim Milk, 1 Optional Calorie

186 Calories, 2 gm Fat, 9 gm Protein, 33 gm Carbohydrate, 221 mg Sodium, 118 mg Calcium, 6 gm Fiber

DIABETIC: 1 Starch, 1 Vegetable, ½ Fat

Nor'eastern Green Bean Casserole

■ ❄ ■

When a storm with harsh winds from the Northeast blows up in New England, the popular wisdom says you're going to get at least three days of rain and wind. Ships at sea make for the nearest harbor, knowing better than to risk their crews against such odds. A supper side dish like this one would surely warm those shivering sailors!

Serves 6

½ cup chopped onion
¼ cup (one 2-ounce jar) chopped
    pimiento, undrained
1 (10 ¾-ounce) can Healthy
    Request Tomato Soup
2 teaspoons yellow mustard

4 cups (two 16-ounce cans) cut
    green beans, rinsed and
    drained
½ cup + 1 tablespoon (2¼
    ounces) shredded Kraft
    reduced-fat Cheddar cheese

Preheat oven to 350 degrees. Spray an 8-by-8-inch baking dish with butter-flavored cooking spray. In a large skillet sprayed with butter-flavored cooking spray, sauté onion for 5 minutes. Stir in undrained pimiento, tomato soup, and mustard. Add green beans and Cheddar cheese. Mix well to combine. Spread mixture into prepared baking dish. Bake for 25 to 30 minutes or until mixture is bubbly and cheese melts. Place baking dish on a wire rack and let set for 5 minutes. Divide into 6 servings.

Each serving equals:
HE: 1½ Vegetable, ½ Protein, ¼ Slider, 10 Optional Calories
98 Calories, 2 gm Fat, 4 gm Protein, 16 gm Carbohydrate, 732 mg Sodium, 108 mg Calcium, 2 gm Fiber
DIABETIC: 1½ Vegetable, ½ Meat

Baked Maple-Glazed Carrots

■ ❄ ■

When you ask someone about New England cooking, the first thing they're apt to say is, *"Hmm, maple syrup on everything!"* Well, I might not go that far, but here's a superb way to bring a special sweetness to this hearty vegetable. While they seem most perfect to serve on a cold, snowy evening, they're good enough to stir up all the time!

Serves 6

4½ cups frozen cut carrots, thawed

¼ cup (1 ounce) chopped walnuts

½ cup Cary's Sugar Free Maple Syrup

1 tablespoon + 1 teaspoon reduced-calorie margarine

2 teaspoons dried onion flakes

1 tablespoon dried parsley flakes

Preheat oven to 350 degrees. Spray an 8-by-8-inch baking dish with butter-flavored cooking spray. Evenly arrange carrots in prepared baking dish. Stir in walnuts. In a small bowl, combine maple syrup and margarine. Stir in onion flakes and parsley flakes. Drizzle syrup mixture evenly over carrots. Cover and bake for 45 minutes. Uncover and continue baking for 10 minutes. Place baking dish on a wire rack and let set for 5 minutes. Divide into 6 servings.

HINT: Thaw carrots by placing in a colander and rinsing under hot water for one minute.

Each serving equals:

HE: 1½ Vegetable, ½ Fat, ¼ Slider, 3 Optional Calories

96 Calories, 4 gm Fat, 2 gm Protein, 13 gm Carbohydrate, 133 mg Sodium, 40 mg Calcium, 3 gm Fiber

DIABETIC: 1½ Vegetable, ½ Fat, ½ Starch/Carbohydrate

Cauliflower with Mustard-Cheese Sauce

■ ■ ■

Farm life isn't easy anywhere, but it's especially tough for those hardy souls in the Northeast, where some mornings you've got to shovel your way to the barn for milking! This kind of savory vegetable skillet is a great example of good old Yankee ingenuity—using a few basic ingredients to warm cold bodies in a hurry.

Serves 4 (⅔ cup)

3 cups boiling water
3 cups frozen cut cauliflower
¾ cup (3 ounces) shredded Kraft
   reduced-fat Cheddar cheese

¼ cup Dijon mustard
¼ cup Kraft fat-free mayonnaise
1 tablespoon dried onion flakes
1 teaspoon dried parsley flakes

In a large saucepan, cook cauliflower in water for 7 to 8 minutes or until just tender. Drain well and return to saucepan. In a medium bowl, combine Cheddar cheese, mustard, mayonnaise, onion flakes, and parsley flakes. Add cheese mixture to cauliflower. Mix well to combine. Return saucepan to stove and continue cooking for 3 to 5 minutes or until cheese melts, stirring constantly.

Each serving equals:

HE: 1½ Vegetable, 1 Protein, 10 Optional Calories

99 Calories, 3 gm Fat, 9 gm Protein, 9 gm Carbohydrate, 692 mg Sodium, 160 mg Calcium, 2 gm Fiber

DIABETIC: 1½ Vegetable, 1 Meat

"Almost" Boston Baked Beans

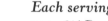

Traditional versions of this much-loved dish often call for molasses and salt pork, which are high in sugar (the first), high in salt (the second), and high in calories (both, unfortunately). But I knew there had to be a way to deliver "almost" that much sweet and tangy goodness in a baked-bean dish—and I vowed not to stop until I figured it out! Here's my solution, simmered for hours in your Crock-Pot, and sure to please. *Serves 6 (½ cup)*

32 ounces (two 16-ounce cans) navy beans, rinsed and drained
1 tablespoon white vinegar
1 cup (one 8-ounce can) Hunt's Tomato Sauce
2 tablespoons Brown Sugar Twin

2 tablespoons pourable Sugar Twin
1 tablespoon yellow mustard
1 cup finely chopped onion
1 full cup (6 ounces) finely diced Dubuque 97% fat-free ham or any extra-lean ham

In a slow cooker container, combine navy beans, vinegar, tomato sauce, Brown Sugar Twin, Sugar Twin, and mustard. Add onion and ham. Mix well to combine. Cover and cook on low heat for 8 hours. Mix well before serving.

Each serving equals:
HE: 2⅓ Protein, 1 Vegetable, 4 Optional Calories

161 Calories, 1 gm Fat, 12 gm Protein, 26 gm Carbohydrate, 946 mg Sodium, 62 mg Calcium, 6 gm Fiber

DIABETIC: 1½ Meat, 1 Starch, 1 Vegetable

Kedgeree

■ ■ ■

The sailors who shipped out from New England ports and traveled the world on great ships came home with tales of the wonders they saw—and they also brought stories of the exotic foods they'd eaten while visiting abroad. This East Indian dish was much loved by those seamen, and so their wives and mothers back home incorporated it into their menus.

Serves 6 (⅔ cup)

⅔ cup Carnation Nonfat Dry
   Milk Powder
½ cup water
2 cups hot cooked rice
2 (6-ounce) cans white tuna,
   packed in water, drained and
   flaked

2 hard-boiled eggs, chopped
2 tablespoons minced fresh
   parsley or 2 teaspoons dried
   parsley flakes
⅛ teaspoon black pepper

In a large saucepan sprayed with butter-flavored cooking spray, combine dry milk powder and water. Stir in rice. Add tuna, chopped eggs, parsley, and black pepper. Mix well to combine. Cook over medium heat for 8 to 10 minutes or until mixture is heated through, stirring occasionally.

HINT: 1. 1¼ cups uncooked instant rice usually cooks to about 2 cups.
2. If you want the look and feel of egg without the cholesterol, toss out the yolk and dice the white.

Each serving equals:
HE: 1⅓ Protein (⅓ limited), ⅔ Bread, ⅓ Skim Milk
159 Calories, 3 gm Fat, 17 gm Protein, 16 gm Carbohydrate, 242 mg Sodium, 113 mg Calcium, 0 gm Fiber
DIABETIC: 2 Meat, 1 Starch

Rinktum-Ditty

■ ■ ■

Here's a New England creation (also known as Rinktum-Tiddy) that's as cozy and comforting as the beloved cheesy supper treat Welsh rarebit back in Olde England! The origin of this traditional dish is a bit of a mystery, but I can imagine some overworked mom stirring it up to please her kids on a chilly fall night. Now, of course, it's perfect for pleasing "kids" of all ages!   *Serves 4*

½ cup finely chopped onion
2 cups (one 16-ounce can) toma-
    toes, coarsely chopped and
    undrained
2 teaspoons pourable Sugar Twin
    or Sprinkle Sweet
1 teaspoon dried parsley flakes
⅛ teaspoon black pepper
1 cup + 2 tablespoons (4½
    ounces) shredded Kraft
    reduced-fat Cheddar cheese

1 egg, beaten, or equivalent in
    egg substitute
8 slices reduced-calorie white
    bread, toasted and lightly
    sprayed with butter-flavored
    cooking spray

In a large skillet sprayed with butter-flavored cooking spray, sauté onion for 6 minutes or until tender. Add undrained tomatoes, Sugar Twin, parsley flakes, and black pepper. Mix well to combine. Stir in Cheddar cheese. Lower heat and simmer for 3 to 4 minutes or until cheese melts. Blend in egg. Continue simmering for 1 minute or until mixture is smooth, stirring constantly. For each serving, place 2 slices of toast on a plate and spoon about ½ cup tomato mixture over top.

Each serving equals:
HE: 1¾ Protein (¼ limited), 1¼ Vegetable, 1 Bread, 1 Optional Calorie
223 Calories, 7 gm Fat, 16 gm Protein, 24 gm Carbohydrate, 691 mg Sodium, 292 mg Calcium, 6 gm Fiber
DIABETIC: 1 Meat, 1 Vegetable, 1 Starch

Fish Cakes with Tartar Sauce

■ ❋ ■

The coastline of New England shaped the menus of that region with the abundant seafood providing the basis for most meals. Traditionally, fish cakes are prepared with cod, but because you may not have it handy, I've created a tasty version using canned tuna. Yes, I know there are plenty of frozen fish cakes available at your supermarket, but for flavor and texture, there's nothing like homemade!

Serves 4

½ cup Kraft fat-free mayonnaise

2 tablespoons sweet pickle relish

2 teaspoons prepared horseradish
   sauce

⅔ cup (1½ ounces) instant
   potato flakes

½ cup boiling water

2 tablespoons Land O Lakes
   no-fat sour cream

1 teaspoon Dijon mustard

2 teaspoons dried parsley
   flakes

½ teaspoon Worcestershire
   sauce

2 (6-ounce) cans white tuna,
   packed in water, drained and
   flaked

In a medium bowl, combine mayonnaise, pickle relish, and horseradish sauce. Cover and refrigerate while preparing fish cakes. In a large bowl, combine potato flakes and boiling water. Stir in sour cream, mustard, parsley flakes, and Worcestershire sauce. Add tuna. Mix well to combine. Using a ½-cup measuring cup as a guide, form mixture into 4 patties. Place patties in a large skillet sprayed with butter-flavored cooking spray. Brown the cakes for 3 to 4 minutes on each side or until golden brown. For each serving, place 1 fish cake on a plate and spoon about 2 tablespoons tartar sauce over top.

HINT: 2 cups cold cooked and flaked cod can be substituted for tuna.

Each serving equals:

HE: 1½ Protein, ½ Bread, ¼ Slider, 17 Optional Calories

158 Calories, 2 gm Fat, 18 gm Protein, 17 gm Carbohydrate, 605 mg Sodium, 33 mg Calcium, 1 gm Fiber

DIABETIC: 3 Meat, 1 Starch

Fireside Chicken and Biscuits

■ ❋ ■

When the wind blows cold and damp from the coast, nothing tastes better than a cozy meal of chicken in rich gravy over flaky biscuits! This is a wonderful company dish that isn't expensive but looks as if you fussed for hours. If you've never served your family fresh biscuits, this is the perfect way to start.

Serves 6

16 ounces skinned and boned uncooked chicken breasts, cut into 24 pieces
2 cups sliced celery
1½ cups sliced carrots
1 cup chopped onion
½ cup water
1 (10¾-ounce) can Healthy Request Cream of Chicken Soup

1 tablespoon dried parsley flakes ☆
⅛ teaspoon black pepper
1 cup + 2 tablespoons Bisquick Reduced Fat Baking Mix
¼ cup skim milk
2 tablespoons Land O Lakes no-fat sour cream

In a large saucepan, combine chicken, celery, carrots, onion, and water. Bring mixture to a boil. Lower heat, cover, and simmer for 20 to 25 minutes or until vegetables are tender. Stir in chicken soup, 2 teaspoons parsley flakes, and black pepper. Preheat oven to 425 degrees. Spray an 8-by-12-inch baking dish with butter-flavored cooking spray. Spread mixture into prepared baking dish In a medium bowl, combine baking mix, remaining 1 teaspoon parsley flakes, skim milk, and sour cream. Drop batter by tablespoonful over chicken mixture to form 6 biscuits. Bake for 12 to 15 minutes or until biscuits are golden brown. Place baking dish on a wire rack and let set for 5 minutes. Divide into 6 servings.

Each serving equals:
HE: 2 Protein, 1½ Vegetable, 1 Bread, ¼ Slider, 19 Optional Calories
236 Calories, 4 gm Fat, 20 gm Protein, 30 gm Carbohydrate, 707 mg Sodium, 82 mg Calcium, 2 gm Fiber
DIABETIC: 2 Meat, 1½ Starch, 1 Vegetable

Creamed Turkey over
Savory Cornbread

■ ❋ ■

The hardy pioneers who settled the New England region are renowned for their thrift, believing that you're supposed to "use it up" or "wear it out" before buying something new. Well, the same is true when it comes to leftovers, and here's a recipe that doesn't taste secondhand in the least! Post–Turkey Day or served the week after Christmas, you'll feel the celebration isn't over yet.   *Serves 8*

½ cup (3 ounces) yellow cornmeal
¾ cup Bisquick Reduced Fat
  Baking Mix
⅓ cup Carnation Nonfat Dry
  Milk Powder
2 tablespoons pourable Sugar
  Twin or Sprinkle Sweet
2 teaspoons dried onion flakes
2 teaspoons dried parsley flakes
1½ cups (one 12-fluid-ounce can)
  Carnation Evaporated Skim
  Milk ☆

6 tablespoons Land O Lakes
  no-fat sour cream
1¼ cups finely chopped celery
¾ cup finely chopped onion
3 cups (16 ounces) diced cooked
  turkey breast
1 (10¾-ounce) can Healthy
  Request Cream of Chicken
  Soup
¼ cup (one 2-ounce jar) chopped
  pimiento, undrained

Preheat oven to 375 degrees. Spray an 8-by-8-inch baking dish with butter flavored cooking spray. In a large bowl, combine cornmeal, baking mix, dry milk powder, Sugar Twin, onion flakes, and parsley flakes. Add ½ cup evaporated skim milk and sour cream. Mix gently to combine. Spread batter into prepared baking dish. Bake for 12 to 15 minutes or until a toothpick inserted near center comes out clean. Meanwhile, in a large skillet sprayed with butter-flavored cooking spray, sauté celery and onion for 6 to 8 minutes. Stir in turkey. Add chicken soup, undrained pimiento, and remaining 1 cup evaporated skim milk. Mix well to combine. Lower heat and simmer while cornbread continues baking, stirring occasionally. Cut cornbread into 8 pieces. For each serving, place 1 piece cornbread on a plate and spoon a full ½ cup turkey mixture over top.

HINT: If you don't have leftovers, purchase a chunk of cooked turkey breast from your local deli.

Each serving equals:

HE: 2 Protein, 1 Bread, ½ Skim Milk, ½ Vegetable, ¼ Slider, 15 Optional Calories

230 Calories, 2 gm Fat, 24 gm Protein, 29 gm Carbohydrate, 54 mg Sodium, 112 mg Calcium, 1 gm Fiber

DIABETIC: 2 Meat, 1½ Starch/Carbohydrate, ½ Skim Milk, ½ Vegetable

Savory Meat Pie

■ ❋ ■

Any cook who could create some culinary magic from a bit of dough and some leftover chunks of meat would surely be a welcome guest in those thrifty New England kitchens, where every morsel of food found its way into a soup or a stew or, in this case, a kind of Cornish pastie like they served across the sea. *Serves 6*

½ cup chopped onion
2 full cups (12 ounces) diced
  cooked lean roast beef
1 cup (one 8-ounce can) sliced
  carrots, rinsed and drained
½ cup frozen peas, thawed
⅓ cup (2 ounces) diced cooked
  potatoes

1 (12-ounce) jar Heinz Fat Free
  Beef Gravy
1 teaspoon dried parsley flakes
⅛ teaspoon black pepper
1 (7.5-ounce) can Pillsbury
  refrigerated biscuits

Preheat oven to 425 degrees. Spray an 8-by-8-inch baking dish with butter-flavored cooking spray. In a large skillet sprayed with butter-flavored cooking spray, sauté onion for 5 minutes. Stir in roast beef, carrots, peas, and potatoes. Add gravy, parsley flakes, and black pepper. Mix well to combine. Bring mixture to a boil, stirring occasionally. Spoon mixture into prepared baking dish. Separate biscuits and cut each into 3 pieces. Evenly sprinkle biscuit pieces over hot meat mixture. Lightly spray biscuit tops with butter-flavored cooking spray. Bake for 15 to 20 minutes. Place baking dish on a wire rack and let set for 5 minutes. Divide into 6 servings.

HINT: 1. If you don't have leftovers, purchase a chunk of lean cooked roast beef from your local deli or use Healthy Choice Deli slices.
2. Thaw peas by placing in a colander and rinsing under hot water for one minute

Each serving equals:
HE: 2 Protein, 1½ Bread, ½ Vegetable, ¼ Slider, 5 Optional Calories
237 Calories, 5 gm Fat, 22 gm Protein, 26 gm Carbohydrate, 735 mg Sodium, 16 mg Calcium, 3 gm Fiber
DIABETIC: 2 Meat, 1½ Starch, ½ Vegetable

Yankee Pot Roast

■ ■ ■

To survive the tough winters and the wet springs of the Northeast required sturdy, filling meals, especially hearty meat dishes that could survive a few extra minutes on the stove. This is a terrific entree for a special Sunday dinner, when the family is gathered round your table for a leisurely meal.   *Serves 6*

3 tablespoons all-purpose flour
1½ pounds lean round steak
⅛ teaspoon black pepper
1 cup water ☆
3 cups (15 ounces) coarsely chopped unpeeled raw potatoes

3 cups coarsely chopped carrots
1 cup coarsely chopped onion
½ cup peeled and coarsely chopped turnips
1 (12-ounce) jar Heinz Fat Free Beef Gravy

Place flour on a plate and coat both sides of steak with flour. In a very large skillet sprayed with butter-flavored cooking spray, brown meat for 3 to 4 minutes on each side. Stir any remaining flour and black pepper into ½ cup water. Pour water mixture evenly over meat. Lower heat, cover, and simmer for 30 minutes. Add potatoes, carrots, onion, and turnips. Mix well to combine. Pour remaining ½ cup water over top. Re-cover and continue simmering for 45 minutes or until vegetables are tender. Remove meat and vegetables to a plate to keep hot. Stir gravy into same skillet. Increase heat and bring gravy to a boil, stirring constantly. Cut meat into 6 pieces. For each serving, place 1 piece meat on a plate, arrange about 1 cup vegetable mixture next to meat, and spoon about ¼ cup gravy over top.

Each serving equals:
HE: 3 Protein, 1½ Vegetable, ⅔ Bread, ¼ Slider, 5 Optional Calories

334 Calories, 6 gm Fat, 40 gm Protein, 30 gm Carbohydrate, 463 mg Sodium, 45 mg Calcium, 4 gm Fiber

DIABETIC: 3 Meat, 1½ Starch, 1½ Vegetable

New England Boiled Dinner

■ ❋ ■

The origin of this traditional dish isn't hard to imagine. With all the chores needed to keep a household running smoothly, it was a perfect solution to a busy cook's dilemma to simply chop up vegetables—carrots, potatoes, parsnips, and cabbage— add some cured meat, light a fire under her big iron pot, and come back hours later to a satisfying stewed meal. In coastal towns, salt cod was often used, but elsewhere corned beef provided the protein.

Serves 4 (full 1½ cups)

1½ cups diced carrots

3 cups (15 ounces) diced raw potatoes

¾ cup chopped onion

¾ cup chopped parsnips (optional)

2 cups water

4 (2.5-ounce) packages Carl Buddig 90% lean corned beef, shredded

2 teaspoons dried parsley flakes

3 cups coarsely chopped cabbage

In a large saucepan, combine carrots, potatoes, onion, parsnips, and water. Bring mixture to a boil. Stir in corned beef and parsley flakes. Lower heat, cover, and simmer for 30 minutes. Add cabbage. Mix well to combine. Re-cover and continue simmering for 30 minutes or until vegetables are tender, stirring occasionally.

Each serving equals:

HE: 3 Vegetable, 2½ Protein, ¾ Bread

203 Calories, 3 gm Fat, 11 gm Protein, 33 gm Carbohydrate, 532 mg Sodium, 68 mg Calcium, 6 gm Fiber

DIABETIC: 3 Meat, 2 Vegetable, 1 Starch

Corned Beef Hash

■ ❋ ■

This dish's origins go much further back than the birth of our nation, as far back as when people began salting and curing fresh meat so they'd have food through leaner times. There's no more beloved dish for St. Patrick's Day dinners, but there's no reason to make this a once-a-year delight when lean corned beef is now so widely available.

Serves 4

1 cup finely chopped onion
2 full cups (12 ounces) finely
   diced cooked potatoes
2 (2.5-ounce) packages Carl
   Buddig 90% lean corned beef,
   shredded

¼ cup (one 2-ounce jar) chopped
   pimiento, undrained
1 tablespoon dried parsley flakes
⅛ teaspoon black pepper

In a large skillet sprayed with butter-flavored cooking spray, sauté onion for 5 minutes. Add potatoes, corned beef, undrained pimiento, parsley flakes, and black pepper. Mix well to combine. Press the mixture flat with a spatula. Cook for 20 to 25 minutes, turning with the spatula after the first 10 minutes, or until crusty. Divide into 4 servings.

Each serving equals:
HE: 1¼ Protein, ¾ Bread, ½ Vegetable

122 Calories, 2 gm Fat, 9 gm Protein, 17 gm Carbohydrate, 483 mg Sodium, 19 mg Calcium, 2 gm Fiber

DIABETIC: 1 Meat, 1 Starch, ½ Vegetable

Red Flannel Hash

■ ❋ ■

Here's another great example of that New England tradition of "recycling" one meal into the next. Take the leftovers of your boiled dinner, add a few ingredients, and you've got a whole new dish. Naming a dish after the red flannel underwear that early settlers wore to keep warm on cold nights seems a bit racy, but once you see the effect the beets have on this hash, you'll know why it made perfect sense! (It's said that Revolutionary War heroes Ethan Allen and his Green Mountain Boys considered this a favorite dish.)   *Serves 6 (scant 1 cup)*

16 ounces ground 90% lean
  turkey or beef
2 cups (one 16-ounce can) diced
  beets, rinsed and drained
2 full cups (12 ounces) diced
  cooked potatoes

1 cup finely chopped onion
⅓ cup Land O Lakes no-fat sour
  cream
1 teaspoon dried parsley flakes
⅛ teaspoon black pepper

In a large bowl, combine meat, beets, potatoes, and onion. Place mixture into a large skillet sprayed with butter-flavored cooking spray. Cook over medium-low heat for 15 to 20 minutes or until meat is cooked through. Stir in sour cream, parsley flakes, and black pepper. Continue cooking for 3 to 4 minutes or until mixture is heated through, stirring occasionally.

Each serving equals:
HE: 2 Protein, 1 Vegetable, ½ Bread, 13 Optional Calories
198 Calories, 6 gm Fat, 16 gm Protein, 20 gm Carbohydrate, 189 mg Sodium, 41 mg Calcium, 2 gm Fiber
DIABETIC: 2 Meat, 1 Vegetable, ½ Starch

Boston Brown Bread

■ ❋ ■

Here's a recipe that's just about as much fun to make as it is to eat! Yes, the secret of this famous bread is that it's prepared in a coffee can, and that instead of baking, you steam it! I tried making this without the can, but it just doesn't have that same wonderful flavor. It's another example of Yankee ingenuity—a scrumptious bread that doesn't need careful watching, so you can get your work done while it "bakes."

Serves 8

⅔ cup Carnation Nonfat Dry
   Milk Powder
½ cup water
⅓ cup dark molasses
1 tablespoon white vinegar
½ cup (3 ounces) yellow
   cornmeal

½ cup + 1 tablespoon
   whole-wheat flour
½ cup + 1 tablespoon rye flour
1½ teaspoons baking soda
½ teaspoon salt
Boiling water

Spray the inside of a 12-ounce coffee can with butter-flavored cooking spray. In a small bowl, combine dry milk powder, water, molasses, and vinegar. Set aside. In a large bowl, combine cornmeal, whole-wheat flour, rye flour, baking soda, and salt. Add molasses-and-milk mixture. Mix gently to combine. Pour mixture into prepared coffee can. Spray a piece of aluminum foil with butter-flavored cooking spray and cover the top of the can with the sprayed side down. Secure foil to can with string. Place the coffee can in a deep saucepan. Pour boiling water down the sides of the pan until the water comes halfway up the side of the coffee can. Simmer over low heat for 1½ hours. Add additional boiling water as necessary to keep water level at halfway point of can. Remove the coffee can from the saucepan and remove the foil. Test with a toothpick. If pick doesn't come out clean, re-cover coffee can and continue steaming for 5 more minutes or until it does come out clean. Place coffee can on a wire rack and cool until the bread pulls away from the side of the can. Tap bread out of can and continue cooling on wire rack. Cut into 8 round slices.

Each serving equals:
HE: 1¼ Bread, ¼ Skim Milk, ¼ Slider, 5 Optional Calories

148 Calories, 0 gm Fat, 5 gm Protein, 32 gm Carbohydrate, 562 mg Sodium, 180 mg Calcium, 4 gm Fiber

DIABETIC: 1½ Starch

Maple Fruit Compote

■ ■ ■

I don't know exactly what magic occurs inside a maple tree during the changing seasons in the Northeast, but whatever it is that creates the sap that New England farmers transform into maple syrup, I'm grateful! This easy stewed fruit dessert works with other canned fruits, but I like this combo best.

Serves 6 (½ cup)

¼ cup Cary's Sugar Free Maple
    Syrup
2 cups (one 16-ounce can) sliced
    pears, packed in fruit juice,
    drained and ½ cup liquid
    reserved

¼ teaspoon ground cinnamon
1 cup (2 small) cored, unpeeled,
    and chopped Red Delicious
    apples

In a medium bowl, combine maple syrup, reserved pear liquid, and cinnamon. Stir in pears and apples. Cover and refrigerate for at least 1 hour. Gently stir again just before serving.

Each serving equals:
HE: 1 Fruit, 7 Optional Calories
60 Calories, 0 gm Fat, 0 gm Protein, 15 gm Carbohydrate, 25 mg Sodium,
10 mg Calcium, 2 gm Fiber
DIABETIC: 1 Fruit

Indian Pudding

■ ❄ ■

This traditional cornmeal pudding is one of the oldest dishes in American history, so you can feel a real connection with the past when you stir it up! This dish is full of flavor and sweetness, and although it takes some time to bake, you don't have to keep a careful eye on your oven while it does. This recipe first appeared in a cookbook way back in 1796 (but without the Cool Whip, of course!).

Serves 8

¾ cup (4½ ounces) yellow cornmeal
4 cups skim milk ☆
½ cup pourable Sugar Twin or Sprinkle Sweet

⅓ cup molasses
1½ teaspoons apple pie spice
½ teaspoon salt
1 cup Cool Whip Lite

Preheat oven to 325 degrees. Spray an 8-by-12-inch baking dish with butter-flavored cooking spray. In a small bowl, combine cornmeal and 1 cup skim milk. In a medium saucepan, heat remaining 3 cups skim milk just to boiling point. Lower heat and gradually stir cornmeal mixture into hot milk, using a wire whisk. Mix well until mixture is smooth. Stir in Sugar Twin, molasses, apple pie spice, and salt. Continue simmering for 2 to 3 minutes, stirring often. Pour batter into prepared baking dish. Bake for 1 to 1½ hours or until a knife inserted near center comes out clean. Place baking dish on a wire rack and let set for 30 minutes. Divide into 8 servings. When serving, top each with 2 tablespoons Cool Whip Lite.

HINT: Also good with ½ cup raisins stirred in before baking.

Each serving equals:
HE: ¾ Bread, ½ Skim Milk, ½ Slider, 16 Optional Calories
158 Calories, 2 gm Fat, 6 gm Protein, 29 gm Carbohydrate, 428 mg Sodium, 234 mg Calcium, 1 gm Fiber
DIABETIC: 1½ Starch, ½ Skim Milk

Apple Betty

■ ❄ ■

Here's an old-fashioned recipe probably first invented by a clever cook looking for a way to use up stale bread (and whose apple orchard was full of ripe fruit, perhaps!). The best apples for this dish would be Rome or McIntosh if you can find them, as they tend to get softer as they bake.   *Serves 6*

3 cups (6 small) cored, peeled, and sliced cooking apples
3 slices reduced-calorie white bread, made into small soft crumbs ☆
¼ cup pourable Sugar Twin or Sprinkle Sweet

2 tablespoons Brown Sugar Twin
1 teaspoon apple pie spice
2 tablespoons reduced-calorie margarine
¾ cup water

Preheat oven to 350 degrees. Spray an 8-by-8-inch baking dish with butter-flavored cooking spray. In a large bowl, combine apples, 1 cup bread crumbs, Sugar Twin, Brown Sugar Twin, and apple pie spice. Spoon mixture into prepared baking dish. Dot with margarine. Pour water over top. Evenly sprinkle remaining bread crumbs over top and lightly spray with butter-flavored cooking spray. Bake for 45 to 50 minutes. Place baking dish on a wire rack and let set for at least 5 minutes. Divide into 6 servings.

Each serving equals:
HE: 1 Fruit, ½ Fat, ¼ Bread, 6 Optional Calories

74 Calories, 2 gm Fat, 1 gm Protein, 13 gm Carbohydrate, 105 mg Sodium, 17 mg Calcium, 3 gm Fiber

DIABETIC: 1 Fruit, ½ Fat

Cape Cod Berry Grunt

■ ❋ ■

I've always loved the nicknames for different types of baked goods, and when I first heard of a "grunt," I just had to know more! It turned out to be a delectable dessert made by dropping biscuit dough on top of boiling hot berries, then steaming or baking the dish. There are wonderful patches of wild blueberries all along the coast of Cape Cod, which surely inspired those regional cooks to create such a scrumptious dish!

Serves 8

3 cups fresh blueberries
1 cup water
½ cup pourable Sugar Twin or
* Sprinkle Sweet*
1½ cups Bisquick Reduced Fat
* Baking Mix*

1 tablespoon + 1 teaspoon
* reduced-calorie margarine*
¼ cup skim milk

Preheat oven to 325 degrees. Spray an 8-by-12-inch baking dish with butter-flavored cooking spray. In a medium saucepan, combine blueberries, water, and Sugar Twin. Cook over medium heat for 6 to 8 minutes or until berries soften, stirring often and being careful not to crush blueberries. Spoon hot blueberry mixture into prepared baking dish. In a large bowl, combine baking mix, margarine, and skim milk. Spoon batter evenly over blueberry mixture. Cover and bake for 30 minutes. Place baking dish on a wire rack and let set for 5 minutes. Divide into 8 servings.

HINT: Good served with New England Nutmeg Sauce (see page 51) or sugar-and fat-free vanilla ice cream.

Each serving equals:
HE: 1 Bread, ½ Fruit, ¼ Fat, 9 Optional Calories

122 Calories, 2 gm Fat, 2 gm Protein, 24 gm Carbohydrate, 291 mg Sodium, 36 mg Calcium, 2 gm Fiber

DIABETIC: 1 Starch, ½ Fruit

Boston Cream Pie

■ ❄ ■

Yes, it's true—Boston cream pie isn't really a pie, but more of a custard-filled cake served in pie-shaped wedges! The Parker House hotel in Boston has been serving this renowned dessert since the 1850s, and there's nothing quite like it. The cake is light, the custard is rich, and the chocolate glaze on top impossible to resist!

Serves 8

1½ cups all-purpose flour

½ cup pourable Sugar Twin or Sprinkle Sweet

1 teaspoon baking powder

½ teaspoon baking soda

⅓ cup Dannon plain fat-free yogurt

¼ cup Kraft fat-free mayonnaise

2¾ cups water ☆

1 tablespoon +1 teaspoon vanilla extract ☆

1 (4-serving) package JELL-O sugar-free instant vanilla pudding mix

1⅓ cups Carnation Nonfat Dry Milk Powder ☆

⅓ cup Cool Whip Free

1 (4-serving) package JELL-O sugar-free chocolate cook-and-serve pudding mix

½ cup (1 ounce) miniature marshmallows

1 tablespoon + 1 teaspoon reduced-calorie margarine

Preheat oven to 350 degrees. Spray two 9-inch round cake pans with butter-flavored cooking spray. In a large bowl, combine flour, Sugar Twin, baking powder, and baking soda. In a small bowl, combine yogurt, mayonnaise, ¾ cup water, and 1 tablespoon vanilla extract. Add yogurt mixture to flour mixture. Mix gently just to combine. Evenly spread batter into prepared cake pans. Bake for 20 to 25 minutes or until a toothpick inserted near center comes out clean. Place cake pans on wire racks and let cool for 10 minutes. Remove cakes from pans and allow to cool completely on wire racks. Place one layer, bottom side up, on a serving plate. In a medium bowl, combine dry instant pudding mix, ⅔ cup dry milk powder, and 1 cup water. Mix well using a wire whisk. Blend in Cool Whip Free. Spread mixture evenly over cake to within ½ inch from edge. Top with second cake layer, top side up. In a medium saucepan, combine dry cook-and-serve pudding mix, remaining ⅔ cup dry milk powder, and remaining 1 cup water. Cook over medium heat until mixture thickens and starts to boil, stirring constantly. Remove from heat. Stir in remaining 1 teaspoon vanilla extract, marshmallows, and margarine. Place saucepan on a wire rack and let set for 4 to 5 minutes, stirring occasionally. Drizzle partially cooled mixture evenly over top of cake layer. Refrigerate for at least 30 minutes. Cut into 8 servings.

Each serving equals:

HE: 1 Bread, ½ Skim Milk, ¼ Fat, ½ Slider, 10 Optional Calories

185 Calories, 1 gm Fat, 8 gm Protein, 36 gm Carbohydrate, 494 mg Sodium, 177 mg Calcium, 1 gm Fiber

DIABETIC: 1½ Starch/Carbohydrate, ½ Skim Milk, ½ Fat

Majestic Lemon Meringue Pie

■ ■ ■

Can you imagine what people must have thought when the very first lemon meringue pie was carried proudly from a fancy hotel or restaurant kitchen? The mountains of fluffy meringue must have looked as spectacular then as they do now! When the occasion is truly special, or you need to dazzle your guests, there's no more splendid way than with this luscious pie. (My daughter-in-law Angie asked me to e-mail the recipe right away!)   *Serves 8*

*1 Pillsbury refrigerated unbaked
    9-inch piecrust*
*2 (4-serving) packages JELL-O
    sugar-free vanilla cook-and-
    serve pudding mix*
*2 (4-serving) packages JELL-O
    sugar-free lemon gelatin*
*⅔ cup Carnation Nonfat Dry
    Milk Powder*
2 cups Diet Mountain Dew
6 egg whites
*½ cup pourable Sugar Twin or
    Sprinkle Sweet*
½ teaspoon vanilla extract

Preheat oven to 425 degrees. Place piecrust in a 9-inch pie plate. Flute edges and prick bottom and sides with tines of a fork. Bake for 9 to 11 minutes or until lightly browned. Place pie plate on a wire rack and allow to cool completely. Lower heat to 350 degrees. Meanwhile, in a medium saucepan, combine dry pudding mixes, dry gelatins, and dry milk powder. Stir in Diet Mountain Dew. Cook over medium heat until mixture thickens and starts to boil, stirring constantly. Pour hot mixture into cooled piecrust. In a large bowl, beat egg whites with an electric mixer until soft peaks form. Add Sugar Twin and vanilla extract. Continue beating until stiff peaks form. Spread meringue mixture evenly over filling mixture, being sure to seal to edges of piecrust. Bake for 12 to 15 minutes or until meringue starts to turn golden brown. Place pie plate on a wire rack and let set for 30 minutes. Refrigerate for at least 2 hours. Cut into 8 servings.

HINT: 1. Egg whites beat best at room temperature.
2. Meringue pie cuts easily if you dip a sharp knife in warm water before slicing.

Each serving equals:
HE: ½ Bread, ¼ Skim Milk, ¼ Protein, 1 Slider, 6 Optional Calories

167 Calories, 7 gm Fat, 5 gm Protein, 21 gm Carbohydrate, 295 mg Sodium, 70 mg Calcium, 1 gm Fiber

DIABETIC: 1½ Starch/Carbohydrate, 1 Fat

Plymouth Rock Cranberry Pie

■ ■ ■

Something quite magical happens when you bake cranberries in a pie with raisins. The berries split open and all those tart juices moisten and combine with the sweetness of the raisins, producing a thick, syrupy, absolutely irresistible filling that's tasty enough to cross an ocean for! Cranberries are a New World discovery—and a great reason for traveling so far!   *Serves 8*

1 (4-serving) package JELL-O   2 cups fresh or frozen cranberries
  sugar-free vanilla cook-and-   ¾ cup raisins
  serve pudding mix   1 Pillsbury refrigerated unbaked
1¼ cups water   9-inch piecrust

Preheat oven to 425 degrees. In a large saucepan, combine dry pudding mix and water. Stir in cranberries and raisins. Cook over medium heat until mixture thickens and cranberries soften, stirring constantly. Place piecrust in an 8-inch pie plate. With sharp knife, carefully cut crust off even with edge of pie plate. Save scraps. Flute edge. Spoon hot cranberry mixture into prepared piecrust. Garnish top with pie crust scraps. Bake for 20 to 25 minutes. Place pie plate on a wire rack and allow pie to cool completely. Cut into 8 servings.

Each serving equals:
HE: 1 Fruit, ½ Bread, ¾ Slider

187 Calories, 7 gm Fat, 1 gm Protein, 30 gm Carbohydrate, 159 mg Sodium, 9 mg Calcium, 1 gm Fiber

DIABETIC: 1 Fruit, 1 Starch/Carbohydrate, 1 Fat

Maple Majestic Apple Pie

■ ❋ ■

There's just something about autumn in New England, where the trees turn the most gorgeous shades of gold and orange. But the star of the season is the grand old maple tree, whose branches seem to explode with the reddest red leaves that even Mother Nature must find dazzling in their glory! Here's a perfect pie to celebrate fall!

Serves 8

1 (4-serving) package JELL-O sugar-free vanilla cook-and-serve pudding mix
¾ cup Cary's Sugar Free Maple Syrup
½ cup water
3 cups (6 small) cored, peeled, and sliced cooking apples
¼ cup raisins

1 (6-ounce) Keebler graham cracker piecrust
2 tablespoons purchased graham cracker crumbs or 2 (2½-inch) graham crackers, made into crumbs
2 tablespoons (½ ounce) chopped walnuts

Preheat oven to 350 degrees. In a medium saucepan, combine dry pudding mix, maple syrup, and water. Add apples and raisins. Mix well to combine. Cook over medium heat for 6 to 8 minutes or until mixture starts to thicken and apples soften, stirring often. Spoon hot mixture into piecrust. Evenly sprinkle cracker crumbs and walnuts over top. Bake for 30 minutes. Place pie plate on a wire rack and let set for 15 minutes. Refrigerate for at least 1 hour. Cut into 8 servings.

Each serving equals:
HE: 1 Fruit, ½ Bread, 1 Slider, 11 Optional Calories
190 Calories, 6 gm Fat, 2 gm Protein, 32 gm Carbohydrate, 256 mg Sodium, 6 mg Calcium, 2 gm Fiber
DIABETIC: 1 ½ Starch/Carbohydrate, 1 Fruit, 1 Fat

Sour Cream Raisin Pie

■ ■ ■

The tradition of covered-dish suppers goes back to our first settlers, and a simple but delicious pie like this one would surely be welcome on any table! Dried fruits were an important source of nourishment for those pioneers, since they could be stored safely for long periods of time.   *Serves 8*

*1 Pillsbury refrigerated unbaked
    9-inch piecrust*
*1 (4-serving) package JELL-O
    sugar-free vanilla cook-and-
    serve pudding mix*
*⅔ cup Carnation Nonfat Dry
    Milk Powder*

1 cup water
1 cup raisins
*½ cup Land O Lakes no-fat sour
    cream*
¼ teaspoon ground nutmeg
½ cup Cool Whip Lite

Preheat oven to 450 degrees. Place piecrust in a 9-inch pie plate and flute edges. In a medium saucepan, combine dry pudding mix, dry milk powder, and water. Stir in raisins. Cook over medium heat until mixture thickens and starts to boil, stirring constantly. Remove from heat. Fold in sour cream and nutmeg. Spoon mixture into prepared piecrust. Bake for 10 minutes. Reduce heat to 350 degrees and continue baking for 20 to 25 minutes. Place pie plate on a wire rack and allow to cool completely. Cut into 8 servings. When serving, top each piece with 1 tablespoon Cool Whip Lite.

Each serving equals:
HE: 1 Fruit, ½ Bread, ¼ Skim Milk, 1 Slider, 5 Optional Calories
231 Calories, 7 gm Fat, 4 gm Protein, 38 gm Carbohydrate, 210 mg Sodium, 95 mg Calcium, 1 gm Fiber
DIABETIC: 1½ Starch/Carbohydrate, 1 Fruit, 1 Fat

Thanksgiving Pumpkin Pie

■ ❈ ■

I don't know if there's a rule book somewhere that says pumpkin pie must be served on Thanksgiving, but if there isn't, there should be! After all, this old-fashioned dessert was likely served at that very first Thanksgiving, and I'm willing to believe that every scrumptious slice served helped cement the friendship of the colonists and the natives who would together build the new land.

Serves 8

1 Pillsbury refrigerated unbaked 9-inch piecrust

1⅓ cups Carnation Nonfat Dry Milk Powder

1½ cups water

2 cups (one 15-ounce can) pumpkin

2 eggs, beaten, or equivalent in egg substitute

½ cup pourable Sugar Twin or Sprinkle Sweet

1½ teaspoons pumpkin pie spice

1 cup Cool Whip Lite

Preheat oven to 450 degrees. Place piecrust in a 9-inch pie plate and flute edges. In a small bowl, combine dry milk powder and water. In a large bowl, combine pumpkin, eggs, and milk mixture. Stir in Sugar Twin and pumpkin pie spice. Pour mixture into prepared piecrust. Bake for 10 minutes. Reduce heat to 350 degrees and continue to bake for 40 to 45 minutes or until a knife inserted near center comes out clean. Place pie plate on a wire rack and allow to cool completely. Cut into 8 servings. When serving, top each piece with 2 tablespoons Cool Whip Lite.

Each serving equals:
HE: ½ Skim Milk, ½ Bread, ½ Vegetable, ¼ Protein (limited), ¾ Slider, 16 Optional Calories

209 Calories, 9 gm Fat, 7 gm Protein, 25 gm Carbohydrate, 180 mg Sodium, 162 mg Calcium, 2 gm Fiber

DIABETIC: 1½ Starch/Carbohydrate, 1 Fat, ½ Skim Milk

Easy Gingerbread Cake

■ ❄ ■

Even during our earliest years as a nation, the women of New England had access to spices from all over the world, since ships called at every major port and brought with them the flavors of the West Indies and even the Far East. This version of gingerbread is a bit different than most, with the addition of tea. You can experiment with different flavors of tea if you wish, though we liked it best with the traditional kind.   *Serves 8*

1½ cups Bisquick Reduced Fat
    Baking Mix
¼ cup pourable Sugar Twin or
    Sprinkle Sweet
2 tablespoons Brown Sugar Twin
1½ teaspoons ground ginger
1 teaspoon ground cinnamon

½ cup Land O Lakes no-fat sour
    cream
1 egg, beaten, or equivalent in
    egg substitute
½ cup molasses
½ cup cold tea

Preheat oven to 350 degrees. Spray a 9-by-9-inch cake pan with butter-flavored cooking spray. In a large bowl, combine baking mix, Sugar Twin, Brown Sugar Twin, ginger, and cinnamon. In a small bowl, combine sour cream, egg, molasses, and tea. Add liquid mixture to dry mixture. Mix gently just to combine. Spread batter into prepared cake pan. Bake for 28 to 32 minutes or until a toothpick inserted near center comes out clean. Place cake pan on a wire rack and allow to cool completely. Cut into 8 servings.

Each serving equals:
HE: 1 Bread, ¾ Slider, 13 Optional Calories
162 Calories, 2 gm Fat, 3 gm Protein, 33 gm Carbohydrate, 299 mg Sodium, 95 mg Calcium, 1 gm Fiber
DIABETIC: 2 Starch/Carbohydrate

New England Nutmeg Sauce

■ ■ ■

Nutmeg is another of those fragrant spices brought to New England by ships that traveled to faraway ports. This sauce makes a wonderful accompaniment for a fresh-baked berry dish or a fruited pie.   *Serves 8 (¼ cup)*

1 (4-serving) package JELL-O
   sugar-free vanilla cook-and-
   serve pudding mix
2 cups water

1 tablespoon + 1 teaspoon
   reduced-calorie margarine
1 teaspoon ground nutmeg

In a medium saucepan, combine dry pudding mix and water. Cook over medium heat until mixture thickens and starts to boil, stirring often. Remove from heat. Stir in margarine and nutmeg. Place saucepan on a wire rack and let set for at least 5 minutes, stirring occasionally. Serve warm.

HINT: Reheat leftovers in microwave.

Each serving equals:
HE: ¼ Fat, 10 Optional Calories
20 Calories, 1 gm Fat, 0 gm Protein, 5 gm Carbohydrate, 80 mg Sodium, 1 mg Calcium, 0 gm Fiber
DIABETIC: 1 Free Food

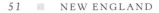

Tart and Tasty Stuffing

■ ❆ ■

From the land of the First Thanksgiving have come many legends about that original festive supper. I don't know when the tradition of stuffing your turkey with fragrant bits of bread and spices originated, but I believe this unusually rich and colorful turkey dressing would have found just as many fans back then as it will today.

Serves 8

1½ cups finely chopped celery
½ cup finely chopped onion
2 cups (one 16-ounce can) Healthy Request Chicken Broth
4 cups (6 ounces) unseasoned bread cubes

1 teaspoon dried sage
2 teaspoons dried parsley flakes
2 cups (one 16-ounce can) tart red cherries, packed in water, drained

Preheat oven to 350 degrees. Spray an 8-by-12-inch baking dish with butter-flavored cooking spray. In a large skillet sprayed with butter-flavored cooking spray, sauté celery and onion for 5 minutes. Stir in chicken broth. Bring mixture to a boil. Add bread cubes, sage, and parsley flakes. Mix well to combine. Fold in cherries. Spread mixture into prepared baking dish. Cover and bake for 30 minutes. Uncover and continue baking for 15 minutes. Place baking dish on a wire rack and let set for 5 minutes. Divide into 8 servings.

HINT: Especially good served with pork.

Each serving equals:
HE: 1 Bread, ½ Fruit, ½ Vegetable, 4 Optional Calories

129 Calories, 1 gm Fat, 5 gm Protein, 25 gm Carbohydrate, 397 mg Sodium, 20 mg Calcium, 2 gm Fiber

DIABETIC: 1 Starch, ½ Fruit, ½ Vegetable

Grape Lemonade

■ ■ ■

In just about every small town from Maine to Massachusetts, every house has a porch for "setting out" and enjoying a well-earned bit of leisure at the end of a tough day. Here's my vote for a light and thirst-quenching drink that's as cooling as a breeze off the Atlantic!   *Serves 8 (1 cup)*

> 1 tub Crystal Light lemonade
>   mix
> 1 (0.14-ounce) package sugar-
>   free grape Kool-Aid

> 8 cups water
> ¼ lemon, including skin and
>   seeds

In a large pitcher, combine dry lemonade mix, dry grape Kool-Aid, and water. Mix well. Coarsely chop lemon. Pour 2 cups lemonade mixture and chopped lemon into a blender container. Cover and process on HIGH for 20 to 30 seconds or until lemon has "almost" disappeared. Pour mixture back into pitcher. Mix well. Serve over ice.

Each serving equals:
HE: 0 Calories
0 Calories, 0 gm Fat, 0 gm Protein, 0 gm Carbohydrate, 10 mg Sodium, 0 mg Calcium, 0 gm Fiber
DIABETIC: Free Food

THE EASTERN
SEABOARD

∎ ∎ ∎

From cities whose skyscrapers sparkle at sunset to quaint ocean-side towns where the loudest noise is the squawking of seagulls, from the rolling hills of rural Pennsylvania to the verdant farms of New Jersey and Maryland, the Eastern Seaboard region celebrates an extraordinary variety of foods. Some dishes reflect an urban sophistication and energy that could only come from New York, Philadelphia, or Washington, D.C. Others speak to a more old-fashioned lifestyle treasured by the Pennsylvania Dutch. And still others have less to do with geography, and much more to say about the unique contributions of the immigrants who arrived on our shores by the millions during the twentieth century (and even earlier!). The foods they shared with their new neighbors from around the world soon formed the menu from which they all began to eat. Their traditions became our traditions, and their family favorites and comfort foods transformed the way a nation cooked and ate.

This region, which is often referred to as the "Middle Atlantic," is definitely one where food is devoured with a particular gusto. Not only that, but locals seem tireless when it comes to talking about food, deciding where to eat, organizing occasions to try new ethnic cuisines, and generally reveling in the constant influx of new flavors brought here by recent arrivals from all over— particularly the Caribbean, Asia, Africa, and Eastern Europe.

I think the expression *foodie* must have originated in this part of the country, because I've rarely met people as interested in what they're eating, where it originated, how to prepare it, and where to get the best version of it!

Maybe that's why, even though I'm from a small town in Iowa, I feel right at home along the Eastern Seaboard. My own relatives came to America from Ireland, England, and Bohemia, originally part of Czechoslovakia. Cliff's family is originally from Scandinavia and Poland, so we're a regular United Nations just in our own family. Our ancestors came here in hopes of giving their children a better life, but while they were committed to building their dream in this new nation, they brought with them wonderful traditions to pass along as well.

Nowhere are those traditions more visible than in the foods they loved best.

I'm especially drawn to the cookery of the Pennsylvania Dutch, perhaps because their "style" is old-fashioned farm cooking, practical and hearty, thrifty and comforting, prepared from foods they grow on their own land or trade for with their neighbors.

The people we call Pennsylvania Dutch are actually descended from German ancestors (people here confused the German word *Deutsch* and called the settlers "Dutch"). They sailed for the New World in search of freedom to practice their religion in an atmosphere of tolerance. The first of these groups arrived on our shores beginning in the late seventeenth century, but thousands more followed in the next hundred years. I was amazed to learn that so many German immigrants settled near Philadelphia that by the 1750s, half of that city's population hailed from Germany. The street signs were both in German and English during that period.

These immigrants were excellent farmers, able to quickly turn the fertile soil of Pennsylvania into a garden of plenty. Because of this, their tables groaned with the bounty of the earth, and their families were very well nourished. The women knew their dishes had to be substantial enough to satisfy the appetites of their hardworking husbands, but they also needed to create a variety of tasty recipes from what they were able to harvest and preserve.

The soups of this region are renowned, and one recipe that really fascinated me was the Pennsylvania Dutch pretzel soup (known as *Shdreis'l Suppe*). It's a terrific example of their skill at creating filling and flavorful soups that are a meal in a bowl! It's very easy, it's very frugal, and outside the region it's not very well known. Did you know that you can still go to the Pennsylvania Dutch country today and roll your own pretzels? My *Lancaster Chicken Corn Soup* is another Pennsylvania Dutch–inspired recipe that is perfect for serving on a cool autumn night for supper. Just add some fresh bread, and you've got a little piece of heaven.

Eating in the Big Apple is an entirely different experience! I've truly enjoyed my visits to New York City over the years (the very first time when I was still in my teens!) It's a food lover's paradise in many ways, and everywhere you walk in its different neighborhoods you get a real sense of people's passion for tasty foods. It seems that just about every country's cuisine is well represented there, so it wasn't easy deciding which favorite New York dishes to feature here.

New York has been home to so many Jewish immigrants over the years. You won't find better deli meats anywhere, and it's still the best place to eat a bagel! To recognize the unique culinary contributions of the Jews, I wanted to include a recipe in this section for *Challah*, a traditional bread that peeks out, beautifully golden crusted, from the window of every Jewish bakery you pass. I was pleasantly surprised that the loaf this recipe produced was as tasty as it was lovely to look at! You'll be surprised how easy it is to make, too!

It's just about impossible to travel through Maryland and not keep running into *Maryland Crab Cakes* on every menu you see! I had them there for the first time and liked them a lot. Some people like these when they're made of almost all crab with very little "binder," but at the kind of truck stops and family restaurants Cliff and I visit, they're prepared in much the same way as my recipe here. I think the reason I enjoy them so much is that they're kind of a variation of two things I really like: turkey dressing (stuffing) and bread pudding.

The selection of recipes in this section also provides healthy versions of some of the most famous dishes served along the Eastern Seaboard: *Coney Island Hot Dogs, Philly Cheese Steak Sandwiches,* and one of the toughest of all to create: *Deli-Style New York Cheesecake!* (This tasted so amazingly good, Rita—my testing assistant—and I both called our husbands and told them to come right home to the test kitchen to try it! They agreed it was out of this world!)

Even if you never get to travel to these great cities, I want you to experience what is most memorable about their most popular foods. Close your eyes when you take a bite, and you'll be transported as if by magic to the cities that never seem to sleep and the pretty country villages where wonderful foods of all kinds say "Welcome!"

THE EASTERN SEABOARD RECIPES

Italian Spaghetti Cauliflower Soup

Lancaster Chicken Corn Soup

Shdreis'l Suppe (Pretzel Soup)

Manhattan Clam Chowder

Scaled-Down U.S. Senate Bean Soup

Tavern Cheese Soup

Vichyssoise

Feta Beet Salad

City Lights Carrot Salad

Jersey Tomato Salad

Greek Tossed Salad

Waldorf Salad

Tossed Pasta Antipasto Salad

Mushrooms à la Russe

Sweet-and-Sour Red Cabbage

Brooklyn Bridge Peas

Pennsylvania Dutch Green Beans

Schnitzel Beans

Green Beans in "Hollandaise"

Eggplant Parmigiana

Creamy Pasta Primavera

Philly Cheese Steak Sandwiches

Coney Island Hot Dogs

Puttin' on the Ritz Fish Fillets

Maryland Crab Cakes

Chicken Divan

Classic Chicken Cacciatore

Creamy Chicken Cordon Bleu
    Skillet

Classic Chicken à la King

Italian Baked Pork Tenders

Deli-Style New York Cheesecake

Raisin Pie (Funeral Pie)

Shoo-Fly Pie

Lady Baltimore Cake

Belgian Waffles with Cherry Sauce

Challah

Gnocchi

Old-Fashioned Scrapple

Italian Spaghetti Cauliflower Soup

A friend visited Ellis Island a few years back, where she watched a short film about the people who arrived in New York from so many other places. It was a bit hard to hear, she told me, because the man next to her was translating the movie into Italian for his mother! This is the kind of substantial meal-in-a-bowl that kept many immigrant families going through hard times—and still would today.

Serves 4 (1⅓ cups)

4 cups (two 16-ounce cans) Healthy Request Chicken Broth
2 cups frozen cauliflower pieces
½ cup chopped onion
1 teaspoon Italian seasoning
1 (2.5-ounce) package Carl Buddig 90% lean pastrami, shredded

⅔ cup (1½ ounces) broken uncooked spaghetti
¼ cup (¾ ounce) grated Kraft fat-free Parmesan cheese

In a large saucepan, combine chicken broth, cauliflower, and onion. Bring mixture to a boil. Lower heat and simmer for 10 minutes, stirring occasionally. Stir in Italian seasoning, pastrami, and uncooked spaghetti. Cover and continue to simmer for 10 minutes or until cauliflower and spaghetti are tender, stirring often. When serving, sprinkle 1 tablespoon Parmesan cheese over top of each bowl.

HINT: If you can't find Carl Buddig 90% lean pastrami, use extra-lean ham.

Each serving equals:
HE: 1¼ Vegetable, ¾ Protein, ½ Bread, ¼ Slider, 3 Optional Calories
102 Calories, 2 gm Fat, 9 gm Protein, 12 gm Carbohydrate, 769 mg Sodium, 20 mg Calcium, 2 gm Fiber
DIABETIC: 1 Vegetable, 1 Meat, ½ Starch

Lancaster Chicken Corn Soup

■ ❄ ■

Thick, hearty soups have always been an immigrant tradition, as they used any available ingredients, bubbled away for hours, and could fill up hungry tummies with the addition of bits of meat, veggies, and milk. Here's a rich chicken soup so full of goodies it's almost a stew, very reminiscent of the Pennsylvania Dutch's cooking tradition. Poor in pocketbook one might be, but never poor in nourishment or spirit!

Serves 4 (1½ cups)

2 cups (one 16-ounce can)
   Healthy Request Chicken
   Broth
1 cup finely chopped celery
½ cup finely chopped onion
1 cup (one 8-ounce can) cream-
   style corn
1½ cups (one 12-fluid-ounce can)
   Carnation Evaporated Skim
   Milk

1½ tablespoons all-purpose flour
1 full cup (6 ounces) diced
   cooked chicken breast
1 cup (one 8-ounce can) whole-
   kernel corn, rinsed and
   drained
1 teaspoon dried parsley flakes
⅛ teaspoon black pepper

In a large saucepan, combine chicken broth, celery, and onion. Bring mixture to a boil. Lower heat, cover, and simmer for 15 minutes. Stir in cream-style corn, evaporated skim milk, and flour. Add chicken, whole-kernel corn, parsley flakes, and black pepper. Mix well to combine. Continue simmering, uncovered, for 6 to 8 minutes or until mixture is heated through, stirring occasionally.

HINT: If you don't have leftovers, purchase a chunk of cooked chicken breast at your local deli.

Each serving equals:
HE: 1½ Protein, 1 Bread, ¾ Skim Milk, ¾ Vegetable, 8 Optional Calories
238 Calories, 2 gm Fat, 23 gm Protein, 32 gm Carbohydrate, 573 mg Sodium, 28 mg Calcium, 2 gm Fiber
DIABETIC: 1½ Meat, 1 Starch, 1 Skim Milk, ½ Vegetable

Shdreis'l Suppe (Pretzel Soup)

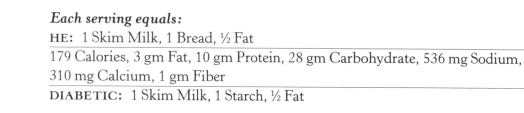

This recipe almost sounds like something a child would invent if given the run of your kitchen, but it's an actual traditional soup served in Pennsylvania Dutch homes! You can use any kind of pretzels in this soup. I've tried it with the straight kind and those formed into curves, and I think I like the curvy ones more. If you're lucky enough to buy your pretzels at a farmers' market (like the one in Union Square Park in Manhattan), pick up an extra bag and try this unusual dish.

Serves 4

1⅓ cups (3 ounces) coarsely broken pretzels
4 cups skim milk

1 tablespoon + 1 teaspoon reduced-calorie margarine

Evenly spoon ⅓ cup pretzels into 4 soup bowls. In a medium saucepan, heat skim milk until hot, but not boiling. Remove from heat. Stir in margarine. Evenly ladle 1 cup hot milk into each bowl. Serve at once.

Each serving equals:
HE: 1 Skim Milk, 1 Bread, ½ Fat
179 Calories, 3 gm Fat, 10 gm Protein, 28 gm Carbohydrate, 536 mg Sodium, 310 mg Calcium, 1 gm Fiber
DIABETIC: 1 Skim Milk, 1 Starch, ½ Fat

Manhattan Clam Chowder

■ ❋ ■

This is my own version of a classic big-city soup, and I think you'll like my little added pleasures, like the bacon and the mushroom soup! Even if you've never been big on clams, give this soup a try, as the flavors blend beautifully into a fragrant and substantial dish that isn't "fishy" at all.   *Serves 4 (1½ cups)*

1 cup chopped onion
1 cup diced celery
2 cups (10 ounces) diced raw potatoes
1½ cups water
1 cup (one 8-ounce can) tomatoes, chopped and undrained

1 (10¾-ounce) can Healthy Request Cream of Mushroom Soup
3 tablespoons Hormel Bacon Bits
1 (4.5-ounce drained weight) can minced clams, undrained

In a large saucepan, combine onion, celery, potatoes, and water. Bring mixture to a boil. Stir in undrained tomatoes. Lower heat, cover, and simmer for 15 minutes or until vegetables are tender. Add mushroom soup, bacon bits, and undrained clams. Mix well to combine. Continue simmering for 6 to 8 minutes or until mixture is heated through, stirring occasionally.

Each serving equals:
HE: 1½ Vegetable, 1 Protein, ½ Bread, ¾ Slider, 8 Optional Calories
155 Calories, 3 gm Fat, 5 gm Protein, 27 gm Carbohydrate, 671 mg Sodium, 108 mg Calcium, 3 gm Fiber
DIABETIC: 1 Vegetable, 1 Meat, 1 Starch/Carbohydrate

Scaled-Down U.S. Senate Bean Soup

■ ■ ■

Did you know that an Idaho senator actually introduced a resolution in the Senate that required the serving of Senate Bean Soup every single day of the year? It's true. Anyone can dine in the Senate restaurant, as long as you contact your elected official in advance, but if a trip to Washington, D.C. isn't on the agenda right now, why not try my healthier version of this Capitol classic? Maybe if I could persuade them to offer my version as well, we'd have a healthier Congress!

Serves 6 (1½ cups)

20 ounces (two 16-ounce cans) navy beans, rinsed and drained
2 cups (one 16-ounce can) Healthy Request Chicken Broth
2 cups water
1 full cup (6 ounces) diced Dubuque 97% fat-free ham or any extra-lean ham

1 cup finely chopped onion
1 cup finely chopped celery
1 cup shredded carrots
1½ cups (8 ounces) diced cooked potatoes
½ teaspoon dried minced garlic
2 teaspoons dried parsley flakes
⅛ teaspoon black pepper
1 bay leaf (optional)

In a large saucepan, combine navy beans, chicken broth, water, ham, onion, celery, and carrots. Bring mixture to a boil. Stir in potatoes, garlic, parsley flakes, black pepper, and bay leaf. Lower heat, cover, and simmer for 30 minutes. Just before serving, discard bay leaf, if used.

Each serving equals:

HE: 2⅓ Protein, 1 Vegetable, ⅓ Bread, 5 Optional Calories

161 Calories, 1 gm Fat, 9 gm Protein, 29 gm Carbohydrate, 631 mg Sodium, 66 mg Calcium, 7 gm Fiber

DIABETIC: 1½ Meat, 1½ Starch, 1 Vegetable

Tavern Cheese Soup

■ ■ ■

Are you one of those fans of luscious cheese soup, someone whose heart beats just a little faster when you spot this irresistible dish on the menu at your favorite pub? Take heart, dear friends. Now you can enjoy the flavors you love with much less fat and many fewer calories! This is a great choice on a cool fall night, when the trees are turning red and gold and there's a chill in the air that whispers "Winter's coming!"   *Serves 6 (1 full cup)*

3 cups (15 ounces) diced raw
   potatoes
1 cup chopped celery
½ cup chopped onion
2 cups (one 16-ounce can)
   Healthy Request Chicken
   Broth
1 cup + 2 tablespoons (4½
   ounces) shredded Kraft
   reduced-fat Cheddar cheese

1 cup Carnation Nonfat Dry
   Milk Powder
1½ cups water
2 teaspoons Worcestershire sauce
1 teaspoon yellow mustard
⅛ teaspoon black pepper

In a large saucepan, combine potatoes, celery, onion, and chicken broth. Bring mixture to a boil. Lower heat and simmer for 20 to 30 minutes or until potatoes are tender. Remove from heat and mash mixture (do not drain) with a potato masher until smooth. Gently stir in Cheddar cheese. In a medium bowl, combine dry milk powder and water. Add milk mixture to potato mixture. Mix well to combine. Stir in Worcestershire sauce, mustard, and black pepper. Return saucepan to heat and continue simmering for 6 to 8 minutes or until mixture is heated through and cheese melts, stirring often.

Each serving equals:

HE: 1 Protein, ½ Skim Milk, ½ Bread, ½ Vegetable

151 Calories, 3 gm Fat, 12 gm Protein, 19 gm Carbohydrate, 593 mg Sodium, 157 mg Calcium, 2 gm Fiber

DIABETIC: 1 Meat, ½ Skim Milk, ½ Starch, ½ Vegetable

Vichyssoise

■ ■ ■

The name is French, but at the heart of this scrumptious soup is the good, old American potato! Traditional recipes thicken this dish with the addition of way too much cream, but just watch me work magic with some evaporated skim milk, some potatoes, and my blender. This is one of those times when having your own herb garden is fun, because you can snip, snip, snip those bits of chives for a garnish.

Serves 6 (1 cup)

1½ cups cleaned and finely chopped leeks
1½ cups finely chopped onion
2 cups (one 16-ounce can) Healthy Request Chicken Broth
½ cup water
3 cups (15 ounces) finely chopped peeled raw potatoes

⅛ teaspoon black pepper
1½ cups (one 12-fluid-ounce can) Carnation Evaporated Skim Milk
6 tablespoons chopped fresh chives

In a large saucepan sprayed with butter-flavored cooking spray, sauté leeks and onion for 6 minutes. Stir in chicken broth and water. Add potatoes and black pepper. Mix well to combine. Cover and cook over medium heat for 15 minutes or until potatoes are tender. Place saucepan on a wire rack and let set for 15 minutes. Pour potato mixture into a blender container, cover, and process on BLEND for 30 seconds. Pour blended mixture into a large bowl. Stir in evaporated skim milk. Cover and refrigerate for at least 2 hours. When serving, top each bowl with 1 tablespoon chives.

Each serving equals:
HE: 1 Vegetable, ½ Skim Milk, ½ Bread, 6 Optional Calories
128 Calories, 0 gm Fat, 7 gm Protein, 25 gm Carbohydrate, 238 mg Sodium, 185 mg Calcium, 2 gm Fiber
DIABETIC: 1 Vegetable, ½ Skim Milk, ½ Starch

Feta Beet Salad

■ ■ ■

It turns out that New Yorkers (and maybe most city dwellers) eat out a lot more often than the rest of us. Some days, they'll eat breakfast, lunch, and dinner in a local coffee shop, which is usually run by a family from Greece. This vividly colored salad honors their contribution to nourishing all those with no time to cook!

Serves 4 (1¼ cups)

4 cups shredded lettuce
¼ cup (1 ounce) chopped
    walnuts
3 tablespoons (¾ ounce)
    crumbled feta cheese

1 cup (one 8-ounce can) diced
    beets, rinsed and drained
½ cup Kraft Fat Free Italian
    Dressing

In a large bowl, combine lettuce, walnuts, feta cheese, and beets. Add Italian dressing. Mix gently to combine. Serve at once.

Each serving equals:
HE: 1½ Vegetable, ½ Protein, ½ Fat, 16 Optional Calories
76 Calories, 4 gm Fat, 2 gm Protein, 8 gm Carbohydrate, 371 mg Sodium, 50 mg Calcium, 2 gm Fiber
DIABETIC: 2 Vegetable, ½ Meat, ½ Fat

City Lights Carrot Salad

■ ■ ■

Just as the skyline sparkles and lights up the night sky, so does this unusual carrot salad help make any meal a feast for the senses! This dish was inspired by that "up-all-night" magical place known as the Big Apple—or New York, New York! I had the pleasure of appearing on *World News Tonight* from there very early one morning, and when I emerged from the studios, the sun wasn't up yet, but the lights were still shining all over town!   *Serves 4 (¾ cup)*

2¾ cups shredded carrots
¼ cup finely chopped green onion
¼ cup (1 ounce) chopped
*   walnuts*
½ cup raisins
⅓ cup Kraft fat-free mayonnaise

2 tablespoons Land O Lakes
*   no-fat sour cream*
Sugar substitute to equal 2
*   teaspoons sugar*
2 teaspoons lemon juice
1 teaspoon dried parsley flakes

In a medium bowl, combine carrots, onion, walnuts, and raisins. In a small bowl, combine mayonnaise, sour cream, sugar substitute, lemon juice, and parsley flakes. Add mayonnaise mixture to carrot mixture. Mix gently to combine. Cover and refrigerate for at least 30 minutes. Gently stir again just before serving.

HINT: To plump up raisins without "cooking," place in a glass measuring cup and microwave on HIGH for 20 seconds.

Each serving equals:
HE: 1½ Vegetable, 1 Fruit, ½ Fat, ¼ Protein, ¼ slider, 2 Optional Calories
156 Calories, 4 gm Fat, 2 gm Protein, 28 gm Carbohydrate, 94 mg Sodium, 48 mg Calcium, 4 gm Fiber
DIABETIC: 1½ Vegetable, 1 Fruit, 1 Fat

Jersey Tomato Salad

■ ■ ■

A friend who grew up in New Jersey told me that nothing ever tasted quite as wonderful as the Jersey beefsteak tomatoes of her childhood—or at least that's how she remembered it! It's true, the Garden State is famous for those big, beautiful, and rosy-red gems, and if you're lucky enough to get your hands on some, good for you. But speaking as someone who's always had a tomato patch, I promise you that this dish is truly tasty made with the best fresh tomatoes you can find!

Serves 6 (⅔ cup)

½ cup Kraft Fat Free Ranch
  Dressing
2 tablespoons Grey Poupon
  Honey Mustard
1 teaspoon dried parsley flakes
4 cups chopped unpeeled fresh
  tomatoes

½ cup finely chopped red onion
½ cup + 1 tablespoon (2¼
  ounces) shredded Kraft
  reduced-fat Cheddar cheese
3 tablespoons Hormel Bacon
  Bits

In a large bowl, combine Ranch dressing, honey mustard, and parsley flakes. Stir in tomatoes and onion. Add Cheddar cheese and bacon bits. Mix gently to combine. Cover and refrigerate for at least 10 minutes. Gently stir again just before serving.

Each serving equals:
HE: 1½ Vegetable, ½ Protein, ½ Slider, 6 Optional Calories
128 Calories, 4 gm Fat, 6 gm Protein, 17 gm Carbohydrate, 462 mg Sodium, 80 mg Calcium, 2 gm Fiber
DIABETIC: 1½ Vegetable, ½ Meat, ½ Starch

Greek Tossed Salad

■ ■ ■

Until I tasted feta cheese, the centerpiece of the classic Greek salad, I thought it was some weird foreign ingredient that would never find its way to DeWitt, Iowa! But our supermarkets keep surprising us with the variety of foods available just about anywhere. Greek salad is a mainstay of diner menus in New York, and popular anywhere Greek food is served, so do give it a try if you haven't yet. You'll be glad you did!

Serves 4

4 cups torn Romaine lettuce
1 cup unpeeled and chopped fresh tomato
¼ cup (1 ounce) sliced ripe olives
1 cup + 2 tablespoons (4.5 ounces) crumbled feta cheese

½ cup Kraft Fat Free Ranch Dressing
2 tablespoons Kraft fat-free mayonnaise
½ teaspoon dried basil
10 Ritz Reduced Fat crackers, made into coarse crumbs

In a large bowl, combine Romaine lettuce, tomato, olives, and feta cheese. In a small bowl, combine Ranch dressing, mayonnaise, and basil. Add dressing mixture to lettuce mixture. Toss gently to combine. For each serving, place 1¼ cups salad on a plate and sprinkle about 1½ tablespoons cracker crumbs over top.

HINT: A self-seal sandwich bag works great for crushing crackers.

Each serving equals:
HE: 1½ Protein, 1½ Vegetable, ½ Bread, ¼ Fat, ½ Slider, 15 Optional Calories
188 Calories, 8 gm Fat, 8 gm Protein, 21 gm Carbohydrate, 705 mg Sodium, 211 mg Calcium, 2 gm Fiber
DIABETIC: 1½ Meat, 1½ Vegetable, 1 Starch

Waldorf Salad

■ ■ ■

Invented by an enterprising chef for the gala opening of New York's Waldorf-Astoria Hotel in 1893, the Waldorf-Astoria salad has appeared in many cookbooks and in many variations. I think this version is just great. It's easy to prepare, it's got that true classic taste and crunch, and it makes a terrific side-dish salad all year long.

Serves 6 (scant ½ cup)

2 cups (4 small) cored, unpeeled, and diced Red Delicious apples
1 teaspoon lemon juice
¼ cup raisins
¾ cup chopped celery
¼ cup (1 ounce) chopped walnuts
½ cup Kraft fat-free mayonnaise
⅓ cup Cool Whip Free

In a large bowl, combine apples and lemon juice. Stir in raisins, celery, and walnuts. Add mayonnaise and Cool Whip Free. Mix well to combine. Cover and refrigerate for at least 30 minutes. Gently stir again just before serving.

HINT: To plump up raisins without "cooking," place in a glass measuring cup and microwave on HIGH for 20 seconds.

Each serving equals:
HE: 1 Fruit, ⅓ Fat, ¼ Vegetable, ¼ Slider, 3 Optional Calories
113 Calories, 5 gm Fat, 2 gm Protein, 15 gm Carbohydrate, 17 mg Sodium, 21 mg Calcium, 2 gm Fiber
DIABETIC: 1 Fruit, ½ Fat, ½ Starch/Carbohydrate

Tossed Pasta Antipasto Salad

■ ■ ■

An antipasto is a classic Italian hors d'oeuvre, and in the fancier restaurants, you may be invited to choose your own selections from an enormous table of platters featuring all kinds of vegetables and meats. In this recipe, I've chosen for you, and stirred in some pretty pasta as well. This is such a colorful dish, your eyes will enjoy it before your fork even reaches your lips! With tricolor rotini, it's just gorgeous.

Serves 8 (1¼ cups)

*1 cup Kraft Fat Free Italian
Dressing* ☆
1 cup sliced fresh mushrooms
*½ cup (2 ounces) sliced ripe
olives*
1 cup chopped red bell pepper
*4 cups cold cooked ziti or rotini
pasta, rinsed and drained*
*2 cups chopped unpeeled fresh
tomatoes*

2 hard-boiled eggs, chopped
*1 (3.5-ounce) package Hormel
reduced-fat pepperoni
slices*
*¾ cup (3 ounces) shredded
Kraft reduced-fat mozzarella
cheese*
*1 cup (one 8-ounce can) arti-
choke hearts, cut into halves
(optional)*

In a large bowl, combine ¾ cup Italian dressing, mushrooms, olives, and red pepper. Stir in pasta. Add tomatoes, chopped eggs, pepperoni slices, mozzarella cheese, and artichoke hearts. Mix well to combine. Cover and refrigerate for at least 30 minutes. Gently stir in remaining ¼ cup Italian dressing.

HINT: 1. 3 cups uncooked pasta usually cooks to about 4 cups.
2. If you want the look and feel of egg without the cholesterol, toss out the yolk and dice the whites.

Each serving equals:
HE: 1¼ Protein (¼ limited), 1 Bread, 1 Vegetable, ¼ Fat, 16 Optional Calories
218 Calories, 6 gm Fat, 13 gm Protein, 28 gm Carbohydrate, 754 mg Sodium, 134 mg Calcium, 2 gm Fiber
DIABETIC: 1½ Starch, 1 Meat, 1 Vegetable, ½ Fat

Mushrooms à la Russe

■ ❋ ■

Inspired by the famous (and regrettably now-closed) Russian Tea Room in New York City, this magnificent dish will dazzle your guests with its luscious, creamy taste and rich flavor! The original recipe included tons of butter and sour cream, but you'll never miss it in this spectacularly tasty delight. Rumor has it the Russian Tea Room may reopen soon, but you can enjoy this imperial marvel at home! *Serves 6*

½ cup finely chopped onion
4 cups (four 4-ounce cans) sliced
   mushrooms, well drained
4½ tablespoons all-purpose flour
⅔ cup Carnation Nonfat Dry
   Milk Powder
1 cup water
¾ cup Land O Lakes no-fat sour
   cream

1 tablespoon reduced-calorie
   margarine
½ cup (1½ ounces) grated
   Kraft fat-free Parmesan
   cheese ☆
1 teaspoon parsley flakes
⅛ teaspoon black pepper
¼ teaspoon Worcestershire
   sauce

Preheat oven to 350 degrees. Spray an 8-by-8-inch baking dish with butter-flavored cooking spray. In a large skillet sprayed with butter-flavored cooking spray, sauté onion for 5 minutes. Stir in mushrooms. In a covered jar, combine flour, dry milk powder, and water. Shake well to blend. Add milk mixture to mushroom mixture. Mix well to combine. Stir in sour cream, margarine, ¼ cup Parmesan cheese, parsley flakes, black pepper, and Worcestershire sauce. Continue cooking until mixture thickens, being careful not to let mixture come to a boil. Spread mixture into prepared baking dish. Evenly sprinkle remaining ¼ cup Parmesan cheese over top. Bake for 20 to 25 minutes or until golden and bubbly. Place baking dish on a wire rack and let set for 5 minutes. Divide into 6 servings.

Each serving equals:
HE: 1½ Vegetable, ⅓ Skim Milk, ⅓ Protein, ¼ Bread, ¼ Fat, ¼ Slider, 10 Optional Calories
121 Calories, 1 gm Fat, 6 gm Protein, 22 gm Carbohydrate, 755 mg Sodium, 52 mg Calcium, 4 gm Fiber
DIABETIC: 1½ Vegetable, 1 Starch/Carbohydrate

Sweet-and-Sour Red Cabbage

■ ■ ■

Here's a truly flavorful way to serve an old standby, a recipe that has its roots in the tradition of German and Eastern European immigrants who settled in New York and Pennsylvania. This is such a beautiful color, it makes a terrific side dish for pork tenders or chicken breasts. Treat yourself to a small box of ground cloves if you happen not to have any in the house—it's definitely worth it, and you're more likely to serve this dish often.

Serves 6 (½ cup)

2 tablespoons reduced-calorie
   margarine
1 cup chopped onion
1½ cups (3 small) cored, peeled,
   and chopped tart cooking
   apples

½ cup water
2 tablespoons Brown Sugar Twin
2 tablespoons cider vinegar
½ teaspoon ground cloves
3½ cups sliced red cabbage

In a large skillet sprayed with butter-flavored cooking spray, melt margarine. Stir in onion and sauté for 5 minutes. Add apples, water, Brown Sugar Twin, vinegar, and cloves. Mix well to combine. Stir in cabbage. Bring mixture to a boil. Lower heat, cover, and simmer for 30 to 40 minutes or until cabbage is tender. Uncover and continue simmering for 10 minutes, stirring occasionally.

Each serving equals:
HE: 1½ Vegetable, ½ Fruit, ½ Fat, 2 Optional Calories

62 Calories, 2 gm Fat, 1 gm Protein, 10 gm Carbohydrate, 54 mg Sodium, 34 mg Calcium, 2 gm Fiber

DIABETIC: 1 Vegetable, ½ Fruit, ½ Fat

Brooklyn Bridge Peas

■ ■ ■

Did you know you can actually walk across the Brooklyn Bridge? It's true! The pedestrian walkway is made of wood, and the view from the middle of the East River is spectacular. I thought this festive veggie blend was worthy of such a great monument to engineering!

Serves 4 (¾ cup)

½ cup chopped onion
½ cup finely chopped celery
2 cups frozen peas, thawed
1 cup (one 4-ounce can) sliced
    mushrooms, undrained

¼ cup (one 2-ounce jar) chopped
    pimiento, undrained
⅛ teaspoon black pepper

In a large skillet sprayed with butter-flavored cooking spray, sauté onion and celery for 8 to 10 minutes or until celery is tender. Add peas, undrained mushrooms, undrained pimiento, and black pepper. Mix well to combine. Lower heat and simmer for 5 minutes, stirring occasionally.

HINT: Thaw peas by placing in a colander and rinsing under hot water for one minute.

Each serving equals:
HE: 1 Bread, 1 Vegetable

80 Calories, 0 gm Fat, 5 gm Protein, 15 gm Carbohydrate, 185 mg Sodium, 34 mg Calcium, 6 gm Fiber

DIABETIC: 1 Starch, 1 Vegetable

Pennsylvania Dutch Green Beans

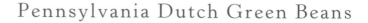

I discovered that by the middle of the 1700s, half the population of Philadelphia was German, and it's clear to see that many German culinary traditions made their way into the tasty foods served by the people known as the Pennsylvania Dutch! The hardworking farm wives of the region planted gardens to ensure they'd have a steady supply of vegetables. Just be glad you don't have to labor over a hot stove for hours to prepare this tangy bean dish.   *Serves 6 (⅔ cup)*

*4 cups frozen cut green beans,
     thawed*
2 cups hot water
½ cup chopped onion
2 tablespoons white vinegar

*1 tablespoon pourable Sugar
     Twin or Sprinkle Sweet*
⅛ teaspoon black pepper
¼ cup Hormel Bacon Bits

In a large saucepan, combine green beans and water. Cook over medium heat for 15 minutes or until tender. Drain. Meanwhile, in a large skillet sprayed with butter-flavored cooking spray, sauté onion for 6 to 8 minutes. Stir in vinegar, Sugar Twin, and black pepper. Add hot green beans and bacon bits. Mix well to combine. Lower heat and simmer for 5 minutes, stirring often.

HINT: Thaw green beans by placing in a colander and rinsing under hot water for one minute.

Each serving equals:
HE: 1½ Vegetable, 18 Optional Calories

53 Calories, 1 gm Fat, 3 gm Protein, 8 gm Carbohydrate, 169 mg Sodium, 37 mg Calcium, 2 gm Fiber

DIABETIC: 1½ Vegetable

Schnitzel Beans

■ ❄ ■

"Schnitzel" usually means a cutlet of meat (as in *Wienerschnitzel,* which is a breaded veal cutlet). This recipe was designed to be served alongside such hearty fare, and because it simmers for a while on top of the stove, you'll find that the ingredients blend together beautifully.   *Serves 6 (¾ cup)*

4 cups frozen cut green beans, thawed
1½ cups chopped onion
2 cups peeled and chopped fresh tomatoes
1 cup water

3 tablespoons Hormel Bacon Bits
1 tablespoon pourable Sugar Twin or Sprinkle Sweet
⅛ teaspoon black pepper

In a large skillet sprayed with butter-flavored cooking spray, combine green beans, onion, tomatoes, and water. Stir in bacon bits, Sugar Twin, and black pepper. Bring mixture to a boil. Lower heat, cover, and simmer for 45 to 60 minutes or until beans are very tender, stirring occasionally.

HINT: Thaw green beans by placing in a colander and rinsing under hot water for one minute.

Each serving equals:
HE: 2½ Vegetable, 14 Optional Calories
77 Calories, 1 gm Fat, 4 gm Protein, 13 gm Carbohydrate, 134 mg Sodium, 46 mg Calcium, 4 gm Fiber
DIABETIC: 2½ Vegetable

Green Beans in "Hollandaise"

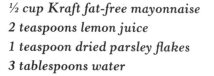

They take vegetables seriously in those fancy restaurants back East. It's not enough to serve a little side dish of cut green beans—oh no! Instead, they like to serve their beans with a big dollop of the French sauce called Hollandaise. The original version has so much fat, it's no wonder everyone there is worried about their cholesterol, but this healthy version should satisfy the urge!   *Serves 4*

½ cup Kraft fat-free mayonnaise
2 teaspoons lemon juice
1 teaspoon dried parsley flakes
3 tablespoons water

1 teaspoon lemon pepper
4 cups (two 16-ounce cans) cut
   green beans, rinsed and
   drained

In a small bowl, combine mayonnaise, lemon juice, and parsley flakes. Set aside. In a large saucepan, combine water and lemon pepper. Stir in green beans. Cover and simmer for 6 to 8 minutes or until mixture is heated through. For each serving, place a full ¾ cup green beans on a plate and spoon about 2 tablespoons mayonnaise mixture over top. Serve at once.

Each serving equals:
HE: 2 Vegetable, ¼ Slider
48 Calories, 0 gm Fat, 1 gm Protein, 11 gm Carbohydrate, 264 mg Sodium, 37 mg Calcium, 2 gm Fiber
DIABETIC: 2 Vegetable

Eggplant Parmigiana

■ ❋ ■

Here's a classic dish that turns up on the menus of most Italian restaurants, especially in New York's Little Italy neighborhood that has been home to so many new arrivals on our shores! It's a sturdy and satisfying dish that makes a great entree and can be served with a small portion of spaghetti, as tradition calls for. This version is especially rich because it features two delectable cheeses, and meat, too!

Serves 6

1 large eggplant
½ teaspoon salt
16 ounces ground 90% lean
  turkey or beef
½ cup chopped onion
2 cups (one 16-ounce can) toma-
  toes, chopped and undrained
2 tablespoons chopped fresh

parsley or 2 teaspoons dried
  parsley flakes
⅛ teaspoon black pepper
¼ cup (¾ ounce) grated Kraft
  fat-free Parmesan cheese
3 (¾-ounce) slices Kraft reduced-
  fat mozzarella cheese

Preheat oven to 350 degrees. Spray an 8-by-8-inch baking dish with butter-flavored cooking spray. Cut eggplant into 12 slices. Sprinkle slices lightly with salt. Let set for 5 minutes. Pat slices dry. In a large skillet sprayed with butter-flavored cooking spray, brown eggplant slices on both sides. Meanwhile, in another large skillet sprayed with butter-flavored cooking spray, brown meat and onion. Stir in undrained tomato, parsley, and black pepper. Lower heat and simmer for 5 minutes. Arrange half of eggplant slices in prepared baking dish. Spoon meat mixture over top. Evenly arrange remaining eggplant slices over meat mixture. Sprinkle Parmesan cheese evenly over eggplant. Cut mozzarella cheese slices in half diagonally. Evenly arrange cheese pieces over top. Bake for 30 minutes. Place baking dish on a wire rack and let set for 5 minutes. Divide into 6 servings.

Each serving equals:
HE: 2⅔ Protein, 1½ Vegetable

192 Calories, 8 gm Fat, 18 gm Protein, 12 gm Carbohydrate, 510 mg Sodium, 104 mg Calcium, 4 gm Fiber

DIABETIC: 2½ Meat, 1½ Vegetable

Creamy Pasta Primavera

■ ■ ■

This light and lovely Italian pasta dish is a fixture on every Little Italy restaurant menu! Don't you just love finding those bits of vegetables nestled in a mound of luscious fettuccine on your plate? This is perfect for those days when you've got no time to cook. I bet most busy New Yorkers would buy precut vegetables at the nearest salad bar.

Serves 4 (1 cup)

1 cup shredded carrots
1½ cups chopped fresh broccoli
1 cup snow peas
*2 cups hot cooked fettuccine,
    rinsed and drained*
*½ cup Kraft Fat Free Ranch
    Dressing*

*¼ cup (¾ ounce) grated Kraft
    fat-free Parmesan cheese*
*2 tablespoons chopped fresh
    parsley or 2 teaspoons dried
    parsley flakes*

In a medium saucepan, cook carrots and broccoli in boiling water for 3 to 4 minutes. Stir in snow peas. Continue cooking for 1 minute. Drain well. Return vegetables to saucepan. Add fettuccine. Mix gently to combine. Stir in Ranch dressing, Parmesan cheese, and parsley. Serve at once.

HINT: 1½ cups broken, uncooked fettuccine usually cooks to about 2 cups.

Each serving equals:
HE: 1¾ Vegetable, 1 Bread, ¼ Protein, ½ Slider, 10 Optional Calories

189 Calories, 1 gm Fat, 7 gm Protein, 38 gm Carbohydrate, 424 mg Sodium, 47 mg Calcium, 6 gm Fiber

DIABETIC: 2 Vegetable, 1½ Starch

Philly Cheese Steak Sandwiches

■ ■ ■

There are many pretenders, they say, but only one true Philly cheese steak sandwich–making style! On my many trips to QVC, whose studios are in a suburb of Philadelphia, I've had the chance to watch as this classic cheese-and-roast-beef delight was prepared a number of different ways. Then I waved my Healthy Exchanges whisk and created a little Philly magic of my own. Even if you never visit the City of Brotherly Love, you can taste what makes the city tick!

Serves 4

2 cups thinly sliced onion
¼ cup water
2 teaspoons Dijon mustard
½ teaspoon dried minced garlic
4 hot dog buns
1 (6-ounce) package Healthy
   Choice 97% fat-free Deli
   Sliced Roast Beef

4 (¾-ounce) slices Kraft reduced-
   fat Swiss cheese
¾ cup (3 ounces) shredded Kraft
   reduced-fat Cheddar cheese

Preheat broiler. In a large skillet sprayed with butter-flavored cooking spray, combine onion and water. Cover and cook over medium heat for 10 minutes or until onions are softened, stirring occasionally. Stir in mustard and garlic. Separate each hot dog bun and arrange on a baking sheet. Lightly spray buns with butter-flavored cooking spray. Broil for 1 to 2 minutes. Separate beef into 4 even piles. Top bottom half of each bun with a pile of roast beef and a slice of Swiss cheese. Evenly spoon about ½ cup onion and 3 tablespoons Cheddar cheese over top of remaining bun halves. Broil for 1 to 2 minutes or until cheese melts. Sandwich each half together, cut in half, and serve at once.

Each serving equals:
HE: 3 Protein, 1 Bread, 1 Vegetable
293 Calories, 9 gm Fat, 26 gm Protein, 27 gm Carbohydrate, 706 mg Sodium, 424 mg Calcium, 3 gm Fiber
DIABETIC: 3 Meat, 1 Starch, 1 Vegetable

Coney Island Hot Dogs

■ ■ ■

I'm sure that the famous hot dogs served in Coney Island taste even better when nibbled right by the ocean, but I wanted you to have the chance to savor them at home! This seaside community comes alive every summer with amusement park rides, thousands of beachgoers, a mermaid parade (!), and of course, all kinds of delicious "takeout" foods. Take a bite of this, then close your eyes and imagine yourself surrounded by those salty breezes! *Serves 8*

8 ounces ground 90% lean turkey or beef
1 cup finely chopped onion
1 cup (one 8-ounce can) Hunt's Tomato Sauce
1 teaspoon chili seasoning
1 tablespoon Brown Sugar Twin
½ teaspoon Worcestershire sauce
1 teaspoon dried parsley flakes
1 (8-count) package Healthy Choice 97% lean Ball Park frankfurters
1 cup hot water
8 hot dog buns

In a large skillet sprayed with butter-flavored cooking spray, brown ground meat and onion. Add tomato sauce, chili seasoning, Brown Sugar Twin, Worcestershire sauce, and parsley flakes. Mix well to combine. Lower heat and simmer while preparing frankfurters, stirring occasionally. In a large saucepan, cook frankfurters in water for 5 minutes or until heated through. Drain well. For each sandwich, place a frankfurter in a bun and spoon about ¼ cup meat sauce over top.

Each serving equals:
HE: 2 Protein, 1 Bread, ¾ Vegetable, 1 Optional Calorie

167 Calories, 3 gm Fat, 13 gm Protein, 22 gm Carbohydrate, 808 mg Sodium, 33 mg Calcium, 2 gm Fiber

DIABETIC: 2 Meat, 1 Starch, 1 Vegetable

Puttin' on the Ritz Fish Fillets

■ ■ ■

If we got our information from Fred-and-Ginger movies, we might be convinced that city folks dress for dinner every night in tuxedos and gowns! Well, even if your favorite dance partner is wearing shorts and sneakers, and you're fixing supper in Boise or Birmingham, here's a terrific way to make plain old fish special. *Serves 4*

¼ cup Kraft Fat Free French Dressing
1 teaspoon dried onion flakes
1 teaspoon dried parsley flakes

16 ounces white fish, cut into 4 pieces
15 Ritz Reduced Fat Crackers, made into fine crumbs

Preheat oven to 500 degrees. Spray a baking sheet with butter-flavored cooking spray. In a saucer, combine French dressing, onion flakes, and parsley flakes. Dip fish pieces into dressing mixture, then coat in cracker crumbs. Place coated fish pieces on prepared baking sheet Drizzle any remaining dressing mixture and cracker crumbs over top. Bake for 10 to 12 minutes or until fish flakes easily. Serve at once.

HINT: A self-seal sandwich bag works great for crushing crackers.

Each serving equals:
HE: 1½ Protein, ¾ Bread, ¼ Slider, 5 Optional Calories
171 Calories, 3 gm Fat, 22 gm Protein, 14 gm Carbohydrate, 344 mg Sodium, 60 mg Calcium, 0 gm Fiber
DIABETIC: 3 Meat, 1 Starch

Maryland Crab Cakes

■ ■ ■

If Maryland had a state food, it would definitely be the crab cake! There's plenty of spectacular seafood that comes from beautiful Chesapeake Bay, but the pride of those blue waters is crab. Here's a terrific version of this recipe classic that even a landlocked Iowan can enjoy! These are tangy enough not to need tartar sauce.

Serves 6 (2 each)

3 tablespoons Kraft fat-free mayonnaise

2 tablespoons yellow mustard

1½ teaspoons Worcestershire sauce

1 egg or equivalent in egg substitute

3 (4.5-ounce drained weight) cans crabmeat, drained and flaked

6 tablespoons Bisquick Reduced Fat Baking Mix

2 teaspoons dried parsley flakes

In a large bowl, combine mayonnaise, mustard, Worcestershire sauce, and egg. Add crabmeat, baking mix, and parsley flakes. Mix well to combine. Using a ¼-cup measuring cup as a guide, form into 12 cakes. Place cakes on a hot griddle sprayed with butter-flavored cooking spray. Brown for 3 to 4 minutes on each side.

Each serving equals:

HE: 2¼ Protein, ⅓ Bread, 5 Optional Calories

106 Calories, 2 gm Fat, 15 gm Protein, 7 gm Carbohydrate, 442 mg Sodium, 85 mg Calcium, 0 gm Fiber

DIABETIC: 2½ Meat, ½ Starch

Chicken Divan

■ ❄ ■

Here's a delectable recipe that was oh-so-dear to the hearts of those 1950s and 1960s brides! What a perfect way to persuade your husband that he married the right woman, and what a lovely dish to serve your new mother-in-law! The definition of a classic is something that's always in fashion, and this creamy chicken dish is as welcome now as it always was!   *Serves 4*

3 cups frozen cut broccoli,
   thawed
1½ cups (8 ounces) diced cooked
   chicken breast
1 (10¾-ounce) can Healthy
   Request Cream of Chicken
   Soup

⅓ cup skim milk
1 teaspoon dried onion flakes
1 teaspoon dried parsley flakes
½ cup + 1 tablespoon (2¼
   ounces) shredded Kraft
   reduced-fat Cheddar cheese

Preheat oven to 375 degrees. Spray an 8-by-8-inch baking dish with butter-flavored cooking spray. Evenly arrange broccoli in prepared baking dish. Sprinkle chicken evenly over broccoli. In a small bowl, combine chicken soup, skim milk, onion flakes, and parsley flakes. Spread soup mixture evenly over chicken. Evenly sprinkle Cheddar cheese over top. Bake for 30 to 35 minutes. Place baking dish on a wire rack and let set for 5 minutes. Divide into 4 servings.

HINT: 1. Thaw broccoli by placing in a colander and rinsing under hot water.
       2. If preferred, a 10-ounce package frozen broccoli spears, thawed, may be substituted for cut broccoli.
       3. If you don't have leftovers, purchase a chunk of cooked chicken breast from your local deli.

Each serving equals:
HE: 2¾ Protein, 1½ Vegetable, ½ Slider, 13 Optional Calories
230 Calories, 6 gm Fat, 28 gm Protein, 16 gm Carbohydrate, 519 mg Sodium, 210 mg Calcium, 4 gm Fiber
DIABETIC: 2½ Meat, 1½ Vegetable, ½ Starch/Carbohydrate

Classic Chicken Cacciatore

■ ✳ ■

A great many immigrants came to the United States from Italy in the first half of the twentieth century, and this is just one of the delicious recipes they brought with them! It's a terrific way to prepare chicken that is tender and super-flavorful. If a classic is a dish that's in it for the long run, this one's gonna stick around forever!

Serves 4

16 ounces skinned and boned uncooked chicken breasts, cut into 4 pieces
2 cups (one 16-ounce can) tomatoes, chopped and undrained
½ cup *Healthy Request* tomato juice or any reduced-sodium tomato juice

1½ teaspoons Italian seasoning
½ teaspoon dried minced garlic
2 teaspoons dried parsley flakes
1 tablespoon pourable Sugar Twin or Sprinkle Sweet
1½ cups chopped onion
1 cup chopped green bell pepper

In a large skillet sprayed with olive oil–flavored cooking spray, brown chicken pieces for 3 minutes on each side. In a large bowl, combine undrained tomatoes, tomato juice, Italian seasoning, garlic, parsley flakes, and Sugar Twin. Stir in onion and green pepper. Spoon vegetable mixture evenly over chicken pieces. Lower heat, cover, and simmer for 30 minutes or until vegetables are tender. When serving, place 1 piece of chicken on a plate and spoon ¾ cup vegetable mixture over top.

Each serving equals:
HE: 3 Protein, 2 ½ Vegetable, 1 Optional Calorie
183 Calories, 3 gm Fat, 25 gm Protein, 14 gm Carbohydrate, 238 mg Sodium, 69 mg Calcium, 3 gm Fiber
DIABETIC: 3 Meat, 2 Vegetable

Creamy Chicken Cordon Bleu Skillet

■ ❋ ■

Every Eastern city worth its glitter features some ritzy French restaurants whose chef was trained at France's great Cordon Bleu cooking school. ("Cordon bleu" actually means blue ribbon!) Well, even if you never learned a syllable of French in school, you'll still come out a winner when you serve this luscious dish. *Serves 4 (1 cup)*

1 cup (5 ounces) diced cooked chicken breast

1 full cup (6 ounces) diced Dubuque 97% fat-free ham, or any extra-lean ham

1 (10¾-ounce) can Healthy Request Cream of Mushroom Soup

¼ cup Land O Lakes no-fat sour cream

⅓ cup water

3 (¾-ounce) slices Kraft reduced-fat Swiss cheese, shredded

2 cups hot cooked noodles, rinsed and drained

1 teaspoon dried onion flakes

In a large skillet sprayed with butter-flavored cooking spray, sauté chicken and ham for 5 minutes. Stir in mushroom soup, sour cream, water, and Swiss cheese. Add noodles and onion flakes. Mix well to combine. Lower heat and simmer for 6 to 8 minutes or until mixture is heated through and cheese melts, stirring occasionally.

HINT: 1. If you don't have leftovers, purchase a chunk of cooked chicken breast from your local deli.
2. 1¾ cups uncooked noodles usually cooks to about 2 cups.

Each serving equals:
HE: 3 Protein, 1 Bread, ½ Slider, 16 Optional Calories

309 Calories, 9 gm Fat, 26 gm Protein, 31 gm Carbohydrate, 959 mg Sodium, 82 mg Calcium, 1 gm Fiber

DIABETIC: 3 Meat, 1½ Starch/Carbohydrate

Classic Chicken à la King

■ ❄ ■

Don't you just love creamy, cozy chicken skillet suppers? My kids always looked forward to the nights when I stirred up this old-fashioned dish that's just as satisfying now as when it was first invented! This version is particularly luscious and oh-so-smooth: perfect for a gathering of friends on your patio or a quick Sunday supper for the family you love.   *Serves 6 (¾ cup)*

1 (12-ounce) jar Heinz Fat Free
*   Chicken Gravy*
1½ cups frozen peas, thawed
¼ cup (one 2-ounce jar) chopped
*   pimiento, undrained*
⅛ teaspoon ground sage

1 teaspoon dried parsley flakes
⅛ teaspoon black pepper
2 full cups (12 ounces) diced
*   cooked chicken breast*
¾ cup Land O Lakes no-fat sour
*   cream*

In a large skillet, combine chicken gravy, peas, and undrained pimiento. Stir in sage, parsley flakes, and black pepper. Add chicken. Mix well to combine. Cook over medium heat for 5 minutes, stirring occasionally. Stir in sour cream. Lower heat and simmer for 3 to 4 minutes or until mixture is heated through, stirring often.

HINT: 1. Thaw peas by placing in a colander and rinsing under hot water for one minute.
2. If you don't have leftovers, purchase a chunk of cooked chicken breast from your local deli.

Each serving equals:

HE: 2 Protein, ½ Bread, ½ Slider, 15 Optional Calories

162 Calories, 2 gm Fat, 22 gm Protein, 14 gm Carbohydrate, 420 mg Sodium, 60 mg Calcium, 2 gm Fiber

DIABETIC: 2 Meat, 1 Starch/Carbohydrate

Italian Baked Pork Tenders

■ ✳ ■

The olives in Italy are so delicious, they produce the most in-demand olive oil in the world! So I knew I had to stir some into this splendidly meaty pork supper that just pleased Cliff no end. And a dish that needs no watching while it bakes is every working mom's best friend! *Magnifico!*   Serves 4

4 (4-ounce) lean tenderized pork tenderloins or cutlets	½ cup (one 2.5-ounce jar) sliced mushrooms, undrained
1 (10¾-ounce) can Healthy Request Tomato Soup	2 tablespoons water
1½ teaspoons Italian seasoning	2 teaspoons dried onion flakes
	¼ cup (1 ounce) sliced ripe olives

Preheat oven to 350 degrees. Spray an 8-by-8-inch baking dish with olive oil–flavored cooking spray. Evenly arrange meat in prepared baking dish. In a medium bowl, combine tomato soup, Italian seasoning, undrained mushrooms, water, onion flakes, and olives. Spoon soup mixture evenly over meat. Cover and bake for 45 minutes. Uncover, and continue baking for 15 minutes, or until meat is tender. When serving, evenly spoon sauce over meat.

Each serving equals:

HE: 3 Protein, ¼ Fat, ¼ Vegetable, ½ Slider, 5 Optional Calories

220 Calories, 8 gm Fat, 26 gm Protein, 11 gm Carbohydrate, 461 mg Sodium, 43 mg Calcium, 1 gm Fiber

DIABETIC: 3 Meat, ½ Starch/Carbohydrate

Deli-Style New York Cheesecake

■ ■ ■

I've traveled all over the country, and I've seen cheesecake on menus just about everywhere, but until you've tasted cheesecake the way it's served in New York City, you haven't had CHEESECAKE! What makes it such a winner? It depends on whom you ask, but I believe it's because it's got a scrumptious crust, a uniquely creamy texture, and a wonderful hint of lemon. I worked hard to get this healthy version just right!

Serves 12

1½ cups purchased graham cracker crumbs or 12 (2½-inch) graham cracker squares, made into crumbs

¼ cup pourable Sugar Twin or Sprinkle Sweet

2 tablespoons reduced-calorie margarine, melted

3 (8-ounce) packages Philadelphia fat-free cream cheese

2 (4-serving) packages JELL-O sugar-free vanilla cook-and-serve pudding mix

1 cup Carnation Nonfat Dry Milk Powder

1 cup water

3 eggs, slightly beaten, or equivalent in egg substitute

½ cup Land O Lakes no-fat sour cream

3 tablespoons lemon juice

2 teaspoons vanilla extract

Preheat oven to 325 degrees. Spray an 8-by-8-inch spring-form pan with butter-flavored cooking spray. In a medium bowl, combine graham cracker crumbs, Sugar Twin, and margarine. Gently press crumbs into prepared pan. In a large bowl, stir cream cheese with a spoon until soft. Add dry pudding mix, dry milk powder, water, and eggs. Mix well using a wire whisk. Blend in sour cream, lemon juice, and vanilla extract. Pour mixture into prepared pan. Gently rotate pan to settle batter. Bake for 50 to 60 minutes or until cake is set 2 inches from the edges, but the center is still pudding-like. Turn oven off, open door, and let cake set in oven for 15 minutes. Place pan on a wire rack and allow to cool completely. Remove sides of pan and refrigerate cake for at least 2 hours. Cut into 12 servings.

HINT: 1. A self-seal sandwich bag works great for crushing graham crackers.
2. When serving, good garnished with 1 tablespoon spreadable fruit and Cool Whip Lite.

Each serving equals:

HE: 1¼ Protein (¼ limited), ⅔ Bread, ¼ Skim Milk, ¼ Fat, 19 Optional Calories

168 Calories, 4 gm Fat, 10 gm Protein, 23 gm Carbohydrate, 433 mg Sodium, 207 mg Calcium, 0 gm Fiber

DIABETIC: 1 Meat, 1 Starch/Carbohydrate, ½ Fat

Raisin Pie (Funeral Pie)

⁕

This very traditional recipe got its name because it was customary to serve it at funerals in the Pennsylvania Dutch country, but I hope you'll consider it for more festive occasions as well. It's light and luscious, made from ingredients you will likely have on hand, and requires very little preparation.   *Serves 8*

1 Pillsbury refrigerated unbaked 9-inch piecrust

1 (4-serving) package JELL-O sugar-free vanilla cook-and-serve pudding mix

1 (4-serving) package JELL-O sugar-free lemon gelatin

2 cups water

1 cup raisins

Let piecrust set at room temperature for 10 minutes. Meanwhile, in a medium saucepan, combine dry pudding mix, dry gelatin, and water. Stir in raisins. Cook over medium heat until mixture thickens and starts to boil, stirring often. Remove from heat. Place saucepan on a wire rack and let set. Cut the piecrust in half on the folded line. Gently roll each half into a ball. Wipe counter with a wet cloth and place a sheet of waxed paper over damp spot. Place one of the balls on the waxed paper. Cover with another piece of waxed paper and roll out into a 9-inch circle, with rolling pin. Carefully remove waxed paper from one side and place crust into an 8-inch pie plate Remove other piece of waxed paper. Evenly spoon pudding mixture into piecrust. Repeat process of rolling out remaining piecrust half. Place second crust over top of pie and flute edges. Make about 8 slashes with a knife to allow steam to escape. Bake at 450 degrees for 10 minutes. Reduce heat to 350 degrees and continue baking for 30 minutes. Place pie plate on a wire rack and allow to cool completely. Cut into 8 servings.

Each serving equals:

HE: 1 Fruit, ½ Bread, ¾ Slider, 5 Optional Calories

191 Calories, 7 gm Fat, 1 gm Protein, 31 gm Carbohydrate, 183 mg Sodium, 10 mg Calcium, 1 gm Fiber

DIABETIC: 1 Fruit, 1 Starch, 1 Fat

Shoo-Fly Pie

■ ■ ■

No one is absolutely sure where this sweet dessert got its name, though most people figure it's called that because the molasses attracted lots of flies! The list of ingredients is intriguing, because it's not all that clear what's *in* this pie's filling, but your tastebuds will be delighted once this pie emerges from your oven. You'll often see this on the menu in restaurants in Pennsylvania's Amish country.

Serves 8

*1 Pillsbury refrigerated unbaked
   9-inch piecrust*
¾ cup all-purpose flour
*½ cup pourable Sugar Twin or
   Sprinkle Sweet*
2 tablespoons Brown Sugar Twin

⅛ teaspoon salt
*2 tablespoons reduced-calorie
   margarine*
½ teaspoon baking soda
⅔ cup hot water
½ cup molasses

Preheat oven to 425 degrees. Place piecrust in a 9-inch pie plate. Flute edges. In a medium bowl, combine flour, Sugar Twin, Brown Sugar Twin, salt, and margarine. Mix with a fork until mixture is crumbly. In a large bowl, dissolve baking soda in water. Stir in molasses. Reserve ¼ cup crumb mixture. Stir remaining crumb mixture into molasses mixture. Pour mixture into prepared piecrust. Evenly sprinkle reserved crumb mixture over top. Bake for 10 minutes. Reduce heat to 350 degrees and continue baking for 20 to 30 minutes or until filling is firm. Place pie plate on a wire rack and allow to cool completely. Cut into 8 servings.

Each serving equals:
HE: 1 Bread, ⅓ Fat, ¾ Slider, 10 Optional Calories

224 Calories, 8 gm Fat, 2 gm Protein, 36 gm Carbohydrate, 258 mg Sodium, 47 mg Calcium, 1 gm Fiber

DIABETIC: 2 Starch/Carbohydrate, 1 Fat

Lady Baltimore Cake

■ ■ ■

Here's a spectacular cake named for one of Maryland's most prominent women of a past century. I found recreating this recipe a real challenge, since the original dessert calls for a boiled frosting just full of sugar. Because Sugar Twin doesn't make a satisfactory syrup, I had to substitute Cool Whip instead. But I'd bet that if Lady Baltimore herself were making this treasured treat today, she'd choose to do it the Healthy Exchanges way! *Serves 12*

1⅓ cups Carnation Nonfat Dry
Milk Powder
1 cup cold water
1 tablespoon white vinegar
1½ cups all-purpose flour
½ cup pourable Sugar Twin or
Sprinkle Sweet
1 teaspoon baking powder

1 teaspoon baking soda
½ cup Kraft fat-free mayonnaise
1 tablespoon vanilla extract ☆
2½ cups Cool Whip Free
¼ cup (1 ounce) chopped pecans
8 maraschino cherries, quartered
¼ cup raisins
¼ cup chopped figs

Preheat oven to 350 degrees. Spray two 9-by-9-inch cake pans with butter-flavored cooking spray. In a small bowl, combine dry milk powder, water, and vinegar. Set aside. In a large bowl, combine flour, Sugar Twin, baking powder, and baking soda. Stir mayonnaise and 2 teaspoons vanilla extract into milk mixture. Add milk mixture to flour mixture. Mix gently to combine. Pour batter into prepared cake pans. Bake for 18 to 22 minutes or until a toothpick inserted in center comes out clean. Place cake pans on wire racks and cool for 10 minutes. Remove cakes from pans and continue to cool completely on wire racks. In a large bowl, combine Cool Whip Free and remaining 1 teaspoon vanilla extract. Add pecans, maraschino cherries, raisins, and figs. Mix gently to combine. To assemble cake, place 1 cake layer on serving plate, spread 1 cup topping mixture over top, arrange remaining cake layer on top, and frost sides and top with remaining topping. Cut into 12 servings. Refrigerate leftovers.

Each serving equals:

HE: ⅔ Bread, ⅓ Skim Milk, ⅓ Fruit, ⅓ Fat, ½ Slider, 2 Optional Calories

146 Calories, 2 gm Fat, 3 gm Protein, 29 gm Carbohydrate, 246 mg Sodium, 80 mg Calcium, 1 gm Fiber

DIABETIC: 2 Starch/Carbohydrate

Belgian Waffles with Cherry Sauce

■ ■ ■

I was raised to believe that waffles were breakfast food, so when I first saw Belgian waffles on a fancy dessert menu, I was intrigued—and very curious about how they were prepared. This is a wonderful choice for a festive occasion, especially when you want to impress the people gathered round the table! It's almost too pretty to eat, but definitely dig in! Take a picture of it if you must, then gobble, gobble it down! *Serves 8*

1 (8-ounce) package Philadelphia fat-free cream cheese

¼ cup + 2 tablespoons pourable Sugar Twin or Sprinkle Sweet ☆

1 tablespoon vanilla extract ☆

1 cup Cool Whip Free

1 (4-serving) package JELL-O sugar-free vanilla cook-and-serve pudding mix

1 (4-serving) package JELL-O sugar-free cherry gelatin

2 cups (one 16-ounce can) tart red cherries, packed in water, drained, and ½ cup liquid reserved

2¼ cups water ☆

½ teaspoon almond extract

4 eggs or equivalent in egg substitute

2 tablespoons reduced-calorie margarine

1 tablespoon Land O Lakes no-fat sour cream

⅔ cup Carnation Nonfat Dry Milk Powder

1½ cups Bisquick Reduced Fat Baking Mix

2 tablespoons (½ ounce) slivered almonds

In a medium bowl, stir cream cheese with a spoon until soft. Stir in ¼ cup Sugar Twin and 1 teaspoon vanilla extract. Add Cool Whip Free. Mix gently to combine. Refrigerate. Meanwhile, in a medium saucepan, combine dry pudding mix, dry gelatin, reserved cherry liquid, and 1½ cups water. Stir in cherries. Cook over medium heat until mixture thickens and starts to boil, stirring often, being careful not to crush the cherries. Remove from heat. Stir in almond extract. Place saucepan on a wire rack while preparing waffles. In a large bowl, combine eggs, margarine, sour cream, and remaining 2 teaspoons vanilla extract. Add dry milk powder and remaining ¾ cup water. Mix well using a wire whisk. Whisk in baking mix and remaining 2 tablespoons Sugar Twin. Bake batter in a Belgian waffle iron according to manufacturer's instructions, making 8 waffles. For each serving, place a waffle on a plate, spread with scant ¼ cup cream cheese filling, spoon about ⅓ cup cherry sauce over top, and garnish with ¾ teaspoon almonds.

Each serving equals:

HE: 1 Bread, 1 Protein (½ limited), ½ Fruit, ½ Fat, ¼ Skim Milk, ½ Slider, 1 Optional Calorie

234 Calories, 6 gm Fat, 12 gm Protein, 33 gm Carbohydrate, 567 mg Sodium, 210 mg Calcium, 1 gm Fiber

DIABETIC: 1½ Starch/Carbohydrate, 1 Meat, ½ Fruit, ½ Fat

Challah

■ ❄ ■

Every time I walked past a Jewish bakery in Manhattan, I just couldn't take my eyes off that beautiful bread called Challah (and pronounced, my friend Barbara tells me, like "Ha"—Ha-lah!) It graces the table every week at Sabbath dinner, and it's as delicious as it looks. I had to figure out the secret of its wonderful texture and its golden crust, so it took a bit of testing before I got it just right. I'm very pleased with the results, and I think you will be too.   *Serves 8*

⅔ cup warm water
1 tablespoon pourable Sugar Twin or Sprinkle Sweet
1 (¼-ounce) package active dry yeast
2 eggs or equivalent in egg substitute ☆
1 tablespoon + 1 teaspoon reduced-calorie margarine, melted

1 teaspoon salt
3 cups all-purpose flour ☆
2 tablespoons cold water
2 teaspoons Sesame seeds (optional)

In a large bowl, combine warm water, Sugar Twin, and dry yeast. Stir just to dissolve yeast. Let set for about 5 minutes or until bubbly. Add 1 egg, margarine, and salt. Mix well using a wire whisk. Whisk in 1 cup flour. Gradually add 1¾ cups flour. Mix well until a soft dough forms. Evenly sprinkle remaining ¼ cup flour on a large piece of aluminum foil. Place dough on floured surface. Knead for 5 to 6 minutes until dough is smooth and elastic. Place dough in a large bowl sprayed with butter-flavored cooking spray. Lightly spray surface of dough. Cover and put in a warm place to rise until dough is doubled, about 1 hour. Punch dough down and divide into 3 large pieces. Roll each piece into a 24-inch-long rope. Loosely braid ropes together, tuck ends under, and pinch to seal. Place on a baking sheet sprayed with butter-flavored cooking spray. Lightly spray top of loaf with butter-flavored cooking spray. Cover and let rise for 40 minutes or until almost doubled. Discard white of remaining egg. In a small bowl, combine egg yolk and water. Brush on top and sides of loaf. Sprinkle sesame seeds over top. Bake in a preheated 375-degree oven for 22 to 26 minutes or until top is lightly browned and bottom sounds

hollow when tapped. Remove loaf from baking sheet and cool on a wire rack. Cut into 8 pieces.

Each serving equals:

HE: 2 Bread, ¼ Protein (limited), ¼ Fat, 2 Optional Calories

199 Calories, 3 gm Fat, 7 gm Protein, 36 gm Carbohydrate, 324 mg Sodium, 21 mg Calcium, 1 gm Fiber

DIABETIC: 2 Starch, ½ Fat

Gnocchi

■ ■ ■

These Italian treats, called "Nyock-ee," are a sort of pasta dumpling, here baked in a cheesy, creamy sauce that's almost too good to be true! My daughter-in-law Pam, who loves fettuccine Alfredo, is the family member I had in mind when I was creating this recipe. I just know she'll love this rich baked entree. Some restaurants serve gnocchi made from potatoes—another tasty idea!   *Serves 8*

⅔ cup *Carnation Nonfat Dry Milk Powder*
¾ cup water
1 tablespoon + 1 teaspoon reduced-calorie margarine
1½ cups all-purpose flour
2 eggs or equivalent in egg substitute
¾ cup (3 ounces) shredded

Kraft reduced-fat Cheddar cheese ☆
⅛ teaspoon black pepper
2 cups boiling water
1 (10¾-ounce) can *Healthy Request Cream of Mushroom Soup*
2 tablespoons *Land O Lakes no-fat sour cream*
1 teaspoon dried parsley flakes

Preheat oven to 350 degrees. Spray an 8-by-8-inch baking dish with butter-flavored cooking spray. In a small bowl, combine dry milk powder and water. Pour mixture into a large saucepan sprayed with butter-flavored cooking spray. Stir in margarine. Cook over medium heat until mixture is hot, but not boiling. Stir in flour, using a wire whisk. Continue cooking for 5 to 6 minutes, stirring constantly. Remove saucepan from heat. Let set for 5 minutes. Add eggs, ¼ cup Cheddar cheese, and black pepper. Mix well to combine. Spread the dough onto a large piece of aluminum foil and cut into 16 pieces. Drop into a large saucepan with boiling water. Cook for 10 minutes. Drain and place pieces in prepared baking dish. In a small bowl, combine mushroom soup, sour cream, remaining ½ cup Cheddar cheese, and parsley flakes. Evenly spoon mixture over Gnocchi and bake for 15 minutes. Divide into 8 servings.

HINT: Be patient—dough is hard to work with.

Each serving equals:
HE: 1 Bread, ¾ Protein (¼ limited), ¼ Skim Milk, ¼ Fat, ¼ Slider, 4 Optional Calories

181 Calories, 5 gm Fat, 9 gm Protein, 25 gm Carbohydrate, 312 mg Sodium, 191 mg Calcium, 1 gm Fiber

DIABETIC: 1½ Starch/Carbohydrate, 1 Meat

Old-Fashioned Scrapple

■ ❄ ■

If you've never heard of scrapple, you're not alone. The dictionary describes it as a kind of mush blended with scraps of meat and broth, then cooked and poured into a mold or pan to set. Later, it's sliced and fried (or in the case of my Healthy Exchanges version, cooked on a griddle sprayed with cooking spray!). It's a good example of how farm wives came up with creative ways to use left-over bits of this and that. I loved testing this recipe, and I think you will be pleasantly surprised at how good it is!

Serves 8

16 ounces ground 90% lean turkey or beef
1¾ cups (one 14½-ounce can) Swanson Beef Broth
1 teaspoon poultry seasoning

½ teaspoon ground sage
½ teaspoon garlic powder
⅛ teaspoon black pepper
¾ cup (4½ ounces) yellow corn-meal

In a medium saucepan, combine meat and beef broth. Bring mixture to a boil. Add poultry seasoning, sage, garlic powder, and black pepper. Mix well to combine. Gradually stir cornmeal into meat mixture, stirring constantly. Lower heat and simmer for 30 minutes, stirring occasionally. Spread mixture into a 9-by-5-inch loaf pan. Cover and refrigerate for at least 6 hours. Cut into 8 slices. Place slices on a hot griddle or large skillet sprayed with butter-flavored cooking spray. Cook for 4 to 6 minutes on each side or until lightly browned.

Each serving equals:
HE: 1½ Protein, ¾ Bread, 4 Optional Calories

145 Calories, 5 gm Fat, 12 gm Protein, 13 gm Carbohydrate, 238 mg Sodium, 3 mg Calcium, 1 gm Fiber

DIABETIC: 1½ Meat, 1 Starch

THE SOUTH

. . .

I first came to know the American South through the cookbooks I collected, and so for me, the notion of Southern hospitality was something I believed in, even if I hadn't yet experienced it for myself. I loved the idea of such a gracious tradition, a world where relatives came to stay for weeks at a time, and meals seemed never ending because of all the visiting that went on across the table!

I envisioned picnics of fried chicken served under willow trees, baked-ham dinners, cornbread and spoon bread and of course grits for breakfast every single day! Luncheon would be served on lovely china, and I could just hear those clinking glasses as neighbors exchanged gossip on a century-old verandah.

At least, that is what I thought Southern cooking was—until I discovered the sizzle and sparkle of Cajun and Creole cuisine that makes Louisiana such a tremendously tasty destination! It was only the beginning of my education in the foods of the South.

The more I read, the more I understood that this part of the nation encompassed many culinary traditions, some inspired by the area's climate and rich soil, which was so welcoming to the growing of crops like corn, rice, sugar, and peanuts (in addition to cotton and tobacco).

I also came to see that much of what was best in Southern cooking developed because of its unique geography and the foods it produced: shellfish "farmed" off the Carolina coast and along the warm curve of the Gulf of Mexico, fish and fowl found in abundance across the region's riverbeds and marshlands, plenty of grazing land for raising cows and hogs for the table. It was, simply, a land of plenty.

Most of all, though, I learned that Southern cooking had everything to do with an attitude, a relaxed sense of having "all the time in the world." Why is it more true across the South than elsewhere in this land? Perhaps it's the area's origins as an agricultural society, where neighbors lived a little too far away to stop by for a quick visit. Instead, every encounter became an occasion to sit back and catch up on everything (accompanied, of course, by a substantial meal!).

Although many of the first settlers of this region came here from England, bringing their customs and traditions with them, other influences were just as strong, especially the French and Spanish who'd first made their homes in Florida or Louisiana but eventually moved inland and across the South.

As years passed, the frontier pushed farther and farther west, into Kentucky and West Virginia, then across Tennessee, and new immigrants arrived to take the places of those who'd first settled in Virginia and Georgia. They came from Scotland and France, Germany and Italy, Ireland and Holland, drawn by dreams of freedom and land for the claiming. As they shared their favorite recipes with neighbors and guests, a kind of cross-pollination began to take place.

This blend of cultures and culinary traditions continued into the 1800s, when more was added to the pot: the flavors of Africa and the West Indies. Over the past two centuries, the mixing of these diverse elements with all the others has produced one of the most intriguing and varied cuisines of anywhere in the world.

In recent years, we've driven across the South a number of times, and I've gotten my best information about Southern recipes by visiting with the people we met, more than by actually visiting restaurants. I always like to learn about what people prepare for themselves and their loved ones at home, and no one is more forthcoming about their favorite dishes than the ladies I was fortunate enough to visit with down there.

We've eaten well wherever we've driven, but the food that most quickly comes to mind from this region is what I would call "Southern green beans." (In this book, I've called my version *Down Home Green Beans*!) They're simmered for ages in their own "likker," or juice, until they're wonderfully soft and mushy. They're often cooked with bits of ham to give them a great smoky flavor, too. Cliff loves his green beans soft, and so he usually orders them for dinner wherever we stop in the South.

Another Southern food both Cliff and I have particularly enjoyed is the baking powder biscuit. None compare to the ones baked in the South, even in the truck stops. They're the best in the world. I think girls learn at their mother's knees how to make them lighter than air!

When I went to New Orleans for my first visit to the IACP convention—that's the International Association of Culinary Professionals—I told myself that for once I should try to be more adventurous. (I'm usually not when it comes to food. Most people who use my recipes appreciate that, since they know I'm not going to recommend quail or squid or caviar!) But, I told myself, why not give a few new foods a taste? So I did. I had a chance to try lots of different foods prepared for us by the chefs of New Orleans, and I have to tell you, they were great. You can eat very well in Cajun and Creole country—all I ask is, just don't pile on the crawdads or spice things up too hot for me.

You may wonder what Creole cooking is, and I did, too. What I discovered is that the Creole people trace their ancestry to the French who settled Louisiana years before the American Revolution. They cooked lots of fish with spices and vegetables, making the most of the region's abundant bounty. Other influences on their cuisine include the region's Choctaw Indians, who taught them to use sassafras leaves to thicken soups and stews, and African slaves, who introduced okra into Creole recipes. Later, the Spanish took over the territory and blended their style of cooking with what already existed. The classic Creole dish is jambalaya, which is a stew quite similar to Spanish paella, a dish that mixes meat and fish with vegetables and spices and is served over rice. (I've created a Healthy Exchanges version that honors this classic without keeping you in the kitchen nearly as long as the original does. Give my *Louisiana Jambalaya* a try!) Creole cooking also made use of my favorite nut, the pecan, turning it into pies and that New Orleans treat, the praline. Here, I've honored that delectable tradition with *Golden Pecan Pie*.

Sweet cooking customs are an intrinsic part of Southern cooking, and you'll discover lots of ways to please your sweet tooth in this group of recipes. After all, in the region that harvested so much sugar cane, how could I be surprised to find beloved recipes for both candied tomatoes and sweet potatoes? (Check out *Deep South Candied Tomatoes* and *Orange-Candied Sweet Potatoes!*)

I'm also very pleased to share such down-home basics as *Red Beans and Rice,* the famous rice-and-black-eyed-peas combination known as *Hoppin' John,* the beloved holiday fruit and coconut salad, *Ambrosia,* and what is possibly Florida's most delicious export to the rest of the country: *Key Lime Pie!*

The warm and hospitable people of the South have always welcomed any excuse for eating well, so you'll find that many of these recipes lend themselves to favorite festive occasions. Whether you've placed a bet on a horse or not, this is a perfect year for a Kentucky Derby party. And oh what delightful brunches and Sunday suppers you're set to "throw," now that you've got tasty, healthy recipes for grits and country ham, not to mention the decadently sweet Southern dessert inspired by Bananas Foster.

Here's my suggestion: Just do as they do all over the South—celebrate with friends and family anytime at all the simple joy of being together!

THE SOUTH RECIPES

Vegetable Cheese Bisque

Plantation Bean Soup

Peanut Soup

Jean Lafitte Salad

Crunchy Carrot Fruit Salad

Confetti Veggie Bites

Down-Home Green Beans

Dixie Carrot Casserole

Fresh Tomato Custard

Deep South Candied Tomatoes

Southern Corn Pudding

Orange-Candied Sweet Potatoes

Hoppin' John

Red Beans and Rice

Dixie Grits Casserole

Brunswick Stew

Derby Day Burgoo

Pulled-Pork Sandwiches

Glazed Country Ham

Louisiana Jambalaya

Creole Wieners

Ambrosia

Good-for-You Bananas Foster

Chocolate Sunrise Pudding Treats

Coconut Pudding

Southern Delight Rice Pudding

Raisin Bread Pudding with Rum
Sauce

Sponge Cake Meringues

Key Lime Pie

Golden Pecan Pie

Dixie Peach Crumb Pie

Peach Praline Custard Pie

Coconut Cake with Coconut
Frosting

Kentucky Scramble

Dropped "Buttermilk" Biscuits

Mammy's Cornbread

Southern Buttermilk Spoon Bread

Vegetable Cheese Bisque

■ ■ ■

Maybe it's the gracious way of life that goes back hundreds of years, or perhaps it's the often sultry climate, but when soup is served in the South, it always feels like a special occasion, a time to linger and savor every sip and bite. This creamy bisque rolls over the tastebuds like silk.

Serves 4 (1 full cup)

2 cups Healthy Request tomato
   juice or any reduced-sodium
   tomato juice
2 tablespoons dried onion flakes
1 cup thinly sliced celery
1 cup shredded carrots

1 (10¾-ounce) can Healthy
   Request Tomato Soup
1 cup skim milk
¾ cup (3 ounces) shredded Kraft
   reduced-fat Cheddar cheese
1 teaspoon dried parsley flakes

In a large saucepan, combine tomato juice, onion flakes, celery, and carrots. Cook over medium heat for 10 to 12 minutes or until vegetables are tender. Stir in tomato soup, skim milk, Cheddar cheese, and parsley flakes. Lower heat and simmer for 6 to 8 minutes or until mixture is heated through and cheese melts, stirring often.

Each serving equals:
HE: 2 Vegetable, 1 Protein, ¼ Skim Milk, ½ Slider, 5 Optional Calories
168 Calories, 4 gm Fat, 10 gm Protein, 23 gm Carbohydrate, 557 mg Sodium, 272 mg Calcium, 2 gm Fiber
DIABETIC: 2 Vegetable, 1 Meat, ½ Starch/Carbohydrate

Plantation Bean Soup

■ ■ ■

Many of the great old houses throughout the South still boast grand kitchens where a huge pot of soup simmering away for hours would look right at home! Because this hearty bean soup uses canned beans instead of dried, you get to skip the soaking step (whew!) and can serve this meal-in-a-bowl less than an hour after you start chopping those onions!   *Serves 6 (1½ cups)*

20 ounces (two 16-ounce cans) great northern beans, rinsed and drained

1 full cup (6 ounces) diced Dubuque 97% fat-free ham or any extra-lean ham

1 cup chopped onion

1 cup chopped celery

2 cups (10 ounces) diced raw potatoes

1 cup peeled and chopped fresh turnips

4 cups water

⅛ teaspoon black pepper

In a large saucepan, combine great northern beans, ham, onion, celery, potatoes, and turnips. Add water and black pepper. Mix well to combine. Bring mixture to a boil. Lower heat and simmer for 30 minutes or until vegetables are tender, stirring occasionally.

Each serving equals:

HE: 2⅓ Protein, 1 Vegetable, ⅓ Bread

166 Calories, 2 gm Fat, 12 gm Protein, 25 gm Carbohydrate, 459 mg Sodium, 23 mg Calcium, 7 gm Fiber

DIABETIC: 1½ Meat, 1 Vegetable, 1 Starch

Peanut Soup

■ ❋ ■

Most Americans think of peanuts solely as a snack food, but they contain a sur-prising amount of protein in every bite! Here, it takes only a small portion of nuts to give this creamy chicken-based soup a rich and peanutty flavor. I've always loved peanut butter, so I thought I'd enjoy a cup of this soup, but I was delighted to discover how delicate the flavor is.   *Serves 6 (⅔ cup)*

½ cup (2 ounces) chopped
  dry-roasted peanuts
1 cup chopped carrots
¾ cup chopped celery
¼ cup chopped green onion
1 (10¾-ounce) can Healthy
  Request Cream of Chicken
  Soup

1½ cups (one 12-fluid-ounce can)
  Carnation Evaporated Skim
  Milk
1 tablespoon chopped fresh
  parsley or 1 teaspoon dried
  parsley flakes
¼ teaspoon dried minced garlic

In a large saucepan sprayed with butter-flavored cooking spray, sauté peanuts, carrots, celery, and green onion for 6 to 8 minutes. Stir in chicken soup and evaporated skim milk. Add parsley and garlic. Mix well to combine. Lower heat and simmer for 10 to 12 minutes, stirring occasionally.

Each serving equals:
HE: ⅔ Fat, ⅔ Vegetable, ½ Skim Milk, ⅓ Protein, ¼ Slider,
10 Optional Calories

149 Calories, 5 gm Fat, 9 gm Protein, 17 gm Carbohydrate, 287 mg Sodium,
212 mg Calcium, 2 gm Fiber

DIABETIC: 1 Fat, ½ Vegetable, ½ Skim Milk, ½ Starch/Carbohydrate

Jean Lafitte Salad

■ ■ ■

The legendary pirate made his home near New Orleans, but rumor is, he left buried treasure on islands all along the coast of Louisiana. Here's one treasure you won't need a map to find, a culinary catch that's perfect for your meat-and-potatoes men.

Serves 4 (1 cup)

½ cup *Kraft Fat Free French Dressing*

½ cup *Kraft fat-free mayonnaise*

2 tablespoons sweet pickle relish

1 cup (5 ounces) diced cooked lean roast beef

1½ cups (8 ounces) diced cooked potatoes

1 cup (one 8-ounce can) sliced carrots, rinsed and drained

1 cup (one 8-ounce can) cut green beans, rinsed and drained

1 hard-boiled egg, chopped

In a large bowl, combine French dressing, mayonnaise, and pickle relish. Add roast beef, potatoes, carrots, and green beans. Mix well to combine. Fold in chopped egg. Cover and refrigerate for at least 15 minutes. Gently stir again just before serving.

HINT: 1. If you don't have leftovers, purchase a chunk of lean cooked roast beef from your local deli or use Healthy Choice Deli slices.

2. If you want the look and feel of egg without the cholesterol, toss out the yolk and dice the white.

Each serving equals:

HE: 1½ Protein (¼ limited), 1 Vegetable, ½ Bread, ¾ Slider, 18 Optional Calories

216 Calories, 4 gm Fat, 14 gm Protein, 31 gm Carbohydrate, 659 mg Sodium, 44 mg Calcium, 4 gm Fiber

DIABETIC: 1½ Meat, 1½ Starch/Carbohydrate, 1 Vegetable

Crunchy Carrot Fruit Salad

■ ■ ■

Just like the soft voice of a true Southern belle, this carrot salad is sweet and a little bit seductive! It's cool, creamy, and crunchy all at once, blending elements together in such a way as to make each one more delectable—not unlike the combination of moonlight and magnolias in a lady's smile!   *Serves 6 (½ cup)*

¼ cup Kraft fat-free mayonnaise
¼ cup Land O Lakes no-fat sour cream
2 cups shredded carrots
1 cup (one 11-ounce can) mandarin oranges, rinsed and drained

½ cup raisins
3 tablespoons (¾ ounce) chopped pecans

In a large bowl, combine mayonnaise and sour cream. Add carrots, mandarin oranges, and raisins. Mix gently to combine. Stir in pecans. Cover and refrigerate for at least 30 minutes. Gently stir again just before serving.

HINT: To plump up raisins without "cooking," place in a glass measuring cup and microwave on HIGH for 20 seconds.

Each serving equals:
HE: 1 Fruit, ⅔ Vegetable, ½ Fat, 17 Optional Calories
106 Calories, 2 gm Fat, 1 gm Protein, 21 gm Carbohydrate, 113 mg Sodium, 30 mg Calcium, 1 gm Fiber
DIABETIC: 1 Fruit, ½ Vegetable, ½ Fat

Confetti Veggie Bites

■ ■ ■

Gone with the Wind was probably my first introduction to Southern hospitality. I loved reading about the house parties and barbecues that were so much a part of plantation social life before the Civil War began. The people of the South still take great pleasure in entertaining and would surely put these tasty morsels on the menu!

Serves 12 (3 each)

1 (8-ounce) can Pillsbury Reduced Fat Crescent Rolls

1 (8-ounce) package Philadelphia fat-free cream cheese

¼ cup Kraft fat-free mayonnaise

2 tablespoons dried basil leaves

1½ cups diced fresh tomatoes

1 cup diced unpeeled cucumbers

½ cup chopped red onion

¾ cup (3 ounces) shredded Kraft reduced-fat mozzarella cheese

Preheat oven to 350 degrees. Pat crescent rolls into an ungreased 9-by-15-inch rimmed baking sheet. Gently press dough to cover bottom of pan, being sure to seal perforations. Bake for 10 to 12 minutes or until golden brown. Place baking sheet on a wire rack and allow to cool. Meanwhile, in a medium bowl, stir cream cheese with a spoon until soft. Stir in mayonnaise and basil leaves. Spread mixture over partially cooled crust. Evenly sprinkle tomatoes, cucumbers, and onion over cream cheese mixture. Sprinkle mozzarella cheese evenly over top. Refrigerate for at least 30 minutes. Cut into 36 pieces.

Each serving equals:

HE: ⅔ Bread, ⅔ Protein, ½ Vegetable, 4 Optional Calories

108 Calories, 4 gm Fat, 6 gm Protein, 12 gm Carbohydrate, 361 mg Sodium, 50 mg Calcium, 0 gm Fiber

DIABETIC: 1 Starch, 1 Meat, ½ Vegetable

Down-Home Green Beans

■ ■ ■

Cliff has probably eaten green beans in every state of the union except for Alaska, but even he agrees that Southern green bean recipes are extra-special! This blend of ham, onion, and potatoes delivers rich and hearty flavor, sure to please the most ravenous appetites. With dishes like this, the South is sure to "rise again"!

Serves 4 (1½ cups)

4 cups fresh or frozen cut green beans
1 full cup (6 ounces) diced Dubuque 97% fat-free ham or any extra-lean ham

½ cup chopped onion
3 cups water
2 cups (10 ounces) diced unpeeled red potatoes
⅛ teaspoon black pepper

In a large saucepan, combine beans, ham, onion, and water. Bring mixture to a boil. Stir in potatoes and black pepper. Lower heat and simmer for 40 to 50 minutes or until vegetables are tender and most of liquid is absorbed, stirring occasionally.

Each serving equals:
HE: 2¼ Vegetable, 1 Protein, ½ Bread

154 Calories, 2 gm Fat, 12 gm Protein, 22 gm Carbohydrate, 46 mg Sodium, 66 mg Calcium, 5 gm Fiber

DIABETIC: 2 Vegetable, 1 Meat, 1 Starch

Dixie Carrot Casserole

■ ❋ ■

Here's a dish that will easily have your family singing for their supper—and checking the timer to see when it's time for this cheesy casserole to emerge from the oven all bubbling and brown! If they tend to push veggies aside, this celebration of carrots will make sure they get the nutrition they need!   *Serves 6*

½ cup chopped onion
4 cups (two 16-ounce cans) sliced
* carrots, rinsed and drained*
1 (10¾-ounce) can Healthy
* Request Cream of Celery Soup*
¾ cup (3 ounces) shredded Kraft
* reduced-fat Cheddar cheese*

1½ cups (2¼ ounces) unseasoned
* dry bread cubes*
2 teaspoons dried parsley flakes
¼ cup skim milk
⅛ teaspoon black pepper

Preheat oven to 350 degrees. Spray an 8-by-8-inch baking dish with butter-flavored cooking spray. In a large skillet sprayed with butter-flavored cooking spray, sauté onion for 5 minutes. Add carrots, celery soup, and Cheddar cheese. Mix well to combine. Continue cooking for 3 to 4 minutes or until cheese starts to melt, stirring occasionally. Spread mixture into prepared baking dish. In a medium bowl, combine bread cubes, parsley flakes, skim milk, and black pepper. Mix just until cubes are moistened. Evenly sprinkle mixture over carrot mixture. Lightly spray top with butter-flavored cooking spray. Bake for 20 to 25 minutes. Place baking dish on a wire rack and let set for 5 minutes. Divide into 6 servings.

HINT: Pepperidge Farm bread cubes work great.

Each serving equals:
HE: 1½ Vegetable, ⅔ Protein, ½ Bread, ¼ Slider, 11 Optional Calories
95 Calories, 3 gm Fat, 5 gm Protein, 12 gm Carbohydrate, 527 mg Sodium, 173 mg Calcium, 2 gm Fiber
DIABETIC: 1½ Vegetable, ½ Meat, ½ Starch

Fresh Tomato Custard

■ ■ ■

When your tomato harvest is at its height, here's a splendid way to celebrate the glories of those rosy globes! From the region that brought us such delights as fried green tomatoes, here's another way to make eating your vegetables a cause for excitement.

Serves 6

2½ cups peeled and sliced fresh tomatoes ☆

1 cup chopped onion

1 cup diced green bell pepper

⅔ cup Carnation Nonfat Dry Milk Powder

1 cup water

3 eggs or equivalent in egg substitute

1 cup + 2 tablespoons (4½ ounces) shredded Kraft reduced-fat Cheddar cheese

1 teaspoon dried basil

⅛ teaspoon black pepper

Preheat oven to 350 degrees. Spray an 8-by-12-inch baking dish with butter-flavored cooking spray. Reserve 6 tomato slices. Evenly arrange remaining slices in prepared baking dish, overlapping as necessary. In a large skillet sprayed with butter-flavored cooking spray, sauté onion and green pepper for 5 minutes. Remove from heat. In a large bowl, combine dry milk powder and water. Add eggs. Mix well to combine. Stir in Cheddar cheese, basil, black pepper, and onion mixture. Spoon egg mixture evenly over tomatoes. Evenly top with reserved tomato slices. Bake for 45 to 50 minutes or until a knife inserted near center comes out clean. Place baking dish on a wire rack and let set for 5 minutes. Divide into 6 servings.

Each serving equals:

HE: 1½ Protein (½ limited), 1½ Vegetable, ⅓ Skim Milk

158 Calories, 6 gm Fat, 14 gm Protein, 12 gm Carbohydrate, 81 mg Sodium, 200 mg Calcium, 2 gm Fiber

DIABETIC: 1½ Vegetable, 1 Meat

Deep South Candied Tomatoes

■ ■ ■

Sure, they *could* serve plain old tomatoes in this region of warm sun and relaxed meals, but why settle for plain when you can eat your veggies stirred up sweet and slow? The ingredients are simple, the work is easy, and the flavor is down-right delectable!

Serves 6

¾ cup finely chopped onion
3 cups (one 28-ounce can)
   tomatoes, chopped and
   undrained
½ cup pourable Sugar Twin or
   Sprinkle Sweet

¼ cup Brown Sugar Twin
¼ teaspoon chili seasoning
⅛ teaspoon black pepper
3 slices reduced-calorie white
   bread, made into small
   crumbs

Preheat oven to 350 degrees. Spray an 8-by-8-inch baking dish with butter-flavored cooking spray. In a large skillet sprayed with butter-flavored cooking spray, sauté onion for 5 minutes. Add undrained tomatoes, Sugar Twin, Brown Sugar Twin, chili seasoning and black pepper. Mix well to combine. Continue cooking for 6 to 8 minutes, stirring occasionally. Spoon hot mixture into pre-pared baking dish. Sprinkle bread crumbs evenly over top. Lightly spray with butter-flavored cooking spray. Bake for 25 to 30 minutes or until crumbs are browned. Place baking dish on a wire rack and let set for 5 minutes. Divide into 6 servings.

Each serving equals:
HE: 1¼ Vegetable, ¼ Bread, 12 Optional Calories
56 Calories, 0 gm Fat, 2 gm Protein, 12 gm Carbohydrate, 240 mg Sodium, 57 mg Calcium, 3 gm Fiber
DIABETIC: 1 Vegetable, ½ Starch/Carbohydrate

Southern Corn Pudding

■ ❋ ■

Corn pudding has been a staple in the Midwest for as long as anyone can remember, but it's also a popular dish when it's served down South. This version is a bit creamier and a bit sweeter than the basic recipe, and even an Iowan like myself enjoyed this fresh take on a beloved favorite. *Serves 6*

2 eggs or equivalent in egg substitute

1½ cups (one 12-fluid-ounce can) Carnation Evaporated Skim Milk

2 tablespoons Land O Lakes no-fat sour cream

1 teaspoon dried parsley flakes

1 tablespoon pourable Sugar Twin or Sprinkle Sweet

⅛ teaspoon black pepper

2½ cups frozen whole-kernel corn, thawed

7 small fat-free saltine crackers, made into fine crumbs

Preheat oven to 350 degrees. Spray an 8-by-8-inch baking dish with butter-flavored cooking spray. In a large bowl, combine eggs, evaporated skim milk, and sour cream. Stir in parsley flakes, Sugar Twin, and black pepper. Add corn. Mix well to combine. Spread mixture into prepared baking dish. Evenly sprinkle cracker crumbs over top. Lightly spray crumbs with butter-flavored cooking spray. Bake for 40 to 45 minutes. Place baking dish on a wire rack and let set for 5 minutes. Divide into 6 servings.

HINT: 1. Thaw corn by placing in a colander and rinsing under hot water for one minute.
2. A self-seal sandwich bag works great for crushing crackers.

Each serving equals:
HE: 1 Bread, ½ Skim Milk, ⅓ Protein (limited), 6 Optional Calories
158 Calories, 2 gm Fat, 10 gm Protein, 25 gm Carbohydrate, 140 mg Sodium, 207 mg Calcium, 2 gm Fiber
DIABETIC: 1 Starch, ½ Skim Milk

Orange-Candied Sweet Potatoes

■ ❄ ■

I'm not sure if the tradition of eating sweet potatoes topped with marshmallows originated in the Deep South or somewhere else in America, but a taste for making the already sweet even sweeter had to have come from there! Even if you've been making this dish for holiday meals, I urge you to try this festive and fruity version. Yum!

Serves 6

3½ cups (18 ounces) sliced
   cooked sweet potatoes
2 tablespoons reduced-calorie
   margarine
¼ cup orange marmalade
   spreadable fruit

2 tablespoons Brown Sugar Twin
¾ cup (1½ ounces) miniature
   marshmallows

Preheat oven to 375 degrees. Spray an 8-by-8-inch baking dish with butter-flavored cooking spray. Evenly arrange sweet potatoes in prepared baking dish. Using a teaspoon, dot potatoes with margarine. In a small bowl, combine spreadable fruit and Brown Sugar Twin. Stir in marshmallows. Spread mixture evenly over top. Bake for 30 minutes. Place baking dish on a wire rack and let set for 5 minutes. Divide into 6 servings.

Each serving equals:

HE: 1 Bread, ⅔ Fruit, ½ Fat, 14 Optional Calories

149 Calories, 1 gm Fat, 1 gm Protein, 34 gm Carbohydrate, 69 mg Sodium, 23 mg Calcium, 1 gm Fiber

DIABETIC: 1 Starch, 1 Fruit, ½ Fat

Hoppin' John

■ ❄ ■

More than one Southern chef has laid claim to the title of the true Hoppin' John, and there's even a restaurant in the Carolinas by that name. Some say he was a plantation cook with a lame leg, and another story calls any Hoppin' John leftovers "Skipping Jenny" after his skipping wife. But whoever the creator was behind this tangy blend of bacon, rice, and black-eyed peas, he surely deserves a place in cookbook heaven!   *Serves 4 (¾ cup)*

1 cup chopped onion
1 cup water
⅔ cup (2 ounces) uncooked
  Minute Rice
¼ cup Hormel Bacon Bits

¼ teaspoon Tabasco sauce
10 ounces (one 16-ounce can)
  black-eyed peas or pinto
  beans, rinsed and drained

In a large saucepan sprayed with butter-flavored cooking spray, sauté onion for 5 minutes. Stir in water, uncooked rice, bacon bits, and Tabasco sauce. Bring mixture to a boil. Lower heat, cover, and simmer for 15 minutes. Stir in peas. Continue simmering for 6 to 8 minutes or until mixture is heated through, stirring often.

Each serving equals:
HE: 1¼ Protein, ½ Bread, ½ Vegetable, ¼ Slider, 5 Optional Calories

146 Calories, 2 gm Fat, 8 gm Protein, 24 gm Carbohydrate, 466 mg Sodium, 26 mg Calcium, 3 gm Fiber

DIABETIC: 1 Meat, 1 Starch, ½ Vegetable

Red Beans and Rice

■ ❋ ■

It's simple, it's just about as cheap as food can be, and it's a mainstay on menus across the South especially in Louisiana (or as they say, "Loos-iana"!). Red Beans and Rice is a terrific basic to have in your recipe repertoire. Even when you think you've got nothing in the house for supper, you've probably got the makings of this in your cupboard. Another fun fact: Red beans and rice are what is known as a complete protein, so you don't have to worry about not having meat for your meal; this dish provides all the amino acids you need.

Serves 4

½ cup chopped onion
½ cup chopped green bell pepper
1 cup (one 8-ounce can) Hunt's
    Tomato Sauce
½ teaspoon dried minced garlic
2 tablespoons Hormel Bacon
    Bits

10 ounces (one 16-ounce can) red
    kidney beans or pinto beans,
    rinsed and drained
2 cups hot cooked rice

In a large skillet sprayed with butter-flavored cooking spray, sauté onion and green pepper for 5 minutes or until tender. Stir in tomato sauce, garlic, bacon bits, and kidney beans. Bring mixture to a boil. Lower heat and simmer for 6 to 8 minutes. For each serving, place ½ cup rice on a plate and spoon ½ cup bean mixture over top.

HINT: 1⅓ cups uncooked instant rice usually cooks to about 2 cups.

Each serving equals:
HE: 1½ Vegetable, 1¼ Protein, 1 Bread, 12 Optional Calories
209 Calories, 1 gm Fat, 10 gm Protein, 40 gm Carbohydrate, 499 mg Sodium, 21 mg Calcium, 8 gm Fiber
DIABETIC: 2 Starch, 1 Meat, 1 Vegetable

Dixie Grits Casserole

■ ❋ ■

When you stop for breakfast in truck stops south of the Mason-Dixon line, you're bound to be offered grits with your eggs, grits with your waffles, and grits with your toast. Why? Because down there a breakfast without grits is no breakfast worth mentioning! If plain old grits don't tickle your ivories, try this delicious casserole that turns a simple grain into a star! *Serves 6*

3 cups hot water
1 cup quick cooking grits
1½ cups (6 ounces) shredded
   Kraft reduced-fat Cheddar
   cheese
2 tablespoons reduced-calorie
   margarine

¼ teaspoon dried minced garlic
¼ teaspoon Tabasco sauce
2 eggs or equivalent in egg
   substitute
¼ cup skim milk

Preheat oven to 350 degrees. Spray an 8-by-8-inch baking dish with butter-flavored cooking spray. In a large saucepan, bring water to a boil. Slowly stir grits into boiling water. Lower heat and simmer for 6 minutes, stirring often. Remove saucepan from heat and fold in Cheddar cheese. Stir in margarine, garlic, and Tabasco sauce. In a small bowl, combine eggs and skim milk. Add milk mixture to grits mixture. Mix well to combine. Spread mixture into prepared baking dish. Bake for 55 to 60 minutes or until golden brown. Place baking dish on a wire rack and let set for 10 minutes. Divide into 6 servings.

Each serving equals:
HE: 1⅔ Protein (⅓ limited), 1 Bread, ½ Fat, 4 Optional Calories
225 Calories, 9 gm Fat, 14 gm Protein, 22 gm Carbohydrate, 73 mg Sodium, 250 mg Calcium, 1 gm Fiber
DIABETIC: 1½ Starch, 1 Meat, ½ Fat

Brunswick Stew

■ ❄ ■

This recipe gets its name from Brunswick County, North Carolina—or so they say. The folks in Brunswick, Georgia, also claim this stew as theirs. And other places have insisted it was inspired by their hometowns. No matter who created it, it now belongs to everyone, and that's as it should be! Legend says the original featured squirrel, but these days it's prepared with chicken and lots of hearty vegetables. It's a sturdy stew, perfect for large gatherings and buffet parties, where it may sit for hours without losing its pizzazz.

Serves 6 (1¾ cups)

2 cups (one 16-ounce can) Healthy Request Chicken Broth

2 full cups (12 ounces) diced cooked chicken breast

1 cup chopped celery

½ cup chopped onion

¼ teaspoon dried minced garlic

2 cups (one 16-ounce can) tomatoes, chopped and undrained

2 cups (10 ounces) diced raw potatoes

1 cup (one 8-ounce can) Hunt's Tomato Sauce

2 cups frozen whole-kernel corn, thawed

2 cups frozen green lima beans, thawed

1 tablespoon pourable Sugar Twin or Sprinkle Sweet

½ teaspoon dried thyme

⅛ teaspoon black pepper

In a large saucepan, combine chicken broth, chicken breast, celery, onion, and garlic. Bring mixture to a boil. Stir in undrained tomatoes, potatoes, and tomato sauce. Lower heat, cover, and simmer for 10 minutes. Add corn, lima beans, Sugar Twin, thyme, and black pepper. Mix well to combine. Continue to simmer for 10 minutes, stirring occasionally.

HINT: 1. If you don't have leftovers, purchase a chunk of cooked chicken breast from your local deli.
2. Thaw corn and lima beans by placing in a colander and rinsing under hot water for one minute.

Each serving equals:

HE: 2½ Vegetable, 2 Protein, 1 Bread, 5 Optional Calories

275 Calories, 3 gm Fat, 25 gm Protein, 37 gm Carbohydrate, 666 mg Sodium, 71 mg Calcium, 7 gm Fiber

DIABETIC: 2 Meat, 1½ Vegetable, 1½ Starch/Carbohydrate

Derby Day Burgoo

■ ■ ■

Even if you've never seen a horse race, it's hard to ignore the glamour and ritual of Kentucky Derby Day! Food is a big part of the annual tradition, and a meaty stew called a burgoo is often served. What's a burgoo? The word's origins are unknown, but this savory dish that's chock-full of meat and veggies has been served at political rallies, community picnics, and major occasions for decades.

Serves 6 (1½ cups)

8 ounces skinned and boned
  uncooked chicken breasts, cut
  into 18 pieces
8 ounces lean round steak, cut
  into 18 pieces
8 ounces lean pork tenderloin,
  cut into 18 pieces
2 cups (one 16-ounce can)
  Healthy Request Chicken
  Broth
2 cups (one 16-ounce can) tomatoes, chopped and undrained

2 teaspoons Worcestershire sauce
⅛ teaspoon black pepper
1 cup frozen whole-kernel corn,
  thawed
1 cup (5 ounces) diced raw
  potatoes
½ cup chopped green bell pepper
1½ cups frozen sliced carrots,
  thawed
1 cup chopped onion
1 cup frozen green lima beans,
  thawed

In a large saucepan sprayed with butter-flavored cooking spray, sauté chicken, steak, and tenderloin pieces for 6 to 8 minutes. Stir in chicken broth, undrained tomatoes, Worcestershire sauce, and black pepper. Add corn, potatoes, green pepper, carrots, onion, and lima beans. Mix well to combine. Bring mixture to a boil. Lower heat, cover, and simmer for 45 to 50 minutes, stirring occasionally.

HINT: Thaw corn, carrots, and lima beans by placing in a colander and rinsing under hot water for one minute.

Each serving equals:
HE: 3 Protein, 2 Vegetable, ½ Bread, 5 Optional Calories
240 Calories, 4 gm Fat, 29 gm Protein, 22 gm Carbohydrate, 402 mg Sodium, 50 mg Calcium, 4 gm Fiber
DIABETIC: 3 Meat, 1 Vegetable, 1 Starch

Pulled-Pork Sandwiches

■ ❄ ■

The expression "pulled pork" simply means that the meat has been cooked so long and is so soft and tender that it can actually be pulled off the bone! Served all over the South and at barbecue restaurants everywhere, these sandwiches are made with large, fresh buns and taste oh-so-smoky-good! *Serves 6*

24 ounces lean cooked roast pork
1 cup Heinz Light Harvest
    Ketchup or any reduced-
    sodium ketchup
2 tablespoons water

1½ teaspoons Tabasco sauce
1 teaspoon dried minced garlic
1 teaspoon dried parsley flakes
6 reduced-calorie hamburger
    buns

Shred pork roast using a knife. In a large skillet sprayed with butter-flavored cooking spray, combine ketchup, water, Tabasco sauce, garlic, and parsley flakes. Stir in shredded pork. Cook over medium-low heat for 8 to 10 minutes or until mixture is heated through, stirring occasionally. For each sandwich, spoon about ⅔ cup meat filling into a hamburger bun.

Each serving equals:

HE: 4 Protein, 1 Bread, ½ Slider

270 Calories, 6 gm Fat, 34 gm Protein, 20 gm Carbohydrate, 538 mg Sodium, 10 mg Calcium, 1 gm Fiber

DIABETIC: 4 Meat, 1½ Starch/Carbohydrate

Glazed Country Ham

■ ■ ■

Baking a ham can be a time-consuming undertaking, so many families enjoy the "real thing" only a few times a year. But with this easy recipe, the sweet and tangy flavors of a true country ham meal can be yours just about anytime at all! I think this glaze is good enough to serve to a Southerner, and that's saying a lot!

Serves 12

1 (3-pound) Dubuque 97% fat-
   free ham or any extra-lean ham
½ cup unsweetened apple juice
½ cup apricot spreadable fruit

2 tablespoons Grey Poupon
   Dijon Country Mustard
1 teaspoon dried parsley flakes

Preheat oven to 350 degrees. Spray an 8-by-8-inch baking dish with butter-flavored cooking spray. Evenly arrange ham in prepared baking dish. In a small bowl, combine apple juice, spreadable fruit, mustard, and parsley flakes. Evenly spread glaze mixture over ham. Bake for 30 minutes, basting occasionally. Place baking dish on a wire rack and let set for 5 minutes. Cut into 12 (⅓-inch) slices.

Each serving equals:

HE: 2⅔ Protein, ¾ Fruit

148 Calories, 4 gm Fat, 18 gm Protein, 10 gm Carbohydrate, 820 mg Sodium, 1 mg Calcium, 0 gm Fiber

DIABETIC: 3 Meat, 1 Fruit

Louisiana Jambalaya

■ ✳ ■

If you can't decide what to have for dinner in New Orleans, this spicy hodge-podge of rice, seafood, and veggies is always a winner! Of course, Cliff is likely to pour half a bottle of Tabasco on his food, while I'm the wimp who would rather savor the natural flavors of this dish's fresh ingredients. I created this recipe for my comfort level, but you can add hot sauce if you want to!

Serves 6 (1½ cups)

3 cups (one 28-ounce can) tomatoes, finely chopped and undrained
1 cup water
1 cup (3 ounces) uncooked Minute Rice
¾ cup finely chopped onion
¾ teaspoon dried thyme

¼ teaspoon dried minced garlic
1½ cups (9 ounces) diced Dubuque 97% fat-free ham or any extra-lean ham
1½ cups frozen peas, thawed
1 (6-ounce package) frozen shrimp
1 tablespoon dried parsley flakes

In a large skillet, combine undrained tomatoes, water, uncooked rice, and onion. Stir in thyme and garlic. Bring mixture to a boil. Lower heat, cover, and simmer for 15 minutes, stirring occasionally. Add ham, peas, shrimp, and parsley flakes. Mix well to combine. Re-cover and continue simmering for 6 to 8 minutes or until mixture is heated through and shrimp is cooked, stirring occasionally.

HINT: 1. Thaw peas and shrimp by placing in a colander and rinsing under hot water for one minute.
2. Canned shrimp, rinsed and drained, may be substituted for frozen.

Each serving equals:
HE: 2 Protein, 1¼ Vegetable, 1 Bread
174 Calories, 2 gm Fat, 15 gm Protein, 24 gm Carbohydrate, 620 mg Sodium, 65 mg Calcium, 4 gm Fiber
DIABETIC: 2 Meat, 1 Vegetable, 1 Starch

Creole Wieners

■ ■ ■

The special charm of Creole food is in its unique blend of cultures. But this lively Louisiana culinary tradition isn't about heat—it's about layers of flavor that seem to deepen as the ingredients embrace ever closer. The inspiration for this recipe might have used andouille or even alligator sausage, but I don't go in for such exotic stuff, so tasty frankfurters will have to do!   *Serves 4*

1 cup finely chopped onion
½ cup finely chopped green bell
  pepper
8 ounces Healthy Choice 97%
  fat-free frankfurters, chopped
2 cups (one 16-ounce can) tomatoes, chopped and undrained

1 teaspoon Worcestershire sauce
1 teaspoon dried parsley flakes
1 tablespoon Brown Sugar Twin
2 tablespoons Hormel Bacon
  Bits
2 cups hot cooked rice

In a large skillet sprayed with butter-flavored cooking spray, sauté onion, green pepper, and frankfurters for 6 to 8 minutes. Stir in undrained tomatoes, Worcestershire sauce, parsley flakes, and Brown Sugar Twin. Add bacon bits. Mix well to combine. Lower heat and simmer for 5 minutes, stirring occasionally. For each serving, place ½ cup rice on a plate and spoon about ¾ cup sauce over top.

HINT: 1⅓ cups uncooked instant rice usually cooks to about 2 cups.

Each serving equals:
HE: 1¾ Vegetable, 1⅓ Protein, 1 Bread, 14 Optional Calories
198 Calories, 2 gm Fat, 13 gm Protein, 32 gm Carbohydrate, 838 mg Sodium, 38 mg Calcium, 2 gm Fiber
DIABETIC: 1½ Vegetable, 1½ Meat, 1 Starch

Ambrosia

■ ■ ■

This appealing fruit salad with a tropical accent has been around for nearly half a century, but it still has star quality so many years later! Children seem to love its melange of festive flavors, but I never yet met a man who didn't smile when a dish of this "food of the goods" was placed before him. *Serves 4*

1 cup (one 8-ounce can) pineapple chunks, packed in fruit juice, undrained
1 teaspoon coconut extract
2 (medium-sized) oranges, peeled, seeded, and cut into chunks

1 cup (1 medium) sliced banana
2 tablespoons flaked coconut

In a medium bowl, combine undrained pineapple and coconut extract. Stir in orange chunks and sliced banana. Evenly spoon mixture into 4 dessert dishes. Top each with 1½ teaspoons coconut.

HINT: To prevent banana from turning brown, mix with 1 teaspoon lemon juice or sprinkle with Fruit Fresh.

Each serving equals:
HE: 1½ Fruit, 8 Optional Calories
93 Calories, 1 gm Fat, 1 gm Protein, 20 gm Carbohydrate, 7 mg Sodium, 31 mg Calcium, 3 gm Fiber
DIABETIC: 1½ Fruit

Good-for-You Bananas Foster

■ ■ ■

Bananas are a wonderful fruit, but too often people simply eat them whole or slice them into gelatin. Not very exciting, right? This festive preparation takes your basic banana and transforms it with just a little effort into an ice cream spectacular that will long be remembered. The natural sweetness of the fruit, blended with the spices and extract, turns this into something glorious!

Serves 4

1 (4-serving) package JELL-O sugar-free vanilla cook-and-serve pudding mix
1 cup water
2 tablespoons Brown Sugar Twin
½ teaspoon ground cinnamon
2 teaspoons reduced-calorie margarine

1½ teaspoons rum extract
2 cups (2 medium) sliced bananas
2 cups Wells' Blue Bunny sugar- and fat-free vanilla ice cream or any sugar- and fat-free ice cream

In a medium saucepan, combine dry pudding mix and water. Stir in Brown Sugar Twin and cinnamon. Cook over medium heat until mixture thickens, stirring constantly. Add margarine, rum extract, and banana slices. Mix well to combine. Continue cooking until bananas start to soften, stirring often. For each serving, place ½ cup ice cream in a dessert dish and spoon about ½ cup banana mixture over top.

Each serving equals:
HE: 1 Fruit, ¼ Fat, 1 Slider, 3 Optional Calories
177 Calories, 1 gm Fat, 5 gm Protein, 37 gm Carbohydrate, 195 mg Sodium, 120 mg Calcium, 2 gm Fiber
DIABETIC: 1 Fruit, 1 Starch/Carbohydrate

Chocolate Sunrise Pudding Treats

■ ■ ■

Whenever Cliff and I have traveled, we've always spent a lot of time on the road in the wee hours of the day. It's less crowded most of the time, and sometimes I'll have an early television or radio program to do, so we don't have a choice. But we've both enjoyed watching the sun come up in all the different, beautiful places around the country. This sweet treat was inspired by a particularly pretty Florida morning.

Serves 4

1 cup (one 8-ounce can) apricot halves, packed in fruit juice, undrained

½ cup unsweetened orange juice

1 (4-serving) package JELL-O sugar-free instant chocolate fudge pudding mix

⅔ cup Carnation Nonfat Dry Milk Powder

½ cup Cool Whip Free

2 tablespoons (½ ounce) chopped pecans

In a blender container, combine undrained apricots and orange juice. Cover and process on BLEND for 10 to 15 seconds or until mixture is smooth. In a large bowl, combine dry pudding mix, dry milk powder, and blended apricot mixture. Mix well using a wire whisk. Blend in Cool Whip Free. Evenly spoon mixture into 4 dessert dishes. Top each with 1½ teaspoons pecans. Refrigerate for at least 15 minutes.

Each serving equals:

HE: ¾ Fruit, ½ Skim Milk, ½ Fat, ½ Slider, 10 Optional Calories

154 Calories, 2 gm Fat, 5 gm Protein, 29 gm Carbohydrate, 400 mg Sodium, 149 mg Calcium, 1 gm Fiber

DIABETIC: 1 Fruit, ½ Skim Milk, ½ Starch/Carbohydrate, ½ Fat

Coconut Pudding

■ ■ ■

As immigrants from the Caribbean and South America arrived on our Southern shores, they brought with them foods that made them feel more at home. This coconut pudding is similar to a dish called flan that is often served in coconut or caramel versions, especially in south Florida. This one fairly sings with a calypso beat, so don't be surprised if you suddenly start vocalizing like Harry Belafonte!

Serves 4

1 (4-serving) package JELL-O sugar-free vanilla cook-and-serve pudding mix
⅔ cup Carnation Nonfat Dry Milk Powder

1¾ cups water
1 teaspoon coconut extract
¼ cup flaked coconut

In a medium saucepan, combine dry pudding mix, dry milk powder, and water. Cook over medium heat until mixture thickens and starts to boil, stirring constantly. Remove from heat. Stir in coconut extract and coconut. Evenly spoon mixture into 4 dessert dishes. Refrigerate for at least 30 minutes.

Each serving equals:
HE: ½ Skim Milk, ¼ Slider, 15 Optional Calories

77 Calories, 1 gm Fat, 4 gm Protein, 13 gm Carbohydrate, 188 mg Sodium, 138 mg Calcium, 0 gm Fiber

DIABETIC: ½ Skim Milk, ½ Fat

Southern Delight Rice Pudding

■ ■ ■

It's creamy, sweet, and as luscious as the soft breezes tugging at the branches of the mimosa tree overhead. Can't you just imagine spooning up this cozy dessert while relaxing in the shade of a beautiful tree? My family really enjoyed this version of a traditional favorite.

Serves 6 (⅔ cup)

2 cups (6 ounces) uncooked
    Minute Rice
1½ cups (one 12-fluid-ounce can)
    Carnation Evaporated Skim
    Milk
1 cup water

½ cup pourable Sugar Twin or
    Sprinkle Sweet
½ cup raisins
½ teaspoon ground cinnamon
1½ teaspoons vanilla extract

In a medium saucepan, combine uncooked rice, evaporated skim milk, water, Sugar Twin, and raisins. Bring mixture to a boil, stirring constantly. Remove from heat. Stir in cinnamon and vanilla extract. Cover and let set for 15 minutes, stirring occasionally. Serve warm or cold.

Each serving equals:

HE: 1 Bread, ⅔ Fruit, ½ Skim Milk, 8 Optional Calories

144 Calories, 0 gm Fat, 6 gm Protein, 30 gm Carbohydrate, 77 mg Sodium, 199 mg Calcium, 1 gm Fiber

DIABETIC: 1 Starch, ½ Fruit, ½ Skim Milk

Raisin Bread Pudding with Rum Sauce

■ ■ ■

Bread pudding is high on the list of my Top Ten desserts, so when I spot it on the menu while Cliff and I are traveling, I'm always curious about how it's been prepared. This Southern-style version features my favorite nut–pecans—and a delightful kiss of rum flavoring (not the real thing!).   *Serves 6*

2 (4-serving) packages JELL-O
    sugar-free vanilla cook-and-
    serve pudding mix ☆
4 cups skim milk ☆
1 teaspoon vanilla extract
½ teaspoon ground cinnamon
8 slices reduced-calorie white
    bread, cubed

¾ cup raisins
3 tablespoons (¾ ounce) chopped
    pecans
1 tablespoon reduced-calorie
    margarine
1½ teaspoons rum extract

Preheat oven to 350 degrees. Spray an 8-by-8-inch baking dish with butter-flavored cooking spray. In a large saucepan, combine 1 package dry pudding mix and 2½ cups skim milk. Cook over medium heat until mixture thickens and starts to boil, stirring constantly. Remove from heat. Stir in vanilla extract and cinnamon. Add bread cubes, raisins, and pecans. Mix well to combine. Spread mixture into prepared baking dish. Bake for 35 to 40 minutes or until golden brown and center springs up when pushed down. Place baking dish on a wire rack while preparing rum sauce. In a medium saucepan, combine remaining dry pudding mix and remaining 1½ cups skim milk. Cook over medium heat until mixture thickens and starts to boil, stirring constantly. Remove from heat. Stir in margarine and rum extract. Divide bread pudding into 6 servings. For each serving, place 1 piece bread pudding on a dessert dish and spoon about ¼ cup warm sauce over top.

Each serving equals:
HE: 1 Fruit, ¾ Fat, ⅔ Skim Milk, ⅔ Bread, ¼ Slider, 7 Optional Calories
233 Calories, 5 gm Fat, 10 gm Protein, 37 gm Carbohydrate, 454 mg Sodium, 244 mg Calcium, 5 gm Fiber
DIABETIC: 1 Fruit, 1 Fat, 1 Starch/Carbohydrate, ½ Skim Milk

Sponge Cake Meringues

■ ■ ■

There's just something about little tartlets topped with fluffy meringue that seems perfect for a ladies' afternoon tea, an occasion where everyone wears a hat! These days, of course, few Southern ladies don hats and crook elbows to drink tea, except when it comes to horse racing. Even if you're skipping the Run for the Roses this year, invite your girlfriends for tea!

Serves 4

4 individual sponge cake dessert cups
1 (4-serving) package JELL-O sugar-free chocolate cook-and-serve pudding mix
⅔ cup Carnation Nonfat Dry Milk Powder
1½ cups water

3 egg whites
⅓ cup pourable Sugar Twin or Sprinkle Sweet
1 teaspoon coconut extract
4 maraschino cherries
1 tablespoon + 1 teaspoon flaked coconut

Preheat oven to 350 degrees. Arrange sponge cakes in 4 (12-ounce) custard cups. In a medium saucepan, combine dry pudding mix, dry milk powder, and water. Cook over medium heat until mixture thickens and starts to boil, stirring often. Evenly spoon mixture over sponge cakes. In a large bowl, beat egg whites with an electric mixer on HIGH until soft peaks form. Add Sugar Twin and coconut extract. Continue beating on HIGH until firm peaks form. Evenly spoon meringue mixture over chocolate pudding in custard cups, being sure to seal to edges of cups. Cut each maraschino cherry into quarters. Evenly sprinkle 4 cherry pieces and 1 teaspoon coconut over top of each cup. Place custard cups on a baking sheet. Bake for 10 to 12 minutes or until peaks start to turn brown. Good served warm or cold.

HINT: Egg whites beat best at room temperature.

Each serving equals:
HE: 1 Bread, ½ Skim Milk, ¼ Protein, ½ Slider, 8 Optional Calories

206 Calories, 2 gm Fat, 10 gm Protein, 37 gm Carbohydrate, 567 mg Sodium, 160 mg Calcium, 1 gm Fiber

DIABETIC: 2 Starch/Carbohydrate, ½ Skim Milk

Key Lime Pie

■ ■ ■

History tells us that the lime wasn't native to Florida but was brought there by Spanish explorers. The climate was perfect and the fruit thrived there for centuries, especially in the Florida Keys (thus, the expression "key lime"). I've seen different types of key lime pies in my travels, but I decided that this recipe produced a classic pie that just sparkled with color and sweetness.

Serves 8

1⅓ cups cold water
2⅔ cups Carnation Nonfat Dry Milk Powder
¾ cup pourable Sugar Twin or Sprinkle Sweet ☆
2 (4-serving) packages JELL-O sugar-free instant vanilla pudding mix
2 (4-serving) packages JELL-O sugar-free lime gelatin

1 (6-ounce) Keebler graham cracker piecrust
6 egg whites
1 teaspoon lime juice
2 tablespoons purchased graham cracker crumbs or two (2½-inch) graham crackers, made into crumbs

Place cold water in a 4-cup glass measuring cup. Stir in dry milk powder until mixture makes a smooth paste. Cover and microwave on HIGH (100% power) for 45 to 60 seconds or until mixture is very hot, but not to the boiling point. Stir in ½ cup Sugar Twin. Mix well to combine. Cover and refrigerate for at least 2 hours before using. Preheat oven to 350 degrees. In a large bowl, combine dry pudding mixes, dry gelatins, and refrigerated milk mixture. Mix well using a wire whisk. Spread mixture into piecrust. In a medium bowl, beat egg whites with an electric mixer until soft peaks form. Add lime juice and remaining ¼ cup Sugar Twin. Continue beating until stiff peaks form. Spread meringue mixture evenly over filling mixture, being sure to seal to edges of piecrust. Evenly sprinkle graham cracker crumbs over top. Bake for 8 to 10 minutes or until meringue starts to turn golden brown. Place pie plate on a wire rack and allow to cool 15 minutes. Refrigerate for at least 2 hours. Cut into 8 servings.

HINT: 1. Egg whites beat best at room temperature.
2. Meringue pie cuts easily if you dip a sharp knife in warm water before slicing.
3. A self-seal sandwich bag works great for crushing graham crackers.

Each serving equals:

HE: 1 Skim Milk, ½ Bread, ¼ Protein, 1 Slider, 19 Optional Calories

221 Calories, 5 gm Fat, 12 gm Protein, 32 gm Carbohydrate, 644 mg Sodium, 280 mg Calcium, 1 gm Fiber

DIABETIC: 1 Skim Milk, 1 Starch/Carbohydrate, 1 Fat

Golden Pecan Pie

■ ❋ ■

If you've ever tasted true pecan pie the way it's served down South, you know that an important ingredient is a sugar or corn syrup that is delicious but very high in sugar and calories. I wanted to share that incredibly good flavor, but I needed to do it in a way that whisks out all the extra. This pie pleases your senses but teases you just a little bit, blending oats and pecans for the filling.

Serves 8

1 Pillsbury refrigerated unbaked
   9-inch piecrust
2 (4-serving) packages JELL-O
   sugar-free vanilla cook-and-
   serve pudding mix
1⅓ cups Carnation Nonfat Dry
   Milk Powder

2½ cups water
¼ cup Brown Sugar Twin
1 tablespoon vanilla extract
½ cup (1½ ounces) quick oats
½ cup (2 ounces) chopped pecans

Preheat oven to 325 degrees. Place piecrust in a 9-inch pie plate. Flute edges. In a medium saucepan, combine dry pudding mix, dry milk powder, and water. Stir in Brown Sugar Twin and vanilla extract. Cook over medium heat until mixture thickens and starts to boil, stirring constantly. Remove from heat. Add oatmeal and pecans. Mix well to combine. Spread mixture into piecrust. Bake for 45 to 55 minutes or until filling is firm in center. Place pie plate on a wire rack and allow to cool completely. Cut into 8 servings.

Each serving equals:

HE: 1 Fat, ¾ Bread, ½ Skim Milk, ¾ Slider, 2 Optional Calories

226 Calories, 10 gm Fat, 6 gm Protein, 28 gm Carbohydrate, 278 mg Sodium, 154 mg Calcium, 1 gm Fiber

DIABETIC: 1½ Starch/Carbohydrate, 1½ Fat, ½ Skim Milk

Dixie Peach Crumb Pie

■ ❋ ■

I don't know if the peaches in Georgia are better than anywhere in the entire U.S. of A., but the people of Georgia think it's true! What is undeniable is that fresh peach pie is worth driving a few thousand miles for—but now you don't have to anymore. I think the crumb topping here is more perfect for peaches than a standard crust. My daughter, Becky, the family peach lover, would agree!

Serves 8

1 (4-serving) package JELL-O sugar-free vanilla cook-and-serve pudding mix
¼ teaspoon ground nutmeg
1¼ cups water
3 cups (6 medium) peeled and sliced fresh peaches
1 (6-ounce) Keebler graham cracker piecrust

6 tablespoons purchased graham cracker crumbs or 6 (2½-inch) graham cracker squares made into crumbs
2 tablespoons (½ ounce) chopped pecans
2 tablespoons pourable Sugar Twin or Sprinkle Sweet

Preheat oven to 375 degrees. In a large saucepan, combine dry pudding mix, nutmeg, and water. Stir in peaches. Cook over medium heat until mixture thickens and peaches start to soften, stirring often. Spoon hot mixture into piecrust. In a medium bowl, combine graham cracker crumbs, pecans, and Sugar Twin. Evenly sprinkle crumb mixture over top. Bake for 30 minutes. Place pie plate on a wire rack and allow to cool completely. Cut into 8 servings.

HINT: A self-seal sandwich bag works great for crushing graham crackers.

Each serving equals:
HE: ¾ Bread, ¾ Fruit, ¼ Fat, ¾ Slider, 2 Optional Calories
174 Calories, 6 gm Fat, 2 gm Protein, 28 gm Carbohydrate, 226 mg Sodium, 5 mg Calcium, 2 gm Fiber
DIABETIC: 1 Starch, 1 Fruit, 1 Fat

Peach Praline Custard Pie

■ ■ ■

If a woman from Georgia agreed to marry a man from Louisiana, this is what they might serve at their engagement party! She's the peach in their pair, and if he knows what's good for him, he'll always be sweet to her—and carry pralines in his pocket just in case!

Serves 8

3 cups (6 medium) peeled and sliced fresh peaches

1 (6-ounce) Keebler graham cracker piecrust

1 (4-serving) package JELL-O sugar-free vanilla cook-and-serve pudding mix

⅔ cup Carnation Nonfat Dry Milk Powder

¼ cup Brown Sugar Twin

1¼ cups water

2 tablespoons purchased graham cracker crumbs or 2 (2½-inch) graham cracker squares, made into crumbs

2 tablespoons (½ ounce) chopped pecans

Preheat oven to 350 degrees. Evenly arrange peach slices in piecrust. In a medium saucepan, combine dry pudding mix, dry milk powder, Brown Sugar Twin, and water. Cook over medium heat until mixture thickens and starts to boil, stirring constantly. Spoon hot mixture evenly over peach slices. Evenly sprinkle graham cracker crumbs and pecans over top. Bake for 30 minutes. Place pie plate on a wire rack and let set for 15 minutes. Refrigerate for at least 1 hour. Cut into 8 servings.

Each serving equals:
HE: ¾ Fruit, ½ Bread, ¼ Skim Milk, ¼ Fat, ¾ Slider, 9 Optional Calories
182 Calories, 6 gm Fat, 4 gm Protein, 28 gm Carbohydrate, 235 mg Sodium, 79 mg Calcium, 2 gm Fiber
DIABETIC: 1½ Starch/Carbohydrate, 1 Fruit, 1 Fat

Coconut Cake with Coconut Frosting

■ ❋ ■

From the part of the country where cotillions still occur, where debutantes dressed in white are presented to society, and where women still (on occasion, anyway) wear hats—here's a truly magnificent dessert as romantic and lovely as a Southern belle! You may be amazed at how little actual coconut it takes to give this treat an intense flavor. But isn't it great to know you can "wallow" in coconut and not compromise your health?

Serves 12

1⅓ cups Carnation Nonfat Dry Milk Powder ☆

2 cups water ☆

1 tablespoon white vinegar

1½ cups Bisquick Reduced Fat Baking Mix

¾ cup pourable Sugar Twin or Sprinkle Sweet

6 tablespoons flaked coconut ☆

¼ cup Land O Lakes no-fat sour cream

⅓ cup Dannon plain fat-free yogurt

1 tablespoon + 1 teaspoon coconut extract ☆

1 (4-serving) package JELL-O sugar-free instant vanilla pudding mix

¾ cup Cool Whip Free

Preheat oven to 350 degrees. Spray a 9-by-9-inch cake pan with butter-flavored cooking spray. In a small bowl, combine ⅔ cup dry milk powder, ¾ cup water, and vinegar. Set aside. In a large bowl, combine baking mix, Sugar Twin, and 3 tablespoons coconut. Stir sour cream, yogurt, and 1 tablespoon coconut extract into milk mixture. Add milk mixture to flour mixture. Mix gently to combine. Spread batter into prepared cake pan. Bake for 25 to 30 minutes or until a toothpick inserted in center comes out clean. Place cake pan on a wire rack and allow to cool for at least 30 minutes. In a large bowl, combine dry pudding mix, remaining ⅔ cup dry milk powder, and remaining 1¼ cups water. Mix well using a wire whisk. Blend in remaining 1 teaspoon coconut extract and Cool Whip Free. Spread mixture evenly over cake. Evenly sprinkle remaining 3 tablespoons coconut over top. Cut into 12 servings. Refrigerate leftovers.

Each serving equals:

HE: ⅔ Bread, ⅓ Skim Milk, ¼ Slider, 17 Optional Calories

118 Calories, 2 gm Fat, 4 gm Protein, 21 gm Carbohydrate, 345 mg Sodium, 131 mg Calcium, 1 gm Fiber

DIABETIC: 1½ Starch/Carbohydrate

Kentucky Scramble

■ ■ ■

Here's what they serve on those laid-back mornings in the heart of horse-racing country: a wonderful combination of scrambled eggs blended with corn, onions, and peppers! Even if you don't feel like serving it for brunch along with mint juleps, you'll enjoy this tasty blend of flavors sure to wake up all your senses. *Serves 6 (1 cup)*

½ cup chopped green bell pepper
¼ cup finely sliced green onion
1½ cups frozen whole-kernel
   corn, thawed
¼ cup (one 2-ounce jar) chopped
   pimiento, undrained
6 tablespoons Hormel Bacon
   Bits

9 eggs or equivalent in egg
   substitute
⅛ teaspoon black pepper
½ teaspoon Tabasco sauce
   (optional)

In a large skillet sprayed with butter-flavored cooking spray, sauté green pepper and onion for 5 minutes or until tender. Stir in corn, undrained pimiento, and bacon bits. In a medium bowl, combine eggs, black pepper, and Tabasco sauce, using a wire whisk. Add egg mixture to vegetable mixture. Mix gently to combine. Lower heat and cook until eggs are set but still creamy, stirring occasionally.

HINT: Thaw corn by placing in a colander and rinsing under hot water for one minute.

Each serving equals:
HE: 1½ Protein (limited), ½ Bread, ¼ Vegetable, ¼ Slider, 5 Optional Calories
181 Calories, 9 gm Fat, 14 gm Protein, 11 gm Carbohydrate, 350 mg Sodium, 40 mg Calcium, 1 gm Fiber
DIABETIC: 2 Meat, ½ Starch

Dropped "Buttermilk" Biscuits

■ ❋ ■

Every cook in the South has her own recipe for biscuits but she isn't often inclined to share her secrets! I've nibbled on biscuits from Alabama to Tennessee, and I figured out my own secret version that is both tasty and healthy. The difference is, of course, that my cooking secrets are an open book!

Serves 8

⅔ cup **Carnation Nonfat Dry Milk Powder**

½ cup water

1 tablespoon *white vinegar*

1½ cups **Bisquick Reduced Fat Baking Mix**

Preheat oven to 425 degrees. In a large bowl, combine dry milk powder, water, and vinegar. Let set for 5 minutes. Add baking mix. Mix well to combine until a soft dough forms. Drop dough by tablespoon onto an ungreased baking sheet to form 8 biscuits. Bake for 6 to 8 minutes or until tops start to turn golden brown. Lightly spray tops with butter-flavored cooking spray. Serve warm.

Each serving equals:

HE: 1 Bread, ¼ Skim Milk

101 Calories, 1 gm Fat, 4 gm Protein, 19 gm Carbohydrate, 292 mg Sodium, 92 mg Calcium, 1 gm Fiber

DIABETIC: 1 Starch

Mammy's Cornbread

■ ❋ ■

It just about goes without saying that if you stay overnight at one of the plantation hotels across the South, you're going to be offered cornbread with your meals. This splendid version remakes a classic buttermilk recipe with a few easy changes. After your first bite, you'll probably agree with the philosophy that cornbread goes with everything!

Serves 8

⅔ cup **Carnation Nonfat Dry Milk Powder**

1 cup **water**

1 tablespoon **white vinegar**

1 cup (6 ounces) **yellow cornmeal**

3 tablespoons **all-purpose flour**

1 tablespoon **pourable Sugar Twin or Sprinkle Sweet**

1 teaspoon **baking powder**

½ teaspoon **baking soda**

1 **egg** or equivalent in egg substitute

¼ cup **Land O Lakes no-fat sour cream**

Preheat oven to 375 degrees. Spray an 8-by-8-inch baking dish with butter-flavored cooking spray. In a small bowl, combine dry milk powder, water, and vinegar. Set aside. In a large bowl, combine cornmeal, flour, Sugar Twin, baking powder, and baking soda. Stir egg and sour cream into milk mixture. Add milk mixture to cornmeal mixture. Mix just to combine. Spread batter into prepared baking dish. Bake for 25 to 30 minutes. Place baking dish on a wire rack and let set for at least 5 minutes. Cut into 8 servings.

Each serving equals:

HE: 1 Bread, ¼ Skim Milk, ¼ Slider, 15 Optional Calories

125 Calories, 1 gm Fat, 6 gm Protein, 23 gm Carbohydrate, 277 mg Sodium, 87 mg Calcium, 1 gm Fiber

DIABETIC: 1½ Starch/Carbohydrate

Southern Buttermilk Spoon Bread

■ ❈ ■

There are so many wonderful bakers in the South, and so many variations on bread that it was hard to choose just a few to include in this book. This "buttermilk" spoon bread is a rich combo of milk, eggs, and cornmeal and uses both baking powder and baking soda to rise, rise, rise! *Serves 6*

1 cup Carnation Nonfat Dry
   Milk Powder
1 cup cold water
1 tablespoon white vinegar
2 cups hot water
1 cup (6 ounces) yellow cornmeal
2 eggs or equivalent in egg
   substitute

2 tablespoons Land O Lakes
   no-fat sour cream
1 teaspoon baking powder
½ teaspoon baking soda
1 teaspoon salt

Preheat oven to 350 degrees. Spray an 8-by-8-inch baking dish with butter-flavored cooking spray. In a small bowl, combine dry milk powder, cold water, and vinegar. Set aside. In a large saucepan, bring hot water to a boil. Gradually stir in cornmeal, using a wire whisk. Lower heat and simmer for 10 minutes, stirring constantly. Place saucepan on a wire rack and let set for 15 minutes. Add milk mixture, eggs, sour cream, baking powder, baking soda, and salt. Mix well to combine. Spread mixture into prepared baking dish. Bake for 40 to 50 minutes. Place baking dish on a wire rack and let set for 5 minutes. Divide into 6 servings.

Each serving equals:
HE: 1¼ Bread, ½ Skim Milk, ⅓ Protein (limited), 10 Optional Calories
170 Calories, 2 gm Fat, 9 gm Protein, 29 gm Carbohydrate, 663 mg Sodium, 64 mg Calcium, 2 gm Fiber
DIABETIC: 1½ Starch, ½ Skim Milk

THE SOUTHWEST

∎ ∎ ∎

I can still remember hearing about the great explorers who, hundreds of years ago, mapped the uncharted regions of the American continent. One of the stories that captured my interest back then (fifth grade or so!) was the tale of Coronado, who was searching for the Seven Cities of Gold. His fabled destination turned out to be just a legend, but he still made a golden discovery: the magnificent desert territory of the Southwest.

The terrain of the Southwest varies throughout the region, as does the weather, which is often unpredictable: hot, dry summer months that parch the land, bitter winters that can quickly cover the mountains of New Mexico with several feet of snow, and sudden spring floods that will soon transform the desert into a garden of Eden, where cactus bloom brilliantly and animals roam freely through a forest of piñon trees.

The Southwest is ranch country, a land of cowboys and cattle drives, campfires and chuck wagons, the glorious Grand Canyon and the heroic history of Texas and the Alamo. The men and women who settled this place found their "home on the range" in its wide open spaces. Even today, it's thrilling to imagine Conestoga wagons heading down the Santa Fe Trail and to envision the last days of the old West, when the great tribes of Apache and Navajo left their special mark on the history and culture of this high-spirited land.

The cuisine of this beautiful, wild region is tremendously varied, but because most of the states in it border on Mexico, many of the most popular Southwestern dishes are strongly influenced by the spices, flavors, and vivid colors of our neighbor to the South. There's lots of meat on the menu, whether it's grilled or barbecued or rolled into tortillas, and there are also a great many luscious fresh vegetables and fruits, most of them grown along the shores of that great river of song and story, the Rio Grande. In some parts of this area, the popular combination of beans, squash, corn, and peppers is known as the Sacred Sisters. You'll also find the ever-present *frijoles,* or pinto beans, stirred into many recipes and served just about anywhere you go.

I did have a few reservations when I was working on this section of *Cooking Healthy Across America.* I'm just not a fan of spicy food, and I was concerned that this region's reputation for smoke-out-your-ears spiciness would make it very hard for me to do the job of choosing the dishes to include.

You see, I won't share a recipe until I've tried it myself—no exceptions. The real test came when I realized that I just had to include *Green Chili Stew* among my Southwest specialties. I didn't really want to, but I knew I *had* to taste it. Rita, who helps me prepare my recipes for testing, told me she wished she'd had a camera to record my astonishment for posterity! When I spooned up a mouthful of this regional classic, I found I was pleasantly surprised by its flavor. So, let me extend an invitation to my fellow "wimps"—you may be delightfully amazed at how good food with just a little heat added can taste!

What's important to remember is that you can enjoy things as spicy as you like—or not! (And here's another fascinating fact: Chilis and chiles are not the same thing! *Chili* is actually the Spanish word for pepper, and not all peppers are hot.)

Another Southwestern culinary adventure starring yours truly involved a popular ingredient—avocados. To me, they looked funny, and I knew that they were full of fat. But since they are part and parcel of Southwestern cooking, I figured I'd have to stir some avocado into at least one recipe. *Albuquerque Chicken Soup* has really won me over.

A little goes a long way, which is good for anyone concerned about calories and fat, but when they are used in this way in *moderation,* I found them down-right scrumptious and very pleasurable!

My truck drivin' man is a particular fan of Tex-Mex food, which is probably why the very first Healthy Exchanges recipe I ever created was something called Mexicalli Pie. Since then, I've always kept him in mind when stirring up any dish with a fiesta flair!

But you don't have to travel any farther than your neighborhood market to stock your Southwestern pantry with the ingredients you'll need to prepare these savory delights at home. Besides being able to purchase packaged tortillas in the refrigerator case, you can find many brands of other ingredients, from salsas to dried chilis of all kinds (and temperatures!)

I'm especially proud of my party recipes in this section, which are perfect for celebrating *Cinco de Mayo* or the local football team's winning record. Stir up a pitcher or two of *Sparkling Grape Sangria* and get your motor humming with my *Blended Magical Margaritas!*

I also want to say a few words about my Southwestern desserts, which feature some of the truly unique flavor combinations of this lively cuisine. If you're fixing a Mexican-themed buffet, you'll certainly hear a round of *olés* from the crowd as they dig in to *Rolled Cinnamon Chocolate Cake.* I think chocolate and cinnamon ignite some special culinary fireworks. And I can save you a trip South with just one slice of *San Antonio Pecan Chocolate Cream Pie,* a dish with a flavor as BIG as Texas!

THE SOUTHWEST RECIPES

Santa Fe Gazpacho

Calico Tomato Soup

Cheddar Corn Chowder

Tortilla Soup

Albuquerque Chicken Soup

"Come and Get It" Chuck Wagon
    Chili

Chili Mac Soup

Grande Garden Salad

Southwestern Vegetable Salad

Crunchy Calico Salad

Ranch Hand Green Bean Bake

Frijoles San Juan

Mexicali Rose Skillet Corn

Tex-Mex Corn Bake

Spanish Limas

Cheesy Three-Bean Pot Pie

El Rancho Fish Fillets

Shrimp in Special Sauce

Shrimp Alfredo Deluxe

Arroz Con Pollo (Chicken with Rice)

Santa Fe Chicken Casserole

Southwest Strata

Picadillo (Castilian Hash)

Cowboy Chicken-Fried Steaks

Green Chili Stew

Rio Grande Pork Tenders

South-of-the-Border Pork Sandwiches

Southwest Corned Beef and Cabbage

Date Caramel Cream

Mexican Chocolate Mousse

San Antonio Pecan Chocolate Cream Pie

Rolled Cinnamon Chocolate Cake

Tex-Mex Munch Mix

Gringo Nachos

Panhandle Cheese Muffins

Alamo Fudge

Blended Magical Margaritas

Sparkling Grape Sangria

Santa Fe Gazpacho

There's no cooler or more refreshing delight on a very hot day than a cold bowl of this blended vegetable soup! Even if, as they say in the Southwest, it's only a "dry heat," this combo will bring down the temperature from the inside out.

Serves 6 (full 1 cup)

2 cups reduced-sodium tomato
   juice ☆
1½ cups chopped unpeeled
   cucumber ☆
2½ cups peeled and chopped
   fresh tomatoes ☆

1 teaspoon chili seasoning
½ teaspoon dried minced garlic
½ cup chopped red onion
½ cup chopped green bell pepper
1 tablespoon Brown Sugar Twin

In a blender container, combine 1 cup tomato juice, ½ cup cucumber, 1 cup tomatoes, chili seasoning, and garlic. Cover and process on BLEND for 15 seconds or until mixture is smooth. Pour mixture into a large bowl. Stir in remaining tomato juice, cucumber, and tomatoes. Add onion, green pepper, and Brown Sugar Twin. Mix well to combine. Cover and refrigerate for at least 2 hours. Gently stir again just before serving.

Each serving equals:
HE: 2 Vegetable, 1 Optional Calorie
44 Calories, 0 gm Fat, 2 gm Protein, 9 gm Carbohydrate, 78 mg Sodium, 19 mg Calcium, 2 gm Fiber
DIABETIC: 2 Vegetable

Calico Tomato Soup

■ ✳ ■

I bet that most of the pioneer women who traveled west along the Santa Fe Trail owned a dress or apron made of calico, but that's not how this soup got its name. Rather, it's in honor of the varied colors and flavors stirred together to create something splendid! *Serves 4 (1 cup)*

1 (10¾-ounce) can Healthy
    Request Tomato Soup
2 cups water
1 teaspoon parsley flakes
¾ cup frozen whole-kernel corn,
    thawed

¾ cup frozen peas, thawed
⅓ cup (1 ounce) uncooked
    Minute Rice
2 teaspoons chili seasoning

In a large saucepan, combine tomato soup, water, and parsley flakes. Bring mixture to a boil. Stir in corn, peas, and uncooked rice. Add chili seasoning. Mix well to combine. Lower heat, cover, and simmer for 10 minutes or until rice is tender, stirring occasionally.

HINT: Thaw corn and peas by placing in a colander and rinsing under hot water for one minute.

Each serving equals:
HE: 1 Bread, ½ Slider, 5 Optional Calories
109 Calories, 1 gm Fat, 3 gm Protein, 22 gm Carbohydrate, 234 mg Sodium, 18 mg Calcium, 3 gm Fiber
DIABETIC: 1½ Starch

Cheddar Corn Chowder

■ ❄ ■

Two of the most popular staples of Southwestern food are cheese and corn, so this recipe was a natural for this book! If you're skeptical about the taste of "healthy" cheese, I think this dish will prove just how scrumptious a little reduced-fat Cheddar can be when blended into a rich chowder that sparkles with flavor.   *Serves 4 (1¼ cups)*

1 cup water
1 cup (5 ounces) diced raw potatoes
¼ cup chopped onion
½ cup thinly sliced celery
¾ cup thinly sliced carrots
1 cup (one 8-ounce can) cream-style corn
½ cup frozen whole-kernel corn, thawed

1½ cups (one 12-fluid-ounce can) Carnation Evaporated Skim Milk
¾ cup (3 ounces) shredded Kraft reduced-fat Cheddar cheese
¼ cup (one 2-ounce jar) chopped pimiento, drained
1 teaspoon dried parsley flakes

In a large saucepan, combine water, potatoes, onion, celery, and carrots. Bring mixture to a boil. Lower heat, cover, and simmer for 10 minutes, or until vegetables are tender. Stir in cream-style corn, whole-kernel corn, and evaporated skim milk. Add Cheddar cheese, pimiento, and parsley flakes. Mix well to combine. Continue simmering for 5 minutes or until cheese melts, stirring occasionally.

HINT: Thaw corn by placing in a colander and rinsing under hot water for one minute.

Each serving equals:
HE: 1 Bread, 1 Protein, ¾ Skim Milk, ¾ Vegetable
244 Calories, 4 gm Fat, 16 gm Protein, 36 gm Carbohydrate, 513 mg Sodium, 451 mg Calcium, 3 gm Fiber
DIABETIC: 1½ Starch, 1 Skim Milk, ½ Meat, ½ Vegetable

Tortilla Soup

■ ■ ■

One of the most popular Southwestern soups, this dish gets its name from the strips of tortillas sliced into a savory chicken-based broth. Here's a case where you can adjust the seasonings to please your family's palate. Remember that a little chili powder and pepper go a long way, so be sure to add just a pinch at a time!

Serves 4 (1¼ cups)

3 (6-inch) corn tortillas, cut into
    ¼-inch strips
½ cup finely chopped onion
2 cups (one 16-ounce can)
    Healthy Request Chicken
    Broth
1 cup water
1 cup peeled and diced fresh
    tomato

1 teaspoon chili seasoning
½ teaspoon dried minced
    garlic
⅛ teaspoon black pepper
2 cups (10 ounces) diced cooked
    chicken breast
1 tablespoon lime juice

In a large skillet sprayed with butter-flavored cooking spray, sauté tortilla strips for 5 minutes or until crisp. Place strips on a paper towel while preparing soup. In a large saucepan sprayed with butter-flavored cooking spray, sauté onion for 5 minutes. Stir in chicken broth, water, tomato, chili seasoning, garlic, and black pepper. Add chicken. Mix well to combine. Bring mixture to a boil. Lower heat and simmer for 10 minutes, stirring occasionally. Remove from heat and stir in lime juice and tortilla strips. Serve at once.

HINT: If you don't have leftovers, purchase a chunk of cooked chicken breast from your local deli.

Each serving equals:
HE: 2½ Protein, ¾ Bread, ¾ Vegetable, 8 Optional Calories

171 Calories, 3 gm Fat, 25 gm Protein, 11 gm Carbohydrate, 321 mg Sodium, 43 mg Calcium, 2 gm Fiber

DIABETIC: 2½ Meat, 1 Vegetable, ½ Starch

Albuquerque Chicken Soup

■ ■ ■

Avocado is good for so much more than the festive green dip known as gua-camole, but I wasn't a fan of it—until now. True, it's higher in calories than many veggies, and it's got more fat as well (the good-for-you kind, in modera-tion), but it provides a wonderful flavor and texture in this creamy chicken soup.

Serves 4 (1 cup)

1 (10¾-ounce) can Healthy
    Request Cream of Chicken
    Soup
1½ cups (one 12-fluid-ounce can)
    Carnation Evaporated Skim
    Milk
½ cup water

1 cup (5 ounces) diced cooked
    chicken breast
1 (medium-sized) avocado,
    peeled, pitted, and chopped
¼ cup (1 ounce) sliced ripe olives
3 tablespoons Hormel Bacon
    Bits

In a medium saucepan, combine chicken soup, evaporated skim milk, water, and chicken. Add avocado and olives. Mix well to combine. Stir in bacon bits. Cook over medium heat for 6 to 8 minutes, or until heated through, stirring often.

HINT: If you don't have leftovers, purchase a chunk of cooked chicken breast from your local deli.

Each serving equals:

HE: 1¼ Protein, 1 Fat, ¾ Skim Milk, ¾ Slider, 4 Optional Calories

232 Calories, 8 gm Fat, 21 gm Protein, 19 gm Carbohydrate, 682 mg Sodium, 14 mg Calcium, 1 gm Fiber

DIABETIC: 1 Meat, 1 Fat, 1 Skim Milk, ½ Starch/Carbohydrate

"Come and Get It" Chuck Wagon Chili

■ ❄ ■

Imagine the clanging sound of the dinner gong echoing across the prairie or desert, and you'll know that no other sound could have been more welcome to those hard-traveling pioneers and cattle drivers! In many parts of the country, chili recipes are made with ground beef, but Southwest versions, especially those out of Texas, require cubed beef. What a great hearty dish to serve for supper no matter where you live!   *Serves 6 (1 full cup)*

1 cup finely chopped onion
1 cup finely chopped green bell
    pepper
2 cups (one 16-ounce can) toma-
    toes, chopped and undrained
1 cup (one 8-ounce can) Hunt's
    Tomato Sauce

1¾ cups (one 14½-ounce can)
    Swanson Beef Broth
2 full cups (12 ounces) diced
    cooked lean roast beef
1 tablespoon chili seasoning
1 teaspoon dried parsley flakes
⅛ teaspoon black pepper

In a large saucepan sprayed with butter-flavored cooking spray, sauté onion and green pepper for 6 to 8 minutes. Add undrained tomatoes, tomato sauce, and beef broth. Mix well to combine. Stir in roast beef, chili seasoning, parsley flakes, and black pepper. Lower heat and simmer for 15 to 20 minutes, stirring occasionally.

HINT: If you don't have leftovers, purchase a chunk of cooked lean roast beef from your local deli or use Healthy Choice Deli slices.

Each serving equals:
HE: 2 Protein, 2 Vegetable, 6 Optional Calories
156 Calories, 4 gm Fat, 19 gm Protein, 11 gm Carbohydrate, 559 mg Sodium, 44 mg Calcium, 3 gm Fiber
DIABETIC: 2 Meat, 2 Vegetable

Chili Mac Soup

■ ❋ ■

If you want to introduce your kids to a wonderful Southwestern soup, why not try this tasty one? The elbow pasta seems to make people of all ages smile—maybe because it's in the shape of a grin! I advise adjusting the spices for the tamest tastebuds at your table—and let your family "hotshots" add more later if they wish!

Serves 4 (1½ cups)

8 ounces ground 90% lean turkey
    or beef
½ cup chopped onion
1 cup (one 8-ounce can) Hunt's
    Tomato Sauce
2 cups Healthy Request tomato
    juice or any reduced-sodium
    tomato juice

10 ounces (one 16-ounce can) red
    kidney beans, rinsed and
    drained
1¼ cups water
2 teaspoons chili seasoning
⅛ teaspoon black pepper
⅓ cup (¾ ounce) uncooked elbow
    macaroni

In a large saucepan sprayed with olive oil–flavored cooking spray, brown meat and onion. Stir in tomato sauce, tomato juice, kidney beans, water, chili seasoning, and black pepper. Add uncooked elbow macaroni. Mix well to combine. Bring mixture to a boil. Lower heat, cover, and simmer for 15 minutes or until macaroni is tender, stirring occasionally.

Each serving equals:

HE: 2¾ Protein, 2¼ Vegetable, ½ Bread

225 Calories, 5 gm Fat, 17 gm Protein, 28 gm Carbohydrate, 815 mg Sodium, 46 mg Calcium, 7 gm Fiber

DIABETIC: 2 Meat, 2 Vegetable, 1 Starch

Grande Garden Salad

■ ■ ■

Here's another salad that will make your family lick their lips and gobble it down! Each forkful brings new surprises, from bits of savory bacon to flashes of tangy dressing, that encourage the lightest appetite. If the peppers look especially good at the market, you might want to blend a bit of red and yellow pepper into this mix.

Serves 4 (¾ cup)

2 cups unpeeled and chopped fresh tomatoes
1 cup chopped green bell pepper
½ cup chopped onion
½ cup Kraft Fat Free Catalina Dressing

¼ cup Hormel Bacon Bits
2 teaspoons chili seasoning
1 tablespoon chopped fresh parsley or 1 teaspoon dried parsley flakes

In a large bowl, combine tomatoes, green pepper, and onion. In a small bowl, combine Catalina dressing, bacon bits, chili seasoning, and parsley. Add dressing mixture to vegetable mixture. Mix well to combine. Cover and refrigerate for at least 30 minutes. Gently stir again just before serving.

Each serving equals:
HE: 1¾ Vegetable, ¾ Slider, 15 Optional Calories

114 Calories, 2 gm Fat, 4 gm Protein, 20 gm Carbohydrate, 619 mg Sodium, 13 mg Calcium, 2 gm Fiber

DIABETIC: 1½ Vegetable, ½ Starch, ½ Meat

Southwestern Vegetable Salad

■ ■ ■

When the sun sets in the Arizona desert, you get to see a rainbow of colors like nowhere else in the world! I wanted this fresh and crunchy salad to reflect that rainbow with a festive blend of flavors that are almost like a sunset on your plate.

Serves 4 (1 cup)

1 cup chopped unpeeled cucumber

1 cup (one 8-ounce can) peas, rinsed and drained

1 cup (one 8-ounce can) diced carrots, rinsed and drained

¼ cup chopped green bell pepper

1 cup unpeeled and chopped fresh tomatoes

¼ cup chopped green onion

¼ cup (1 ounce) sliced ripe olives

½ cup Kraft fat-free mayonnaise

1 teaspoon lemon juice

1 tablespoon chili sauce

Sugar substitute to equal 1 teaspoon sugar

1 teaspoon prepared horseradish sauce

In a large bowl, combine cucumber, peas, carrots, and green pepper. Stir in tomatoes, onion, and olives. In a small bowl, combine mayonnaise, lemon juice, chili sauce, sugar substitute, and horseradish sauce. Add dressing mixture to vegetable mixture. Mix gently to combine. Cover and refrigerate for at least 30 minutes. Gently stir again just before serving.

Each serving equals:

HE: 1¾ Vegetable, ½ Bread, ¼ Fat, ¼ Slider, 2 Optional Calories

89 Calories, 1 gm Fat, 3 gm Protein, 17 gm Carbohydrate, 521 mg Sodium, 41 mg Calcium, 4 gm Fiber

DIABETIC: 1 Vegetable, 1 Starch/Carbohydrate, ½ Fat

Crunchy Calico Salad

■ ■ ■

One of the most popular traditions of Southwest cooking is variety on the plate, and this colorful salad delivers both crunch and sparkle to any meal. The dressing is creamy and tangy, a perfect foil to the firm texture of these favorite vegetables.

Serves 6 (full ¾ cup)

2 cups (one 16-ounce can) whole-kernel corn, rinsed and drained

2 cups finely chopped romaine lettuce

1 cup diced carrots

1¼ cups diced unpeeled cucumber

¼ cup sliced green onion

½ cup Kraft Fat Free Ranch Dressing

2 tablespoons Kraft fat-free mayonnaise

1 tablespoon Dijon mustard

⅛ teaspoon dried minced garlic

In a large bowl, combine corn, romaine lettuce, carrots, cucumber, and onion. In a medium bowl, combine Ranch dressing, mayonnaise, Dijon mustard, and garlic. Pour dressing mixture over vegetables. Mix well to combine. Cover and refrigerate for at least 30 minutes. Gently stir again just before serving.

Each serving equals:

HE: 1 Vegetable, ⅔ Bread, ¼ Slider, 17 Optional Calories

100 Calories, 0 gm Fat, 2 gm Protein, 23 gm Carbohydrate, 436 mg Sodium, 23 mg Calcium, 3 gm Fiber

DIABETIC: 1 Vegetable, 1 Starch

Ranch Hand Green Bean Bake

■ ❄ ■

Cliff was so excited when he poked into my kitchen while I was stirring up this recipe. He loves salsa, he loves green beans, he loves cheese (well, what man doesn't?), and he really loves Doritos! This is a fun veggie casserole with enough taste and satisfaction to please the most ravenous working man around your house!

Serves 6

1 (10¾-ounce) can Healthy
   Request Tomato Soup
½ cup chunky salsa (mild,
   medium, or hot)
4 cups (two 16-ounce cans) cut
   green beans, rinsed and
   drained

1 cup + 2 tablespoons (4½
   ounces) shredded Kraft
   reduced-fat Cheddar cheese ☆
1 cup (2¼ ounces) coarsely
   crushed Doritos WOW Nacho
   Cheesier Chips

Preheat oven to 350 degrees. Spray an 8-by-8-inch baking dish with butter-flavored cooking spray. In a large bowl, combine tomato soup and salsa. Stir in green beans and ¾ cup Cheddar cheese. Spread mixture into prepared baking dish. Evenly sprinkle nacho chips over bean mixture. Sprinkle remaining 6 tablespoons Cheddar cheese evenly over top. Bake for 25 to 30 minutes. Place baking dish on a wire rack and let set for 5 minutes. Divide into 6 servings.

Each serving equals:
HE: 1½ Vegetable, 1 Protein, ½ Bread, ¼ Slider, 10 Optional Calories
152 Calories, 4 gm Fat, 8 gm Protein, 21 gm Carbohydrate, 736 mg Sodium, 197 mg Calcium, 3 gm Fiber
DIABETIC: 1½ Vegetable, 1 Meat, ½ Starch/Carbohydrate

Frijoles San Juan

■ ❄ ■

Beans are a wonderful source of protein, and they're also a thrifty choice for an entree when you're watching your budget (and aren't we all?). This skillet dish is ready in just minutes and provides real flavor fireworks in a side dish serving.

Serves 4 (¼ cup)

10 ounces (one 16-ounce can) pinto beans, rinsed and drained
½ cup chunky salsa (mild, medium, or hot)

½ teaspoon dried minced garlic
½ cup +1 tablespoon (2¼ ounces) shredded Kraft reduced-fat Cheddar cheese

In a large bowl, slightly mash pinto beans with a potato masher or fork. Stir in salsa and garlic. Pour mixture into a large skillet sprayed with butter-flavored cooking spray. Cook over medium heat for 10 minutes. Add Cheddar cheese. Mix well to combine. Lower heat and simmer for 5 minutes, stirring occasionally.

Each serving equals:
HE: 2 Protein, ¼ Vegetable

115 Calories, 3 gm Fat, 8 gm Protein, 14 gm Carbohydrate, 428 mg Sodium, 160 mg Calcium, 3 gm Fiber

DIABETIC: 1 Meat, 1 Starch

Mexicali Rose Skillet Corn

■ ■ ■

Was there a legendary female known as Mexicali Rose, an irresistible woman whose charm was as great as her smile? I just like to think that such a lady shared her cooking expertise throughout the Southwest, and that this recipe is her legacy to the rest of us. *Olé!*   *Serves 6 (½ cup)*

¾ cup finely chopped celery
¼ cup finely chopped onion
½ cup finely chopped green bell pepper
¼ cup (one 2-ounce jar) chopped pimiento, undrained

1 tablespoon reduced-calorie margarine
⅛ teaspoon black pepper
3 cups frozen whole-kernel corn, thawed
1 teaspoon dried parsley flakes

In a large skillet sprayed with butter-flavored cooking spray, sauté celery, onion, and green pepper for 5 minutes. Stir in undrained pimiento, margarine, and black pepper. Add corn and parsley flakes. Mix well to combine. Lower heat, cover, and simmer for 5 minutes, stirring occasionally.

HINT: Thaw corn by placing in a colander and rinsing under hot water for one minute.

Each serving equals:
HE: 1 Bread, ½ Vegetable, ¼ Fat
97 Calories, 1 gm Fat, 2 gm Protein, 20 gm Carbohydrate, 28 mg Sodium, 7 mg Calcium, 2 gm Fiber
DIABETIC: 1 Starch, ½ Vegetable, ½ Fat

Tex-Mex Corn Bake

■ ❋ ■

This easy corn casserole tastes of real smoky barbecue flavor (one of the trade secrets of Brown Sugar Twin you may not have known!) and makes a terrific side dish all year round! There's something so hearty about baked corn that just warms your tummy and satisfies the hungriest men at the table.   *Serves 6*

¾ cup finely chopped onion
1¾ cups (one 15-ounce can)
* Hunt's Tomato Sauce*
¼ cup finely chopped
* celery*

1 tablespoon chili seasoning
1 tablespoon Brown Sugar Twin
⅛ teaspoon black pepper
3 cups frozen whole-kernel corn,
* thawed*

Preheat oven to 350 degrees. Spray an 8-by-8-inch baking dish with olive oil–flavored cooking spray. In a large skillet sprayed with olive oil–flavored cooking spray, sauté onion for 5 minutes. Stir in tomato sauce, celery, chili seasoning, Brown Sugar Twin, and black pepper. Add corn. Mix well to combine. Spread mixture into prepared baking dish. Bake for 45 to 50 minutes. Place baking dish on a wire rack and let set for 5 minutes. Divide into 6 servings.

HINT: Thaw corn by placing in a colander and rinsing under hot water for one minute.

Each serving equals:
HE: 1½ Vegetable, 1 Bread, 1 Optional Calorie

104 Calories, 0 gm Fat, 3 gm Protein, 23 gm Carbohydrate, 442 mg Sodium, 21 mg Calcium, 3 gm Fiber

DIABETIC: 1 Vegetable, 1 Starch

Spanish Limas

■ ❄ ■

Maybe lima beans have never awakened any excitement in your tastebuds, or perhaps your mom rarely served them at home. Let me be the one to convince you that these sturdy, starchy legumes can be incredibly tasty when baked in a creamy, tangy tomato sauce and topped with cheese! *Serves 6*

1½ cups chopped onion
1 cup chopped green bell pepper
2 cups (one 16-ounce can) tomatoes, chopped and undrained
10 ounces (one 16-ounce can) lima or butter beans, rinsed and drained

1 teaspoon Worcestershire sauce
⅛ teaspoon black pepper
1⅓ cups (5¼ ounces) shredded Kraft reduced-fat Cheddar cheese ☆

Preheat oven to 350 degrees. Spray an 8-by-8-inch baking dish with butter-flavored cooking spray. In a large skillet sprayed with butter-flavored cooking spray, sauté onion and green pepper for 6 to 8 minutes. Stir in undrained tomatoes. Lower heat and simmer for 10 minutes, stirring occasionally. Add lima beans, Worcestershire sauce, and black pepper. Mix well to combine. Layer half of bean mixture and half of Cheddar cheese in prepared baking dish. Repeat layers. Bake for 20 to 30 minutes. Place baking dish on a wire rack and let set for 5 minutes. Divide into 6 servings.

Each serving equals:
HE: 2 Protein, 1½ Vegetable
148 Calories, 4 gm Fat, 12 gm Protein, 16 gm Carbohydrate, 297 mg Sodium, 250 mg Calcium, 4 gm Fiber
DIABETIC: 1½ Meat, 1 Vegetable, ½ Starch

Cheesy Three-Bean Pot Pie

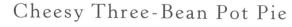

Don't think of homemade pot pie as too much trouble for a busy cook. The taste of a fresh crust is really something special—one bite will confirm that! Serve this with a refreshing glass of Sparkling Grape Sangria (see page 184), and you'll feel as if you're dining at sunset in the Sangre de Cristo Mountains of New Mexico.

Serves 8

¾ cup all-purpose flour

1½ cups (6 ounces) shredded Kraft reduced-fat Cheddar cheese ☆

1½ teaspoons baking powder

1 egg, slightly beaten, or equivalent in egg substitute

⅓ cup skim milk

½ cup chopped onion

½ cup chopped green bell pepper

10 ounces (one 16-ounce can) red kidney beans, rinsed and drained

2 cups (one 16-ounce can) cut green beans, rinsed and drained

2 cups (one 16-ounce can) wax beans, rinsed and drained

1 cup (one 8-ounce can) Hunt's Tomato Sauce

2 teaspoons chili seasoning

Preheat oven to 375 degrees. Spray a deep-dish 10-inch pie plate with olive oil–flavored cooking spray. In a medium bowl, combine flour, ½ cup Cheddar cheese, baking powder, egg, and skim milk. Mix well to combine. Pour mixture into prepared pie plate. Spread mixture evenly over bottom and up sides of pie plate. In a large skillet sprayed with olive oil–flavored cooking spray, sauté onion and green pepper for 5 minutes. Stir in kidney beans, green beans, wax beans, tomato sauce, and chili seasoning. Add ½ cup Cheddar cheese. Mix well to combine. Spoon mixture evenly over batter. Evenly sprinkle remaining ½ cup Cheddar cheese over top. Bake for 25 to 30 minutes or until edges are puffy and lightly browned. Place pie plate on a wire rack and let set for 5 minutes. Cut into 8 servings.

Each serving equals:

HE: 1¾ Protein, 1¾ Vegetable, ½ Bread, 4 Optional Calories

172 Calories, 4 gm Fat, 11 gm Protein, 23 gm Carbohydrate, 471 mg Sodium, 246 mg Calcium, 4 gm Fiber

DIABETIC: 1½ Vegetable, 1 Meat, 1 Starch

El Rancho Fish Fillets

■ ■ ■

Here's a baked fish dish with a real fiesta flair that's sure to please! This is good with any white fish from flounder and sole to halibut and cod. The topping keeps the fish wonderfully moist, and the aroma from the oven will gather the troops even without a call to dinner.   *Serves 4*

16 ounces white fish, cut into 4
*   pieces*
1 cup chunky salsa (mild,
*   medium, or hot)*
1 teaspoon dried parsley flakes

⅓ cup (1½ ounces) shredded
*   Kraft reduced-fat Cheddar*
*   cheese*
¼ cup Land O Lakes no-fat sour
*   cream*

Preheat oven to 350 degrees. Spray an 8-by-8-inch baking dish with butter-flavored cooking spray. Rinse fish pieces under cold water and gently pat dry. Evenly arrange fish pieces in prepared baking dish. In a small bowl, combine salsa and parsley flakes. Evenly spread mixture over fish pieces. Sprinkle Cheddar cheese evenly over top. Bake for 20 minutes. For each serving, place 1 piece of fish on a plate, evenly spoon sauce over top, and garnish with 1 table-spoon sour cream.

Each serving equals:

HE: 2 Protein, ½ Vegetable, 15 Optional Calories

134 Calories, 2 gm Fat, 20 gm Protein, 9 gm Carbohydrate, 621 mg Sodium, 125 mg Calcium, 0 gm Fiber

DIABETIC: 3 Meat, ½ Vegetable

Shrimp in Special Sauce

■ ■ ■

It comes as a surprise to many people to hear that shrimp is harvested along Texas's Gulf of Mexico shoreline. But those sweet, warm waters produce terrific seafood, and so shrimp is a welcome treat across the region. This rich skillet preparation can be served in any way you choose, though I think I prefer it over rice.

Serves 4 (½ cup)

2 tablespoons reduced-calorie
  margarine
1 (6-ounce) package frozen
  shrimp, thawed
1 cup chopped onion
1½ cups (one 12-fluid-ounce can)
  Carnation Evaporated Skim
  Milk
3 tablespoons all-purpose flour

¼ cup Heinz Light Harvest
  Ketchup or any reduced-
  sodium ketchup
1 teaspoon chili seasoning
2 tablespoons chopped fresh
  parsley or 2 teaspoons dried
  parsley flakes
½ teaspoon dried minced
  garlic

In a large skillet sprayed with butter-flavored cooking spray, melt margarine. Stir in shrimp and onion. Sauté for 6 to 8 minutes. In a covered jar, combine evaporated skim milk and flour. Shake well to blend. Pour milk mixture into shrimp mixture. Add ketchup, chili seasoning, parsley, and garlic. Mix well to combine. Lower heat and simmer for 5 minutes or until sauce thickens, stirring often.

HINT: 1. Thaw shrimp by placing in a colander and rinsing under hot water for one minute.
2. Good over toast, pasta, or rice.

Each serving equals:
HE: 1½ Protein, ¾ Skim Milk, ¾ Fat, ½ Vegetable, ¼ Bread, 15 Optional Calories

179 Calories, 3 gm Fat, 17 gm Protein, 21 gm Carbohydrate, 318 mg Sodium, 312 mg Calcium, 1 gm Fiber

DIABETIC: 1½ Meat, 1 Skim Milk, 1 Fat, ½ Vegetable

Shrimp Alfredo Deluxe

■ ■ ■

Here's a recipe worthy of America's newest family playland, Las Vegas! The brand-new hotels that have been rising in this desert mecca feature so many nongambling activities, Vegas has become a fun destination for just about everyone. It's a city where big is better, and the more deluxe, the more delightful, so this dish will fit right in!

Serves 4 (1 cup)

⅔ cup Carnation Nonfat Dry
  Milk Powder
1 cup water
2 tablespoons Kraft Fat Free
  Italian Dressing
¼ cup (¾ ounce) grated Kraft
  fat-free Parmesan cheese

1½ cups thinly sliced unpeeled
  zucchini
2 cups hot cooked fettuccine noodles, rinsed and drained
2 (4.5-ounce drained weight)
  cans small shrimp, rinsed and
  drained

In a large skillet, combine dry milk powder, water, and Italian dressing. Add Parmesan cheese and zucchini. Mix well to combine. Cook over medium heat for 3 to 4 minutes, stirring often. Stir in noodles and shrimp. Mix well to combine. Continue cooking for 2 to 3 minutes, stirring often.

HINT: 1½ cups broken uncooked fettuccine noodles usually cooks to about 2 cups.

Each serving equals:
HE: 2½ Protein, 1 Bread, ¾ Vegetable, ½ Skim Milk, 4 Optional Calories
238 Calories, 2 gm Fat, 23 gm Protein, 32 gm Carbohydrate, 329 mg Sodium, 188 mg Calcium, 2 gm Fiber
DIABETIC: 3 Meat, 1½ Starch/Carbohydrate, ½ Skim Milk

Arroz Con Pollo (Chicken with Rice)

■ ❋ ■

It appears on every Spanish and Mexican restaurant menu, and with good reason. Chicken and rice are staples in that ethnic cuisine. It's one of the first things I ordered when I encountered this kind of food, and I wanted to share my affection for this "comfort food" basic that is always a happy choice for dinner.

Serves 6 (¾ cup)

1 cup chopped onion
16 ounces skinned and boned
    uncooked chicken breasts, cut
    into 18 pieces
½ teaspoon dried minced garlic
½ teaspoon paprika
2 teaspoons dried parsley flakes
⅛ teaspoon black pepper

2 cups (one 16-ounce can)
    Healthy Request Chicken
    Broth
1⅓ cups (4 ounces) uncooked
    Minute Rice
¼ cup (one 2-ounce jar) chopped
    pimiento, undrained
1 cup frozen peas, thawed

In a large skillet sprayed with olive oil–flavored cooking spray, sauté onion for 5 minutes. Stir in chicken pieces, garlic, paprika, parsley flakes, and black pepper. Continue cooking for 10 to 12 minutes or until chicken pieces are browned, stirring occasionally. Add chicken broth. Mix well to combine. Bring mixture to a boil. Stir in uncooked rice, undrained pimiento, and peas. Lower heat and simmer for 15 minutes or until most of liquid is absorbed and rice is tender, stirring occasionally.

HINT: Thaw peas by placing in a colander and rinsing under hot water for one minute.

Each serving equals:
HE: 2 Protein, 1 Bread, ⅓ Vegetable, 5 Optional Calories
174 Calories, 2 gm Fat, 20 gm Protein, 19 gm Carbohydrate, 213 mg Sodium, 27 mg Calcium, 2 gm Fiber
DIABETIC: 2 Meat, ½ Starch/Carbohydrate

Santa Fe Chicken Casserole

■ ❄ ■

If you've never been to Santa Fe, it's a fantastic place to put on your "someday" itinerary, especially if you love music, theatre, art, and gorgeous scenery! The lifestyle is very laid-back, but the food in even the most casual restaurants there is very tasty. Cliff really enjoyed the Dorito crunch on top of this tangy, creamy combo. *Serves 4*

1 (10¾-ounce) can Healthy Request Cream of Chicken Soup

2 tablespoons Land O Lakes no-fat sour cream

1 teaspoon chili seasoning

1 cup (one 8-ounce can) whole-kernel corn, rinsed and drained

1 cup (one 8-ounce can) cut green beans, rinsed and drained

1 cup (one 8-ounce can) sliced carrots, rinsed and drained

⅓ cup (1½ ounces) shredded Kraft reduced-fat Cheddar cheese

1½ cups (8 ounces) diced cooked chicken breast

¼ cup (¾ ounce) crushed Dorito's WOW Nacho Chips

Preheat oven to 350 degrees. Spray an 8-by 8 inch baking dish with olive oil–flavored cooking spray. In a large bowl, combine chicken soup, sour cream, and chili seasoning. Add corn, green beans, and carrots. Mix well to combine. Stir in Cheddar cheese and chicken. Spread mixture evenly into prepared baking dish. Evenly sprinkle Nacho chips over top. Bake for 25 to 30 minutes. Place baking dish on a wire rack and let set for 5 minutes. Divide into 4 servings.

HINT: If you don't have leftovers, purchase a chunk of cooked chicken breast from your local deli.

Each serving equals:

HE: 2½ Protein, 1 Vegetable, ¾ Bread, ½ Slider, 5 Optional Calories

254 Calories, 6 gm Fat, 24 gm Protein, 26 gm Carbohydrate, 822 mg Sodium, 133 mg Calcium, 3 gm Fiber

DIABETIC: 2½ Meat, 1 Vegetable, 1 Starch

Southwest Strata

■ ❋ ■

This spicy, meaty, cheesy casserole makes an easy supper on the patio under a stunning red-gold sunset! As the canyons darken and the stars come out, you'll win cheers from the crowd after every bite. This recipe gives me a chance to deliver true "sausage" flavor without an ounce of the real thing.   *Serves 6*

8 ounces ground 90% lean turkey
   or beef
⅔ cup chopped onion
⅓ cup chopped green bell pepper
¼ teaspoon ground sage
¼ teaspoon garlic powder
¼ teaspoon poultry seasoning
¼ teaspoon black pepper
8 slices reduced-calorie bread,
   cut into 1-inch cubes

1 cup + 2 tablespoons (4½
   ounces) shredded Kraft
   reduced-fat Cheddar cheese
2 cups skim milk
1 cup chunky salsa (mild,
   medium, or hot)
3 eggs, beaten, or equivalent in
   egg substitute

Preheat oven to 350 degrees. Spray an 8-by-8-inch baking dish with butter-flavored cooking spray. In a large skillet sprayed with butter-flavored cooking spray, brown meat, onion, and green pepper. Stir in sage, garlic powder, poultry seasoning, and black pepper. Evenly arrange half of bread cubes in prepared baking dish. Sprinkle half of meat mixture and half of Cheddar cheese over top. Repeat layers. In a medium bowl, combine skim milk, salsa, and eggs. Pour mixture evenly over mixture in baking dish. Bake for 50 to 60 minutes or until a knife inserted near center comes out clean. Place baking dish on a wire rack and let set for 5 minutes. Divide into 6 servings.

HINT: Strata can be prepared, covered, and refrigerated for up to 24 hours before baking.

Each serving equals:
HE: 2½ Protein (½ limited), ⅔ Bread, ⅔ Vegetable, ⅓ Skim Milk

257 Calories, 9 gm Fat, 21 gm Protein, 23 gm Carbohydrate, 635 mg Sodium, 281 mg Calcium, 4 gm Fiber

DIABETIC: 2 Meat, 1 Starch, 1 Vegetable

Picadillo (Castilian Hash)

■ ❋ ■

No, I didn't make a mistake on the ingredients for this Spanish-inspired dish that incorporates nuts and raisins into a ground meat dish. Some adventurous chef once decided that they might work well together, and I was more than a bit surprised to discover that it's true! One of the best reasons for a regional cookbook like this is to expand your culinary horizons, and this dish will do it!

Serves 6 (¾ cup)

16 ounces ground 90% lean turkey or beef
1¾ cups (one 14½-ounce can) Swanson Beef Broth
1 cup finely chopped onion
1½ cups (7.5 ounces) diced raw potatoes
1 cup (one 8-ounce can) Hunt's Tomato Sauce

1 tablespoon (¼ ounce) chopped almonds
3 tablespoons raisins
1 tablespoon Brown Sugar Twin
1 tablespoon chili seasoning
¼ teaspoon dried minced garlic
1 teaspoon dried parsley flakes

In a large skillet, combine meat and beef broth. Cook over medium heat for 10 minutes or until meat is browned, stirring often. Add onion, potatoes, and tomato sauce. Mix well to combine. Stir in almonds, raisins, Brown Sugar Twin, chili seasoning, garlic, and parsley flakes. Continue cooking for 10 minutes or until potatoes are tender, stirring often.

Each serving equals:
HE: 2 Protein, 1 Vegetable, ¼ Bread, ¼ Fruit, 12 Optional Calories

191 Calories, 7 gm Fat, 16 gm Protein, 16 gm Carbohydrate, 561 mg Sodium, 20 mg Calcium, 2 gm Fiber

DIABETIC: 2 Meat, 1 Vegetable, ½ Starch/Carbohydrate

Cowboy Chicken-Fried Steaks

■ ❄ ■

I have a feeling that when you're riding the range and driving cattle, you're ready to eat just about anything when it's time for dinner! Still, some very tasty recipes have been inspired by those heroic cowboys over the years, including this version of that regional favorite, chicken-fried steak. Just wait till you taste the gravy!

Serves 4

1 tablespoon + 1 teaspoon
   reduced-calorie margarine
6 tablespoons all-purpose flour ☆
1 teaspoon chili seasoning
2 tablespoons skim milk
4 (4-ounce) lean tenderized
   minute or cube steaks

1½ cups (one 12-fluid-ounce can)
   Carnation Evaporated Skim
   Milk
½ cup water
1 teaspoon dried parsley flakes
⅛ teaspoon black pepper

In a large skillet sprayed with butter-flavored cooking spray, melt margarine. Meanwhile, in a shallow dish, combine 3 tablespoons flour and chili seasoning. Pour skim milk into another shallow dish. Coat steaks first in skim milk, then in flour mixture. Evenly arrange coated steaks in skillet. Brown for 3 to 5 minutes on each side. Remove steaks and keep warm. In a covered jar, combine evaporated skim milk, water, and remaining 3 tablespoons flour. Shake well to blend. Pour milk mixture into same skillet steaks were cooked in. Stir in parsley flakes and black pepper. Cook over medium heat until gravy thickens, stirring often. For each serving, place 1 steak on a plate and spoon about ½ cup gravy over top.

Each serving equals:
HE: 3 Protein, ¾ Skim Milk, ½ Bread, ½ Fat, 3 Optional Calories
262 Calories, 6 gm Fat, 34 gm Protein, 18 gm Carbohydrate, 204 mg Sodium, 19 mg Calcium, 0 gm Fiber
DIABETIC: 3 Meat, 1 Skim Milk, ½ Starch, ½ Fat

Green Chili Stew

■ ❄ ■

Anyone who knows me knows that I consider myself a "wimp" when it comes to spicy food. I prefer my salsa mild and a light touch with the chili powder. (Cliff, on the other hand, likes smoke coming out of his ears!) But I knew this book wouldn't be complete without a recipe for this favorite, and so I decided to risk it. I was pleasantly surprised by the tang those chilis provided, and I bet you will be too!

Serves 6 (¾ cup)

2 cups (one 16-ounce can) tomatoes, chopped and undrained
1 cup (one 8-ounce jar) green chilies, undrained
1 teaspoon garlic powder

1 teaspoon chili seasoning
1 teaspoon dried parsley flakes
⅛ teaspoon black pepper
2 full cups (12 ounces) diced cooked lean roast pork

In a large saucepan, combine undrained tomatoes, undrained green chilies, garlic powder, chili seasoning, parsley flakes, and black pepper. Stir in roast pork. Bring mixture to a boil. Lower heat, cover, and simmer for 15 to 20 minutes, stirring occasionally.

HINT: 1. If you want it even "hotter", you can always add more green chilies or jalapeño chilies.
2. If you don't have leftovers, purchase a chunk of lean cooked roast pork from your local deli.

Each serving equals:
HE: 2 Protein, 1 Vegetable
129 Calories, 5 gm Fat, 16 gm Protein, 5 gm Carbohydrate, 302 mg Sodium, 93 mg Calcium, 2 gm Fiber
DIABETIC: 2 Meat, 1 Vegetable

Rio Grande Pork Tenders

■ ❄ ■

Grilling and barbecuing are two of the most popular cooking methods in this region, but let's face it, sometimes the weather isn't good enough to prepare dinner outside. I worked a little bit of magic with my spice blend, and I think you'll be delighted at how much saucy flavor this recipe captures in your top-of-the-stove skillet!

Serves 4

4 (4-ounce) lean tenderized pork tenderloins
1¾ cups (one 14½-ounce can) stewed tomatoes, chopped and undrained
¾ cup chopped onion

¼ cup (1 ounce) pimiento-stuffed olives
1 tablespoon Brown Sugar Twin
1 teaspoon chili seasoning
⅛ teaspoon black pepper

In a large skillet sprayed with butter-flavored cooking spray, lightly brown meat for 3 to 4 minutes on each side. In a medium bowl, combine undrained tomatoes, onion, olives, Brown Sugar Twin, chili seasoning, and black pepper. Spoon mixture evenly over meat. Lower heat, cover, and simmer for 30 minutes or until meat is tender. When serving, evenly spoon sauce over meat.

Each serving equals:
HE: 3 Protein, 1¼ Vegetable, ¼ Fat, 1 Optional Calorie

190 Calories, 6 gm Fat, 24 gm Protein, 10 gm Carbohydrate, 390 mg Sodium, 48 mg Calcium, 2 gm Fiber

DIABETIC: 3 Meat, 1 Vegetable

South-of-the-Border Pork Sandwiches

■ ■ ■

Cliff made an interesting comment about the food we sampled in Mexico versus the meals we had while traveling through the Southwest. He felt that in general the food on this side of the border was spicier and more to his liking. But he gave two thumbs up to this fruity, spicy way of serving one of his favorite roast meats!

Serves 4

2 full cups (12 ounces) finely diced lean cooked roast pork
½ cup chunky salsa (mild, medium, or hot)
¼ cup apricot spreadable fruit
1 teaspoon dried parsley flakes
4 reduced-calorie hamburger buns

In a large skillet sprayed with butter-flavored cooking spray, combine pork, salsa, spreadable fruit, and parsley flakes. Cook over medium heat for 6 to 8 minutes or until mixture is heated through, stirring occasionally. For each sandwich, spoon about ½ cup meat mixture into a hamburger bun

Each serving equals:
HE: 3 Protein, 1 Bread, 1 Fruit, ¼ Vegetable

262 Calories, 6 gm Fat, 26 gm Protein, 26 gm Carbohydrate, 359 mg Sodium, 18 mg Calcium, 1 gm Fiber

DIABETIC: 3 Meat, 1 Bread, 1 Fruit

Southwest Corned Beef and Cabbage

■ ✳ ■

I'm not sure if very many Irish immigrants found their way to the American Southwest, though it's intriguing to think about when you taste this recipe. It takes a classic and stirs in a little desert heat to create a savory new sensation! If you're a fan of corned beef and you're ready for a little adventure, fix this one tonight.

Serves 4 (¾ cup)

3 cups shredded cabbage
1 cup chopped onion
½ cup chopped green bell
   pepper
1 (10¾-ounce can) Healthy
   Request Tomato Soup

1 tablespoon chili seasoning
¼ cup (one 2-ounce jar) chopped
   pimiento, undrained
2 (2.5-ounce) packages Carl
   Buddig 90% lean corned beef,
   shredded

In a large skillet sprayed with butter-flavored cooking spray, sauté cabbage, onion, and green pepper for 6 to 8 minutes. Stir in tomato soup, chili seasoning, and undrained pimiento. Add corned beef. Mix well to combine. Lower heat and simmer for 10 minutes, stirring occasionally.

Each serving equals:

HE: 2¼ Vegetable, 1¼ Protein, ½ Slider, 5 Optional Calories

131 Calories, 3 gm Fat, 9 gm Protein, 17 gm Carbohydrate, 716 mg Sodium, 43 mg Calcium, 3 gm Fiber

DIABETIC: 1½ Vegetable, 1 Meat, ½ Starch/Carbohydrate

Date Caramel Cream

■ ■ ■

Many Americans think of dates as some foreign fruit, but they grow in the Southwest and provide an amazing amount of sweet flavor in this intriguing recipe. The custard is so luscious, and the bits of dates and nuts a true taste treat in every spoonful. If you've got a hankering for something a little different tonight, make a date to serve this!

Serves 4

1 (4-serving) package JELL-O sugar-free vanilla cook-and-serve pudding mix
2 tablespoons Brown Sugar Twin
1½ cups (one 12-fluid-ounce can) Carnation Evaporated Skim Milk

½ cup sliced dates
1 teaspoon vanilla extract
¼ cup (1 ounce) chopped walnuts
¼ cup Cool Whip Lite

In a medium saucepan, combine dry pudding mix, Brown Sugar Twin, and evaporated skim milk. Stir in dates. Cook over medium heat until mixture thickens and starts to boil, stirring constantly. Remove from heat. Add vanilla extract and walnuts. Mix well to combine. Pour mixture into 4 dessert dishes. Refrigerate for at least 1 hour. Just before serving, top each with 1 tablespoon Cool Whip Lite.

Each serving equals:

HE: 1 Fruit, ¾ Skim Milk, ½ Fat, ¼ Protein, ¼ Slider, 12 Optional Calories

217 Calories, 5 gm Fat, 8 gm Protein, 35 gm Carbohydrate, 230 mg Sodium, 298 mg Calcium, 2 gm Fiber

DIABETIC: 1 Fruit, 1 Skim Milk, ½ Fat, ½ Starch/Carbohydrate

Mexican Chocolate Mousse

■ ■ ■

It's pretty and it's refreshing, two important elements when you're planning just the right finale for a spicy Southwestern meal. But this special chocolate mousse dessert is full of unexpected surprises, like those bits of almond hidden among the folds of creamy chocolate.

Serves 4

1 (4-serving) package JELL-O sugar-free instant chocolate pudding mix
⅔ cup Carnation Nonfat Dry Milk Powder
1¼ cups water
¾ cup Dannon plain fat-free yogurt

½ cup Cool Whip Free ☆
1 teaspoon almond extract
¾ teaspoon ground cinnamon ☆
1 tablespoon (¼ ounce) chopped almonds

In a large bowl, combine dry pudding mix, dry milk powder, and water. Mix well using a wire whisk. Blend in yogurt. Add ¼ cup Cool Whip Free, almond extract, and ½ teaspoon cinnamon. Mix gently to combine. Evenly spoon mixture into 4 dessert dishes. Top each with 1 tablespoon Cool Whip Free. Lightly sprinkle remaining cinnamon and ¾ teaspoon almonds over top of each. Refrigerate for at least 15 minutes.

Each serving equals:
HE: ¾ Skim Milk, ½ Slider, 14 Optional Calories

125 Calories, 1 gm Fat, 7 gm Protein, 22 gm Carbohydrate, 422 mg Sodium, 204 mg Calcium, 1 gm Fiber

DIABETIC: 1 Skim Milk, ½ Starch/Carbohydrate

San Antonio Pecan Chocolate Cream Pie

■ ❈ ■

Pecans are native to this country and grow in many parts of the U.S., but the nuts grown in the region near San Antonio, Texas, are especially fine. These have always been my "nut of choice" and I still enjoy them often, though used in moderation. Invite all the chocolate lovers you know to sit down for a piece of this festive pie!

Serves 8

2 (4-serving) packages JELL-O
   sugar-free chocolate cook-and-
   serve pudding mix
1⅓ cups Carnation Nonfat Dry
   Milk Powder
2½ cups water
1 teaspoon vanilla extract
1 teaspoon ground cinnamon

¼ cup (1 ounce) chopped
   pecans ☆
1 (6-ounce) Keebler chocolate
   piecrust
2 (2½-inch) chocolate graham
   cracker squares, made into
   crumbs

Preheat oven to 350 degrees. In a medium saucepan, combine dry pudding mixes, dry milk powder, and water. Cook over medium heat until mixture thickens and starts to boil, stirring constantly. Remove from heat. Stir in vanilla extract, cinnamon, and 3 tablespoons pecans. Spread mixture into piecrust. In a small bowl, combine graham cracker crumbs and remaining 1 tablespoon pecans. Evenly sprinkle crumb mixture over top. Bake for 25 to 30 minutes. Place pie plate on a wire rack and let set for 15 minutes. Refrigerate for at least 2 hours. Cut into 8 servings.

HINT: A self-seal sandwich bag works great for crushing graham crackers.

Each serving equals:
HE: ½ Skim Milk, ½ Bread, ½ Fat, 1 Slider, 2 Optional Calories

203 Calories, 7 gm Fat, 6 gm Protein, 29 gm Carbohydrate, 277 mg Sodium, 143 mg Calcium, 1 gm Fiber

DIABETIC: 1½ Starch/Carbohydrate, 1 Fat, ½ Skim Milk

Rolled Cinnamon Chocolate Cake

■ ❋ ■

Some combinations are unique to certain cuisines and cultures, so when you're offered a blend of chocolate and cinnamon, you know to shout *olé!* Here's a festive jelly-roll-style cake that is amazingly rich and fragrant as it bakes.   *Serves 8*

4 eggs or equivalent in egg substitute
½ cup pourable Sugar Twin or
   Sprinkle Sweet
1 teaspoon vanilla extract
¾ cup Bisquick Reduced Fat
   Baking Mix
¼ cup unsweetened cocoa
1 (4-serving) package JELL-O
   sugar-free instant chocolate
   pudding mix

⅔ cup Carnation Nonfat Dry Milk
   Powder
½ teaspoon ground cinnamon
1⅓ cups water
¼ cup (1 ounce) chopped walnuts
½ cup Cool Whip Lite

Preheat oven to 400 degrees. Spray a 15-by-10-by-1-inch jelly-roll pan with butter-flavored cooking spray. Line bottom of pan with waxed paper, then spray paper with butter-flavored cooking spray. In a large bowl, beat eggs with an electric mixer on HIGH until thick and creamy. Stir in Sugar Twin and vanilla extract. Add baking mix and cocoa. Mix gently to combine. Spread batter evenly in prepared pan. Bake for 5 to 7 minutes or until the center springs back when lightly pressed. Loosen cake around the edges with a knife. Invert the pan onto a clean tea towel and peel off waxed paper. Starting at short end, roll up the cake and towel together. Place on a wire rack and allow to cool completely. Just before unrolling, prepare filling. In a large bowl, combine dry pudding mix, dry milk powder, cinnamon, and water. Mix well using a wire whisk. Stir in walnuts. Unroll cake and carefully remove towel. Evenly spread pudding mixture over top and reroll cake. Cut into eight 1¼-inch pieces and top each piece with 2 tablespoons Cool Whip Lite.

Each serving equals:
HE: ⅔ Protein, (½ limited), ½ Bread, ¼ Skim Milk, ¼ Fat, ¼ Slider,
18 Optional Calories

154 Calories, 6 gm Fat, 7 gm Protein, 18 gm Carbohydrate, 359 mg Sodium,
107 mg Calcium, 1 gm Fiber

DIABETIC: 1 Starch/Carbohydrate, 1 Fat, ½ Meat

Tex-Mex Munch Mix

■ ■ ■

Here's a wonderful snack for young and old! It may have been inspired by cooks on both sides of the Rio Grande, but these days, Americans everywhere are spicing things up whenever they get the chance. *Serves 4 (1½ cups)*

6 cups warm air-popped popcorn
I Can't Believe Its Not Butter
Spray

1 tablespoon chili seasoning
¾ cup (3 ounces) shredded Kraft
reduced-fat Cheddar cheese

In a very large bowl, lightly coat popcorn with I Can't Believe It's Not Butter! Spray. Add chili seasoning. Mix well to combine. Stir in Cheddar cheese. Store leftovers in an airtight container.

HINT: Four tablespoons unpopped popcorn usually makes about 6 cups popped popcorn, if prepared in an air popper.

Each serving equals:
HE: 1 Protein, ½ Bread
104 Calories, 4 gm Fat, 7 gm Protein, 10 gm Carbohydrate, 179 mg Sodium, 141 mg Calcium, 2 gm Fiber
DIABETIC: 1 Meat, ½ Starch

Gringo Nachos

■ ■ ■

When your family's favorite basketball team is scheduled to play, here's a top choice for nibbling in front of that big-screen TV! This simple recipe can be easily doubled or tripled for large groups, but it might be best to offer those spicy chilis in a separate bowl.

Serves 4

10 ounces (one 16-ounce can) pinto beans, rinsed and drained

1 teaspoon chili seasoning

½ cup chunky salsa (mild, medium, or hot)

24 oven-baked corn tortilla chips

1 cup peeled and chopped fresh tomato

½ cup thinly sliced pickled jalapeño chilies (optional)

1 cup + 2 tablespoons (4½ ounces) shredded Kraft reduced-fat Cheddar cheese

Preheat oven to 400 degrees. In a medium saucepan, mash pinto beans with a fork. Stir in chili seasoning and salsa. Cook over medium heat until mixture is hot, stirring often. Remove from heat. Spoon 1 full tablespoon bean mixture on top of each tortilla chip and arrange chips in a single layer on a large baking sheet. Evenly sprinkle tomato and chilies over chips. Sprinkle Cheddar cheese evenly over top. Bake for 3 to 5 minutes. Divide into 4 servings. Serve hot.

Each serving equals:

HE: 2¾ Protein, 1 Bread, 1 Vegetable

206 Calories, 6 gm Fat, 13 gm Protein, 25 gm Carbohydrate, 836 mg Sodium, 268 mg Calcium, 5 gm Fiber

DIABETIC: 2 Meat, 1 Starch, 1 Vegetable

Panhandle Cheese Muffins

■ ❄ ■

Whether the day's agenda calls for fixing fences, herding cattle, or just watching over some feisty children, a nourishing breakfast or brunch is a very good idea. These creamy, cheesy muffins smell so good while they're baking, it's tempting to keep pulling open the oven door, but DON'T! Patience will be rewarded, I promise.

Serves 8

1½ cups Bisquick Reduced Fat
    Baking Mix
¾ cup (3 ounces) shredded Kraft
    reduced-fat Cheddar cheese
1 tablespoon pourable Sugar
    Twin or Sprinkle Sweet
1 teaspoon dried onion flakes

1 teaspoon dried parsley flakes
½ cup skim milk
¼ cup Land O Lakes no-fat sour
    cream
¼ cup (one 2-ounce jar) chopped
    pimiento, undrained

Preheat oven to 375 degrees. Spray 8 wells of a 12-hole muffin pan with butter-flavored cooking spray or line with paper liners. In a large bowl, combine baking mix, Cheddar cheese, Sugar Twin, onion flakes, and parsley flakes. Add skim milk, sour cream, and undrained pimiento. Mix just until combined. Evenly spoon batter into prepared muffin wells. Bake for 22 to 26 minutes or until a toothpick inserted in center comes out clean. Place muffin pan on a wire rack and let set for 5 minutes. Remove muffins from pan and continue cooling on wire rack.

Each serving equals:

HE: 1 Bread, ½ Protein, 14 Optional Calories

123 Calories, 3 gm Fat, 5 gm Protein, 19 gm Carbohydrate, 369 mg Sodium, 123 mg Calcium, 1 gm Fiber

DIABETIC: 1 Starch, ½ Meat

Alamo Fudge

■ ■ ■

Some things in life are worth fighting for, like freedom and justice—and this spectacular fudge that's got a flavor as big as Texas! What a luscious treat to enjoy or offer at the PTA bake sale—and you'll be relieved to notice that a "serving" means two delectable pieces.

Serves 16 (2 pieces)

2⅔ cups Carnation Nonfat Dry Milk Powder

½ cup water

½ cup cornstarch

1 cup pourable Sugar Twin or Sprinkle Sweet

1 cup (4 ounces) mini chocolate chips

1 (8-ounce) package Philadelphia fat-free cream cheese

¼ cup vanilla extract

½ cup (2 ounces) chopped pecans

Spray an 8-by-12-inch baking dish with butter-flavored cooking spray. In a large saucepan, combine dry milk powder, water, cornstarch, Sugar Twin, and chocolate chips. Cook over medium heat until mixture thickens and chocolate chips are melted, stirring constantly. Remove from heat. Add cream cheese and vanilla extract. Mix well using a wire whisk until well blended. Stir in pecans. Spread mixture evenly into prepared baking dish. Refrigerate for 2 hours or until firm. Cut into 32 pieces. Refrigerate leftovers.

Each serving equals:

HE: ½ Skim Milk, ½ Fat, ¼ Protein, ½ Slider, 18 Optional Calories

152 Calories, 4 gm Fat, 10 gm Protein, 19 gm Carbohydrate, 177 mg Sodium, 298 mg Calcium, 0 gm Fiber

DIABETIC: 1 Starch/Carbohydrate, ½ Skim Milk, ½ Fat

Blended Magical Margaritas

■ ■ ■

Some people say that the ideal accompaniment to a south-of-the-border meal is beer, while others may choose a Tequila Sunrise. But the margarita is the number-one choice of Mexican food fans, and here's my delightfully teetotaling take on this beloved beverage!

Serves 4 (1 cup)

¼ cup + 1 tablespoon lime
    juice ☆
1 teaspoon salt
2 cups Diet Mountain Dew

2 tablespoons pourable Sugar
    Twin or Sprinkle Sweet
2 cups ice cubes

Pour 1 tablespoon lime juice in a small bowl. Sprinkle salt on a piece of waxed paper. Dip the rims of 4 tall glasses into lime juice, then into salt. Place the glasses in the freezer for 15 minutes or until "frost" sets. Just before serving, in a blender container, combine remaining ¼ cup lime juice, Diet Mountain Dew, and Sugar Twin. Cover and process on BLEND for 10 seconds. Add ice cubes, a couple at a time, re-cover, and process on BLEND for 30 to 40 seconds or until mixture is blended. Evenly spoon into frosted glasses. Serve at once.

HINT: Use either fresh lime juice or the lime juice that comes in a plastic lime from the Produce section of store. DO NOT use bottled lime juice!

Each serving equals:

HE: 3 Optional Calories

4 Calories, 0 gm Fat, 0 gm Protein, 1 Carbohydrate, 596 mg Sodium, 2 mg Calcium, 0 gm Fiber

DIABETIC: Free Food

Sparkling Grape Sangria

∎ ∎ ∎

Spanish tradition suggests that fruited wine punches are the perfect choice for celebrations, but I don't see any reason to miss out on this delightful tradition just because you prefer non-alcoholic refreshment. This is great for a summer party, when the grapes are at their sweetest and most vivid green!

Serves 6 (1 full cup)

1 cup seedless green grapes	*2 cups club soda*
1⅓ cups unsweetened grape juice	*6 lime slices*
2⅔ cups Diet Sprite or Diet Rite	*6 lemon slices*
white grape soda	*1 cup ice cubes*

Arrange grapes in a single layer in an 8-by-8-inch dish. Freeze for 20 to 30 minutes or until frosty and partially frozen. In a large pitcher, combine grape juice, white grape soda, and club soda. Refrigerate until grapes are partially frozen. Gently stir grapes, lime slices, lemon slices, and ice cubes into juice mixture. Serve at once.

Each serving equals:

HE: 1 Fruit

56 Calories, 0 gm Fat, 0 gm Protein, 14 gm Carbohydrate, 19 mg Sodium, 17 mg Calcium, 0 gm Fiber

DIABETIC: 1 Fruit

THE WEST

■ ■ ■

Ever since I was a child studying American history, just the words *the West* have had a kind of magical effect on me. I was fascinated by the tales of the pioneers traveling by wagon train for so many months. I admired their courage and endurance, and I wondered what it must have been like to see the new territories they passed through. Imagine your first glimpse of the Rocky Mountains, so majestic and forbidding, and just think of how terrifying it must have been to cross the Missouri and Colorado rivers in order to reach the new land.

But I also thought how thrilling it would have been for them to see the great Pacific Ocean after all those dusty weeks on the road, and how magnificent the lush green valleys of California would have looked to those brave dreamers. Those American originals, those sturdy and intrepid men and women, had traveled west in search of opportunity, in hopes of claiming land of their own. What they found was a world of remarkable beauty, where abundant wildlife and fertile fields promised a future that they could shape for the generations to come after them.

The West has been home to a wonderful diversity of cultures and peoples, and the food of this region reflects that uniqueness and variety. What I like best about Western cooking is that people here seem open to anything and everything. You won't find traditionalists in this part of the country. More often than not, change begins in the West and works its way east. You really see it in their cooking, not to mention in other areas like music, books, and clothing trends.

I think part of the reason this region develops so many innovative types of dishes is that their ingredients are so fresh, and everything under the sun is growing out there! It just hits their porch first. Most of this region, especially Southern California, has a growing season that lasts all year long. It's true that with modern methods of shipping produce coast-to-coast, we can all share in such bounty, but there's nothing like eating grapes and oranges only hours after they've been picked, or biting into the very freshest asparagus and tomatoes when we're digging out from a foot of snow in DeWitt, Iowa!

So when I was researching the recipes for this section, I kept that pioneer spirit in mind, and that regional appreciation for what's new and what's best in our markets. I wanted to share food traditions as diverse as Mexican and Chinese as well as those island flavors that whisper "Hawaii" with every sip and taste. Years before I ever got to see it for myself, I'd traveled to the West through reading cookbooks that celebrated its cuisine, and it came alive to me with every recipe I read.

Even though I'm not a big fan of shellfish (except shrimp, which I love), I wanted to visit San Francisco, ride the cable cars, and gaze out at the the beautiful bridge that symbolizes that lovely place. The *Golden Gate Carrot Cake* I created for this book is as sweet and special as my memories of that first visit to the "city on the bay." And my *San Francisco Minestrone* will warm you on the foggiest day of the year. It's a beautiful city and a great place to eat if you are lucky enough to visit there. Just as in the ballad made famous by Tony Bennett, I did leave a bit of my heart in San Francisco!

Because so many of our nations's most spectacular national parks are in the West, I selected a few recipes perfect for your family's visit to those beautiful settings. Don't set off for Yosemite or Yellowstone without first packing some of my *Crunchy Trail Mix,* and definitely bring the fixings for my *High Country Camper's Breakfast* if your itinerary calls for a visit to Zion or Bryce National Parks. You'll have enough energy for a day of hiking and rock climbing if you're so inclined, or just for strolling and taking photographs for the family scrapbook.

Doesn't thinking about those wide-open spaces make you hungry for hearty food like my *Sierra Beef and Rice Supper?* This is cattle country, and I can easily imagine the camp cook clanging the dinner bell to call the cowboys over to the campfire for a stick-to-your-ribs meal under a setting sun.

Cliff and I have enjoyed several visits to Hawaii, and we've eaten well every single time! So this section contains a number of recipes inspired by those meals, including at least one memorable luau. Cliff still talks about his first sight of the pit-cooked pig that is the centerpiece for these feasts, and the great taste of the barbecued-pork sandwiches they served from it.

The West has been a favorite spot for both of us, and I think I could be happy living in San Diego. Maybe, when we all go to heaven, that's what it'll be like—no insects, rarely too hot or too cold, rarely does it rain on your special events. Everywhere you look, there's every shade of green you can imagine, and such beautiful blue skies. When it's wintry here at home, I remember those wonderful southwesterly breezes—not so much that it blows your hat off, but just enough for a refreshing coolness as it hits your face.

I just can't imagine God changing anything in heaven!

THE WEST RECIPES

Tomato, Spinach, and Basil Soup

San Francisco Minestrone

Hawaiian Peanut-Carrot Salad

Orange-Romaine Salad

Green Bean Salad with Creamy
  Mustard Dressing

Pineapple-Kiwi Fruit Salad

Endless Sunset Grape Salad

Creamy Fruit Mold

Heavenly Butterscotch Isle Apple
  Salad

Winter Apple Salad

Sweet-and-Sour Carrots

Escalloped Carrots

Garlic Mashed Potatoes

Scrambled Eggs Foo Yung

Egg Mushroom Sauce over Muffins

California Harvest Pizza

Creamed Tuna and Peas on Toast
  Triangles

Toasted Tuna Salad Sandwiches

Vegas-Style Shrimp Cocktail

Sierra Beef and Rice Supper

South Seas Meatloaf

Pepper and Olive Steak

Hawaiian Ham-Filled Tomatoes

Chipped Beef and Potato Skillet

Pineapple Coconut Bars

Pineapple Tarts

Waikiki Lemon Coconut Cream Pie

Hawaiian Strawberry Crumb Pie

Maraschino Cherry Spice Cake

Golden Gate Carrot Cake

Date Nut Muffins

Paradise Banana Bread

Crunchy Trail Mix

Denver Cheese Omelet

High Country Camper's Breakfast

Olive-Nut Spread

Lanai Sunset Punch

Big Island Piña Colada

Tomato, Spinach, and Basil Soup

■ ❊ ■

Herbs are an important part of West Coast cooking, though most recipes created out there call for fresh instead of dried. I enjoy the taste of fresh basil, but it's hard to keep it on hand when we travel so much, so I've experimented to find the right proportions for dried. Make sure you refresh your supply of spices about once a year, because they can lose some of their "kick" over time.

Serves 4 (1 cup)

½ cup chopped onion
1½ cups (one 12-fluid-ounce can)
  Carnation Evaporated Skim
  Milk
1 tablespoon all-purpose flour
1¾ cups (one 15-ounce can)
  Hunt's Tomato Sauce
1 cup water

2 teaspoons pourable Sugar Twin
  or Sprinkle Sweet
1 teaspoon dried basil
⅛ teaspoon black pepper
2 cups shredded fresh spinach
  leaves
¼ cup (¾ ounce) grated Kraft
  fat-free Parmesan cheese

In a large saucepan sprayed with butter-flavored cooking spray, sauté onion for 5 minutes or until tender. In a covered jar, combine evaporated skim milk and flour. Shake well to blend. Stir milk mixture into sautéed onion. Add tomato sauce, water, Sugar Twin, basil, and black pepper. Mix gently to combine. Lower heat and simmer for 10 minutes, stirring often. Stir in spinach. Continue simmering for 3 minutes, stirring occasionally. When serving, top each bowl with 1 tablespoon Parmesan cheese.

Each serving equals:
HE: 2½ Vegetable, ¾ Skim Milk, ¼ Protein, 8 Optional Calories
132 Calories, 0 gm Fat, 9 gm Protein, 24 gm Carbohydrate, 907 mg Sodium, 311 mg Calcium, 3 gm Fiber
DIABETIC: 2 Vegetable, 1 Skim Milk

San Francisco Minestrone

■ ✳ ■

A hearty soup filled with veggies and rice struck me as the perfect foggy day lunchtime treat! I've crossed the Golden Gate when you couldn't see the other side, when there was a definite chill in the air. What a comfort a bowl of this would be, especially coupled with a tasty sandwich on sourdough bread—yum!

Serves 6 (1½ cups)

16 ounces ground 90% lean
   turkey or beef
1 cup chopped onion
1 cup sliced carrots
1 cup finely sliced celery
2 cups (one 16-ounce can) tomatoes, chopped and undrained
3 cups water

⅔ cup (2 ounces) uncooked
   Minute Rice
2 cups shredded spinach leaves
1½ teaspoons dried basil
⅛ teaspoon black pepper
½ cup + 1 tablespoon (2¼
   ounces) shredded Kraft
   reduced-fat Cheddar cheese

In a large saucepan sprayed with butter-flavored cooking spray, brown meat and onion. Add carrots, celery, undrained tomatoes, and water. Mix well to combine. Bring mixture to a boil. Lower heat, cover, and simmer for 15 minutes. Stir in uncooked rice, spinach, basil, and black pepper. Re-cover and continue simmering for 10 minutes or until rice and vegetables are tender. When serving, top each bowl with 1½ tablespoons Cheddar cheese.

Each serving equals:

HE: 2½ Protein, 2 Vegetable, ⅓ Bread

212 Calories, 8 gm Fat, 18 gm Protein, 17 gm Carbohydrate, 319 mg Sodium, 128 mg Calcium, 3 gm Fiber

DIABETIC: 2 Meat, 1½ Vegetable, ½ Starch

Hawaiian Peanut-Carrot Salad

■ ■ ■

The colors of a sunrise over Diamond Head are like nothing else in the world! This salad reminded me of those rosy, golden streaks in the sky. If you don't have the time (or the right appliance) to shred your own fresh carrots, don't skip this recipe—buy them already shredded and packaged in your grocer's veggie department! It may cost a little more, but your good health is worth it.

Serves 6 (¾ cup)

3 cups shredded carrots
½ cup raisins
¼ cup (1 ounce) chopped dry-roasted peanuts
1 cup (one 8-ounce can) crushed pineapple, packed in fruit juice, undrained

½ cup Kraft fat-free mayonnaise
2 tablespoons Peter Pan reduced-fat peanut butter

In a large bowl, combine carrots, raisins, and peanuts. In a medium bowl, combine undrained pineapple, mayonnaise, and peanut butter. Add pineapple mixture to carrot mixture. Mix well to combine. Cover and refrigerate for at least 15 minutes. Gently stir again just before serving.

HINT: To plump up raisins without "cooking," place in a glass measuring cup and microwave on HIGH for 20 seconds.

Each serving equals:
HE: 1 Fruit, 1 Vegetable, ⅔ Fat, ⅓ Protein
160 Calories, 4 gm Fat, 3 gm Protein, 28 gm Carbohydrate, 220 mg Sodium, 29 mg Calcium, 3 gm Fiber
DIABETIC: 1 Fruit, 1 Vegetable, 1 Fat, ½ Starch/Carbohydrate

Orange-Romaine Salad

■ ■ ■

This sweet and tangy salad is my salute to the warm and wonderful California sun! Pick the best head of lettuce you can find, wash the leaves carefully to get out the bits of sand, then dry them thoroughly so you won't end up with a soggy salad. Somehow it just seems easier to "get your greens" in this part of the nation.

Serves 6 (1 cup)

¼ cup orange marmalade spreadable fruit	6 cups torn romaine lettuce
½ cup Kraft Fat Free French Dressing	1 cup (one 11-ounce can) mandarin oranges, rinsed and drained
1 teaspoon dried onion flakes	3 tablespoons (¾ ounce) chopped pecans
1 teaspoon dried parsley flakes	

In a large bowl, combine spreadable fruit, French dressing, onion flakes, and parsley flakes. Add romaine lettuce, oranges, and pecans. Toss gently to coat. Serve at once.

Each serving equals:

HE: 1 Fruit, 1 Vegetable, ½ Fat, ¼ Slider, 13 Optional Calories

102 Calories, 2 gm Fat, 1 gm Protein, 20 gm Carbohydrate, 205 mg Sodium, 27 mg Calcium, 2 gm Fiber

DIABETIC: 1 Fruit, 1 Vegetable, ½ Fat

Green Bean Salad with Creamy Mustard Dressing

■ ■ ■

California cooks are renowned for their fresh and inventive salad dressings. While I often mix a bottled version with a few added ingredients, there's something to be said about creating an aromatic and flavorful dressing from scratch! It's worth experimenting with a couple different Dijon brands to find the one you like best.

Serves 4 (1 cup)

4 cups (two 16-ounce cans) whole green beans, rinsed and drained
½ cup sliced fresh mushrooms
¼ cup (1 ounce) chopped walnuts
¼ cup Kraft fat-free mayonnaise
2 tablespoons Land O Lakes no-fat sour cream
2 teaspoons Dijon mustard
⅛ teaspoon black pepper

In a large bowl, combine green beans, mushrooms, and walnuts. In a small bowl, combine mayonnaise, sour cream, mustard, and black pepper. Add mayonnaise mixture to bean mixture. Mix gently to combine. Cover and refrigerate for at least 30 minutes. Gently stir again just before serving.

Each serving equals:
HE: 2¼ Vegetable, ½ Fat, ¼ Protein, 18 Optional Calories
96 Calories, 4 gm Fat, 3 gm Protein, 12 gm Carbohydrate, 286 mg Sodium, 52 mg Calcium, 3 gm Fiber
DIABETIC: 2 Vegetable, 1 Fat

Pineapple-Kiwi Fruit Salad

■ ■ ■

Can you remember when we'd never even seen a kiwi fruit? It's not that many years ago that this exotic egg-shaped delight, popular in tropical regions like Hawaii, was first widely introduced around the country. I recall someone describing it then as a cross between strawberries and bananas in flavor. It certainly looked a bit odd, but it tasted great then—and still does!

Serves 6 (⅔ cup)

1 (4-serving) package JELL-O sugar-free instant vanilla pudding mix
⅔ cup Carnation Nonfat Dry Milk Powder
1 cup (one 8-ounce can) crushed pineapple, packed in fruit juice, undrained

¾ cup Diet Mountain Dew
¾ cup Dannon plain fat-free yogurt
¾ cup Cool Whip Free
2 cups (4 medium) peeled and diced kiwi

In a large bowl, combine dry pudding mix, dry milk powder, undrained pineapple, and Diet Mountain Dew. Mix well using a wire whisk. Blend in yogurt and Cool Whip Free. Add kiwi. Mix gently to combine. Cover and refrigerate for at least 15 minutes. Gently stir again just before serving.

Each serving equals:
HE: 1 Fruit, ½ Skim Milk, ¼ Slider, 12 Optional Calories

120 Calories, 0 gm Fat, 4 gm Protein, 26 gm Carbohydrate, 289 mg Sodium, 159 mg Calcium, 2 gm Fiber

DIABETIC: 1 Fruit, ½ Skim Milk

Endless Sunset Grape Salad

■ ■ ■

There's an intriguing difference in watching the sun set when you're on an island, I've noticed—and remember, I live in one of the flattest places in the nation. But sunset in Hawaii seems to go on for hours, first in the sky, and then in the water. Days may last longer in Alaska in the summer, but sunsets are beautifully long in our fiftieth state!   *Serves 6 (½ cup)*

½ cup Kraft fat-free mayonnaise
¼ cup Cool Whip Free
2 tablespoons orange marmalade
*   spreadable fruit*
1½ cups (9 ounces) seedless red
*   grapes*

½ cup (3 ounces) seedless green
*   grapes*
¾ cup chopped celery
3 tablespoons (¾ ounce) chopped
*   pecans*

In a medium bowl, combine mayonnaise, Cool Whip Free, and spreadable fruit. Add red grapes, green grapes, celery, and pecans. Mix well to combine. Cover and refrigerate for at least 30 minutes. Gently stir again just before serving.

HINT: Apricot spreadable fruit may be substituted for orange marmalade.

Each serving equals:
HE: 1 Fruit, ½ Fat, ¼ Vegetable, 18 Optional Calories
94 Calories, 2 gm Fat, 1 gm Protein, 18 gm Carbohydrate, 189 mg Sodium, 13 mg Calcium, 1 gm Fiber
DIABETIC: 1 Fruit, ½ Fat

Creamy Fruit Mold

■ ■ ■

This is one of the prettiest molded salads I've created in quite some time; its creamy, fresh flavor reminded me of pleasant walks along the sandy shores of the coast. For a woman who spent most of her life in Iowa, a stroll by the ocean can be a truly spiritual experience!

Serves 8

1 (4-serving) package JELL-O sugar-free vanilla cook-and-serve pudding mix
1 (4-serving) package JELL-O sugar-free orange gelatin
1 cup Diet Mountain Dew
½ cup (4 ounces) Philadelphia fat-free cream cheese

½ cup Land O Lakes no-fat sour cream
2 cups (two 11-ounce cans) mandarin oranges, rinsed and drained
2 cups (2 medium) sliced bananas
¼ cup (1 ounce) chopped pecans

In a medium saucepan, combine dry pudding mix, dry gelatin, and Diet Mountain Dew. Cook over medium heat until mixture thickens and starts to boil, stirring often. Remove from heat. Add cream cheese. Mix well to combine, using a wire whisk. Place saucepan on a wire rack and let set for 15 minutes. Stir in sour cream. Add mandarin oranges, bananas, and pecans. Mix well to combine. Spread mixture into a 4-cup ring mold. Cover and refrigerate until set, about 4 hours. Unmold and cut into 8 servings.

HINT: 1. To prevent bananas from turning brown, mix with 1 teaspoon lemon juice or sprinkle with Fruit Fresh.
2. You can use an 8-by-8-inch dish if you don't have a ring mold. Just cut set salad into 8 servings.

Each serving equals:
HE: 1 Fruit, ½ Fat, ¼ Protein, ¼ Slider, 10 Optional Calories

114 Calories, 2 gm Fat, 3 gm Protein, 21 gm Carbohydrate, 152 mg Sodium, 73 mg Calcium, 2 gm Fiber

DIABETIC: 1 Fruit, ½ Fat, ½ Starch/Carbohydrate

Heavenly Butterscotch Isle Apple Salad

■ ■ ■

If you've ever taken a glass-bottomed boat trip around California's Catalina Island, you know what a little piece of heaven that can be! Here's a lovely and cool salad combo that would be just the ticket as part of a summer luncheon overlooking the Pacific Ocean.

Serves 6

1 (4-serving) package JELL-O
    sugar-free instant butterscotch
    pudding mix
⅔ cup Carnation Nonfat Dry
    Milk Powder
1 cup (one 8-ounce can) crushed
    pineapple, packed in fruit
    juice, undrained

¼ cup water
¾ cup Cool Whip Free
1 teaspoon coconut extract
2 cups (4 small) cored,
    unpeeled, and diced Red
    Delicious apples
2 tablespoons flaked coconut

In a large bowl, combine dry pudding mix, dry milk powder, undrained pineapple, and water. Mix well using a wire whisk. Blend in Cool Whip Free and coconut extract. Add apples. Mix well to combine. Evenly spoon mixture into 6 salad dishes. Sprinkle 1 teaspoon coconut evenly over top of each. Refrigerate for at least 15 minutes.

Each serving equals:
HE: 1 Fruit, ⅓ Skim Milk, ¼ Slider, 17 Optional Calories
108 Calories, 0 gm Fat, 3 gm Protein, 24 gm Carbohydrate, 277 mg Sodium, 101 mg Calcium, 1 gm Fiber
DIABETIC: 1 Fruit, ½ Starch/Carbohydrate

Winter Apple Salad

■ ■ ■

Even though you can usually get great fruit all year long in West Coast markets, I like a salad that you can serve even if nothing looks ripe but the apples! This creamy-crunchy blend is a perfect side dish for pork, but it's tasty with just about any entree.

Serves 6 (½ cup)

1 (4-serving) package JELL-O sugar-free vanilla cook-and-serve pudding mix
1 cup water
¼ cup cider vinegar
2 teaspoons reduced-calorie margarine

2 cups (4 small) cored, unpeeled, and diced Red Delicious apples
1 cup finely chopped celery
¼ cup raisins
¼ cup (1 ounce) chopped walnuts

In a medium saucepan, combine dry pudding mix and water. Cook over medium heat until mixture thickens and starts to boil, stirring constantly. Remove from heat. Stir in vinegar and margarine. Place saucepan on a wire rack and allow to cool completely, stirring occasionally. In a large bowl, combine apples, celery, raisins, and walnuts. Add cooled dressing mixture. Mix gently to combine. Cover and refrigerate for at least 30 minutes. Gently stir again just before serving.

HINT: To plump up raisins without "cooking," place in a glass measuring cup and microwave on HIGH for 20 seconds.

Each serving equals:
HE: 1 Fruit, ½ Fat, ⅓ Vegetable, ¼ Slider, 3 Optional Calories
95 Calories, 3 gm Fat, 1 gm Protein, 16 gm Carbohydrate, 110 mg Sodium, 19 mg Calcium, 2 gm Fiber
DIABETIC: 1 Fruit, ½ Fat

Sweet-and-Sour Carrots

■ ❈ ■

Someone once defined California as a place where people want it all—and will do just about anything to get it! Well, this exceptionally pleasant side dish might satisfy such a demanding populace—it's crunchy and smooth, fruity and tangy, an exciting blend of flavors and textures that covers all the bases.

Serves 6 (⅔ cup)

2 cups water

5 cups sliced fresh or frozen
   carrots

¾ cup chopped green bell pepper

¼ cup chopped green onion

¼ cup Kraft Fat Free Catalina
   Dressing

3 tablespoons grape spreadable
   fruit

In a medium saucepan, bring water to a boil. Add carrots and cook for 7 to 8 minutes or until just tender. Stir in green pepper and green onion. Continue cooking for 2 minutes. Drain. In same saucepan, combine Catalina dressing and spreadable fruit. Add drained vegetables. Mix gently to combine. Continue cooking for 5 minutes or until mixture is heated through, stirring occasionally.

Each serving equals:

HE: 2 Vegetable, ½ Fruit, 17 Optional Calories

76 Calories, 0 gm Fat, 1 gm Protein, 18 gm Carbohydrate, 126 mg Sodium, 22 mg Calcium, 2 gm Fiber

DIABETIC: 2 Vegetable, ½ Starch/Carbohydrate

Escalloped Carrots

■ ■ ■

These sturdy vegetables are grown just about everywhere, but in California they seem to appear as if by magic on most restaurant plates and in *every* sandwich! Here's a handy way to serve carrots when all you've got is a few cans in your pantry, yet you're still getting a healthy wallop of Vitamin A!   *Serves 6*

½ cup finely chopped onion
3 tablespoons all-purpose flour
⅔ cup Carnation Nonfat Dry
   Milk Powder
1 cup water
½ teaspoon yellow mustard
1 teaspoon dried parsley flakes

4 cups (two 16-ounce cans) sliced
   carrots, rinsed and drained ☆
6 (¾-ounce) slices Kraft reduced-
   fat Cheddar cheese ☆
3 tablespoons (¾ ounce) purchased dried fine bread crumbs

Preheat oven to 350 degrees. Spray an 8-by-8-inch baking dish with butter-flavored cooking spray. In a large skillet sprayed with butter-flavored cooking spray, sauté onion for 5 minutes. In a covered jar, combine flour, dry milk powder, and water. Shake well to blend. Pour mixture into skillet with onion. Add mustard and parsley flakes. Mix well to combine. Continue cooking until mixture thickens, stirring constantly. Spoon half of carrots into prepared baking dish. Arrange 3 of the cheese slices over top. Repeat layers. Evenly spoon onion sauce over top. Sprinkle bread crumbs evenly over sauce. Light spray top with butter-flavored cooking spray. Bake for 25 to 30 minutes. Place baking dish on a wire rack and let set for 5 minutes. Divide into 6 servings.

Each serving equals:

HE: 1½ Vegetable, 1 Protein, ⅓ Bread, ⅓ Skim Milk

139 Calories, 3 gm Fat, 8 gm Protein, 20 gm Carbohydrate, 709 mg Sodium, 271 mg Calcium, 3 gm Fiber

DIABETIC: 1½ Vegetable, 1 Meat, ½ Starch/Carbohydrate

Garlic Mashed Potatoes

■ ❄ ■

Creamy, garlicky mashed potatoes are so satisfying, they could almost be a meal by themselves! Many California supermarkets feature buttery-tasting spuds called Yukon Gold potatoes that are just perfect for mashing, so if you can find them, treat yourself. But the simple truth is, any good potato will taste great when prepared this way.   *Serves 4 (1 full cup)*

4 cups (20 ounces) unpeeled
   diced raw potatoes
1 *garlic clove, minced*
1½ *cups water*
⅓ *cup Carnation Nonfat Dry*
   Milk Powder

¼ *cup Land O Lakes no-fat sour*
   cream
1 *teaspoon dried parsley flakes*

In a medium saucepan, combine potatoes, garlic, and water. Bring mixture to a boil. Lower heat, cover, and simmer for 10 to 12 minutes or until potatoes are tender. Drain potatoes and reserve ⅓ cup liquid. Return potatoes to saucepan. Add reserved liquid and dry milk powder. Using an electric mixer on HIGH, whip potatoes until fluffy. Stir in sour cream and parsley flakes.

HINT: Use more garlic if desired, or for convenience ½ teaspoon dried minced
      garlic can be used instead of clove.

Each serving equals:
HE: 1 Bread, ¼ Skim Milk, 15 Optional Calories
148 Calories, 0 gm Fat, 6 gm Protein, 31 gm Carbohydrate, 60 mg Sodium,
102 mg Calcium, 2 gm Fiber
DIABETIC: 1½ Starch

Scrambled Eggs Foo Yung

■ ■ ■

There's an enormous (and growing) Asian population along the West Coast these days, but Chinese food has appeared on American menus for more than a century! Here's a splendid but simple way to prepare this old-time favorite at home. Do try to use the fresh bean sprouts, as the canned ones aren't nearly as good.

Serves 6

6 eggs or equivalent in egg substitute

1 full cup (6 ounces) finely diced cooked chicken breast

1 cup minced green onion

2 cups fresh bean sprouts

¼ cup reduced-sodium soy sauce ☆

2 cups (one 16-ounce can) Healthy Request Chicken Broth

2 tablespoons cornstarch

In a large bowl, beat eggs until slightly thick. Stir in chicken, onion, beans sprouts, and 2 tablespoons soy sauce. Pour batter into a large hot skillet sprayed with butter-flavored cooking spray. Cook for 5 minutes, stirring occasionally. Meanwhile, in a covered jar, combine chicken broth, cornstarch, and remaining 2 tablespoons soy sauce. Shake well to blend. Pour mixture into a medium saucepan sprayed with butter-flavored cooking spray. Cook over medium heat until mixture thickens, stirring occasionally. For each serving, place ¾ cup egg mixture on a plate and spoon ⅓ cup sauce over top.

HINT: 1. If you don't have leftovers, purchase a chunk of cooked chicken breast from your local deli.
2. Cooked pork or shrimp may be substituted for chicken.

Each serving equals:

HE: 2 Protein (1 limited), 1 Vegetable, 15 Optional Calories

162 Calories, 6 gm Fat, 18 gm Protein, 9 gm Carbohydrate, 573 mg Sodium, 39 mg Calcium, 1 gm Fiber

DIABETIC: 2 Meat, 1 Vegetable

Egg-Mushroom Sauce over Muffins

■ ■ ■

A hot breakfast on a chilly morning is always a morale-booster, so dishes like this one are popular in the higher ranges of the West, where snow often arrives even as people are sunbathing an hour or so away! This looks fancy when you serve it, but you and I will know just how easy to fix it really is.   *Serves 4*

1½ cups sliced fresh mushrooms
1½ cups (one 12-fluid-ounce can)
   Carnation Evaporated Skim
   Milk
3 tablespoons all-purpose flour
¾ cup (3 ounces) shredded Kraft
   reduced-fat Cheddar cheese

2 teaspoons dried parsley flakes
⅛ teaspoon black pepper
2 hard-boiled eggs, chopped
2 English muffins, split and
   toasted

In a large skillet sprayed with butter-flavored cooking spray, sauté mushrooms for 2 to 3 minutes. In a covered jar, combine evaporated skim milk and flour. Shake well to blend. Pour milk mixture into skillet with mushrooms. Add Cheddar cheese, parsley flakes, and black pepper. Mix well to combine. Continue cooking until mixture thickens and cheese melts, stirring often. Stir in chopped eggs. For each serving, place a toasted muffin half on a plate and spoon about ½ cup sauce over top.

HINT: If you want the look and feel of egg without the cholesterol, toss out the yolks and dice the whites.

Each serving equals:
HE: 1½ Protein (½ limited), 1¼ Bread, ¾ Skim Milk, ¾ Vegetable
263 Calories, 7 gm Fat, 19 gm Protein, 31 gm Carbohydrate, 454 mg Sodium, 486 mg Calcium, 1 gm Fiber
DIABETIC: 1 Meat, 1 Starch, 1 Skim Milk, ½ Vegetable

California Harvest Pizza

■ ❋ ■

It's a land of sunshine and abundance, so why not create a scrumptious home-baked pizza that sings out the state's culinary glories? I'm such a fan of the ready-made French loaf dough that I use it all the time to create easy, healthy, and downright delicious recipes like this one.   *Serves 8*

1 (11-ounce) can Pillsbury refrig-
    erated French loaf
1 cup (one 8-ounce can) Hunt's
    Tomato Sauce
1 tablespoon pourable Sugar
    Twin or Sprinkle Sweet
1 teaspoon dried basil
2 cups chopped fresh tomatoes

1 cup chopped unpeeled zucchini
1 cup shredded carrots
½ cup (2 ounces) sliced ripe
    olives
¾ cup (3 ounces) shredded Kraft
    reduced-fat mozzarella cheese
¾ cup (3 ounces) shredded Kraft
    reduced-fat Cheddar cheese

Preheat oven to 400 degrees. Unroll French loaf and pat into a 10-by-15-inch rimmed baking sheet. Lightly spray top with olive oil–flavored cooking spray. Bake for 5 minutes. In a small bowl, combine tomato sauce, Sugar Twin, and basil. Spread sauce mixture evenly over partially baked crust. Evenly arrange tomatoes, zucchini, carrots, and olives over sauce. Sprinkle mozzarella cheese and Cheddar cheese evenly over top. Continue baking for 8 to 10 minutes or until vegetables are tender and cheeses melt. Place baking sheet on a wire rack and let set for 5 minutes. Cut into 8 servings.

Each serving equals:
HE: 1½ Vegetable, 1 Bread, 1 Protein, ¼ Fat, 1 Optional Calorie
181 Calories, 5 gm Fat, 10 gm Protein, 24 gm Carbohydrate, 659 mg Sodium,
161 mg Calcium, 2 gm Fiber
DIABETIC: 1½ Vegetable, 1 Starch, 1 Meat, ½ Fat

Creamed Tuna and Peas on Toast Triangles

■ ❄ ■

When the days grow long and you want to stay outside as late as possible, here's an easy light supper that takes almost no time to fix! If the pool beckons, or the tennis court still has enough light to play, then take a quick meal break and head on back to the game.

Serves 4

1 (6-ounce) can white tuna, packed in water, drained and flaked

1 cup frozen peas, thawed

¼ cup (one 2-ounce jar) chopped pimiento, undrained

1 (10¾-ounce) can Healthy Request Cream of Mushroom Soup

¼ cup Land O Lakes no-fat sour cream

1 teaspoon dried onion flakes

1 teaspoon dried parsley flakes

4 slices reduced-calorie white bread

In a medium saucepan, combine tuna, peas, undrained pimiento, and mushroom soup. Stir in sour cream, onion flakes, and parsley flakes. Cook over medium heat until mixture is heated through, stirring occasionally. Meanwhile, toast bread and cut each slice in half diagonally. For each serving, place 2 toast halves on a plate and spoon a scant ⅔ cup tuna mixture over top.

HINT: Thaw peas by placing in a colander and rinsing under hot water for one minute.

Each serving equals:
HE: 1 Bread, ¾ Protein, ½ Slider, 16 Optional Calories
182 Calories, 2 gm Fat, 17 gm Protein, 24 gm Carbohydrate, 605 mg Sodium, 124 mg Calcium, 5 gm Fiber
DIABETIC: 1½ Starch/Carbohydrate, 1½ Meat

Toasted Tuna Salad Sandwiches

■ ■ ■

If you're wondering about the favorite lunchtime munch of West Coast kids, all I can tell you is that I did an informal survey on our last visit west. "Tuna" was the answer I got, so here's a way to make this American classic even more appealing to little and big appetites! *Serves 4*

1 (6-ounce) can white tuna,
   packed in water, drained and
   flaked
⅓ cup Kraft fat-free mayonnaise
1 teaspoon yellow mustard

¼ cup (1 ounce) sliced ripe olives
¼ cup (one 2-ounce jar) chopped
   pimiento, drained
8 slices reduced-calorie whole
   wheat bread

In a medium bowl, combine tuna, mayonnaise, and mustard. Add olives and pimiento. Mix gently to combine. For each sandwich, spread about ½ cup tuna mixture between 2 slices of bread. Place sandwich on a hot griddle or in a large skillet sprayed with butter-flavored cooking spray. Brown for 3 to 4 minutes. Lightly spray top with butter-flavored cooking spray, flip over and continue browning for 3 to 4 minutes. Serve warm.

Each serving equals:

HE: 1 Bread, ¾ Protein, ¼ Fat, 13 Optional Calories

171 Calories, 3 gm Fat, 15 gm Protein, 21 gm Carbohydrate, 608 mg Sodium, 49 mg Calcium, 5 gm Fiber

DIABETIC: 1½ Meat, 1 Starch, ½ Fat

Vegas-Style Shrimp Cocktail

■ ■ ■

If someone told me you can get anything in Las Vegas, I think I'd probably believe him or her—it's just that kind of place! The resort of all resorts is smack in the middle of the desert, but they fly the shrimp in every day, and here's my version of how it's most often served.

Serves 6

16 ounces frozen shrimp,
    cooked, cooled, and peeled
3 tablespoons lemon juice
¾ cup chili sauce
½ cup Heinz Light Harvest
    Ketchup or any reduced-
    sodium ketchup
1 tablespoon prepared horse-
    radish sauce

1 tablespoon finely chopped
    onion
3 tablespoons finely chopped
    celery
⅛ teaspoon black pepper
1 cup finely shredded lettuce

In a large bowl, combine shrimp and lemon juice. Cover and refrigerate for at least 30 minutes. In a medium bowl, combine chili sauce, ketchup, and horse-radish sauce. Stir in onion, celery, and black pepper. Cover and refrigerate for at least 30 minutes. For each serving, spoon about 2 full tablespoons lettuce into 6 dishes, evenly divide the chilled shrimp among the dishes and spoon about 3 tablespoons sauce over top of each.

Each serving equals:
HE: 2½ Protein, ¼ Vegetable, ½ Slider, 15 Optional Calories
125 Calories, 1 gm Fat, 17 gm Protein, 12 gm Carbohydrate, 694 mg Sodium, 34 mg Calcium, 1 gm Fiber
DIABETIC: 2½ Meat, ½ Starch/Carbohydrate

Sierra Beef and Rice Supper

■ ❄ ■

This spectacular California mountain range divides the state right down the middle, and whether there's snow on the mountaintops or just gorgeous peaks silhouetted against a bright blue sky, you know you're in one of God's favorite places! Here's an easy skillet supper to stir up on one of those nights when you've spent a little extra time gazing at the scenery—and now you need dinner in a hurry!

Serves 6 (1 cup)

16 ounces ground 90% lean turkey or beef
1½ cups finely chopped celery
1 (10¾-ounce) can Healthy Request Cream of Mushroom Soup

1¼ cups water
2 cups (6 ounces) uncooked Minute Rice
1 teaspoon dried parsley flakes
½ cup Land O Lakes no-fat sour cream

In a large skillet sprayed with butter-flavored cooking spray, sauté meat and celery for 8 to 10 minutes. Stir in mushroom soup and water. Add uncooked rice and parsley flakes. Mix well to combine. Lower heat, cover, and simmer for 6 to 8 minutes or until rice is tender, stirring occasionally. Stir in sour cream. Continue simmering for 2 to 3 minutes, stirring occasionally.

Each serving equals:
HE: 2 Protein, 1 Bread, ½ Vegetable, ½ Slider, 8 Optional Calories
243 Calories, 7 gm Fat, 16 gm Protein, 29 gm Carbohydrate, 306 mg Sodium, 80 mg Calcium, 1 gm Fiber
DIABETIC: 2 Meat, 1½ Starch/Carbohydrate, ½ Vegetable

South Seas Meatloaf

■ ❄ ■

Recipes that taste of the tropics hint at why those brave explorers were willing to sail for months through uncharted waters in search of paradise! Hawaii is a state where the unexpected often seems just right, so even if you don't think pineapple belongs in a meatloaf, try it—you never know what's over the next horizon until you take a chance.

Serves 6

1 cup (one 8-ounce can) crushed
    pineapple, packed in fruit
    juice, undrained
½ cup finely chopped onion
½ cup finely chopped green bell
    pepper
1 tablespoon pourable Sugar
    Twin or Sprinkle Sweet
1 teaspoon dried parsley flakes

6 tablespoons purchased graham
    cracker crumbs or 6 (2½-inch)
    graham cracker squares, made
    into crumbs
16 ounces ground 90% lean
    turkey or beef
⅓ cup Heinz Light Harvest
    Ketchup or any reduced-
    sodium ketchup

Preheat oven to 350 degrees. Spray a 9-by-5-inch loaf pan with butter-flavored cooking spray. In a large bowl, combine undrained pineapple, onion, green pepper, Sugar Twin, parsley flakes, and graham cracker crumbs. Add meat. Mix well to combine. Pat mixture into prepared loaf pan. Spoon ketchup evenly over top. Bake for 50 to 55 minutes. Place loaf pan on a wire rack and let set for 5 minutes. Cut into 6 servings.

HINT: A self-seal sandwich bag works great for crushing graham crackers.

Each serving equals:
HE: 2 Protein, ⅓ Bread, ⅓ Fruit, ⅓ Vegetable, 14 Optional Calories
187 Calories, 7 gm Fat, 14 gm Protein, 17 gm Carbohydrate, 120 mg Sodium, 15 mg Calcium, 1 gm Fiber
DIABETIC: 2 Meat, 1 Starch/Carbohydrate

Pepper and Olive Steak

■ ❄ ■

It's gotta be the sunshine, because the peppers for sale in California just seemed gigantic to me when I first wandered through the famous Farmers' Market in Los Angeles! This flavorful and speedy skillet style of preparing minute steaks is one of Cliff's favorites, though he's inclined to turn up the heat a bit with more pepper (the black kind!).   *Serves 4*

4 (4-ounce) lean tenderized minute or cube steaks
1 cup chopped onion
1 cup chopped green bell pepper
1 cup chopped red bell pepper
1¾ cups (one 14½-ounce can) Swanson Beef Broth

3 tablespoons all-purpose flour
½ teaspoon dried minced garlic
¼ cup (1 ounce) pimiento-stuffed olives, chopped
⅛ teaspoon black pepper

In a large skillet sprayed with olive oil–flavored cooking spray, lightly brown steaks for 2 to 3 minutes on each side. Remove from skillet and keep warm. In same skillet, sauté onion, green pepper, and red pepper for 5 minutes. In a covered jar, combine beef broth and flour. Shake well to blend. Stir broth mixture into skillet with vegetables. Add garlic, olives, and black pepper. Mix well to combine. Evenly arrange steaks in skillet and spoon vegetable mixture over top. Lower heat, cover, and simmer for 15 minutes or until meat is tender. When serving, spoon about ⅔ cup vegetable mixture over each steak.

Each serving equals:
HE: 3 Protein, 1½ Vegetable, ¼ Bread, ¼ Fat, 8 Optional Calories
197 Calories, 5 gm Fat, 29 gm Protein, 9 gm Carbohydrate, 552 mg Sodium, 24 mg Calcium, 2 gm Fiber
DIABETIC: 3 Meat, 1 Vegetable

Hawaiian Ham-Filled Tomatoes

■ ■ ■

I've been asked if they put pineapple in *everything* in Hawaii, and of course the answer is no. But pineapple is one of that state's most important crops, and so it's only smart to create recipes that put that flavorful fruit to work and show it off best! This is a terrific luncheon dish that looks as if you fussed for hours (but we know you didn't have to!). *Serves 4*

1 full cup (6 ounces) finely chopped Dubuque 97% fat-free ham or any extra-lean ham
1 cup (one 8-ounce can) crushed pineapple, packed in fruit juice, drained, and 2 table-spoons liquid reserved

½ cup finely chopped celery
2 tablespoons (½ ounce) chopped pecans
½ cup Kraft fat-free mayonnaise
4 (medium-sized) fresh ripe tomatoes

In a large bowl, combine ham, pineapple, celery, and pecans. Add mayonnaise and reserved pineapple liquid. Mix well to combine. Cut each tomato length-wise to form 8 wedges, leaving attached at bottom. Spread wedges slightly apart. Spoon about ½ cup ham mixture into center of each tomato. Cover and refrigerate for at least 15 minutes or until ready to serve.

Each serving equals:
HE: 1¼ Vegetable, 1 Protein, ½ Fruit, ½ Fat, ¼ Slider
136 Calories, 4 gm Fat, 8 gm Protein, 17 gm Carbohydrate, 594 mg Sodium, 22 mg Calcium, 2 gm Fiber
DIABETIC: 1 Vegetable, 1 Meat, ½ Fruit, ½ Fat, ½ Starch/Carbohydrate

Chipped Beef and Potato Skillet

■ ❄ ■

Here's another camping favorite, though it's also a satisfying supper when cooked on your stovetop instead of over a campfire! Cliff has loved chipped beef since he was a boy, and so I knew this recipe would please his trucker's taste-buds. My kids used to travel with him during the summers growing up, so I bet it would delight them too.   *Serves 4 (1½ cups)*

1 (5-ounce) jar Hormel lean
    dried chipped beef
1½ cups chopped onion
3 cups (15 ounces) diced raw
    potatoes
1½ cups (one 12-fluid-ounce can)
    Carnation Evaporated Skim
    Milk

3 tablespoons all-purpose flour
1 cup boiling water
1 teaspoon dried parsley flakes
⅛ teaspoon black pepper

Rinse and shred chipped beef. In a large skillet sprayed with butter-flavored cooking spray, sauté chipped beef, onion, and potatoes for 6 to 8 minutes. In a covered jar, combine evaporated skim milk and flour. Shake well to blend. Stir milk mixture into potato mixture. Add water, parsley flakes, and black pepper. Mix well to combine. Lower heat and simmer for 15 to 20 minutes or until potatoes are tender and sauce thickens, stirring occasionally.

Each serving equals:

HE: 1¼ Protein, 1 Bread, ¾ Skim Milk, ¾ Vegetable

214 Calories, 2 gm Fat, 19 gm Protein, 30 gm Carbohydrate, 672 mg Sodium, 282 mg Calcium, 3 gm Fiber

DIABETIC: 1 Meat, 1 Starch, ½ Skim Milk, ½ Vegetable

Pineapple Coconut Bars

■ ❋ ■

Seeing your first palm tree in person is an experience never to forget, and the towering palms that grow in California and Hawaii remind us what big taste we can get from just a sprinkling of coconut! These festive bars deliver true tropical flavor.

Serves 8 (2 each)

¼ cup reduced-calorie margarine

2 tablespoons Land O Lakes no-fat sour cream

½ cup pourable Sugar Twin or Sprinkle Sweet

2 eggs or equivalent in egg substitute

1 cup (one 8-ounce can) crushed pineapple, packed in fruit juice, undrained

1 teaspoon coconut extract

1 cup + 2 tablespoons Bisquick Reduced Fat Baking Mix

6 tablespoons purchased graham cracker crumbs or 6 (2½-inch) graham crackers, made into crumbs

¼ cup flaked coconut

Preheat oven to 350 degrees. Spray a 9-by-9-inch cake pan with butter-flavored cooking spray. In a large bowl, combine margarine, sour cream, and Sugar Twin. Stir in eggs, undrained pineapple, and coconut extract. Add baking mix, graham cracker crumbs, and coconut. Mix gently just to combine. Spread batter evenly into prepared cake pan. Bake for 25 to 30 minutes. Place cake pan on a wire rack and let set for 10 minutes. Cut into 16 bars.

HINT: A self-seal sandwich bag works great for crushing graham crackers.

Each serving equals:

HE: ¾ Bread, ¾ Fat, ¼ Protein (limited), ¼ Fruit, 17 Optional Calories

154 Calories, 6 gm Fat, 4 gm Protein, 21 gm Carbohydrate, 325 mg Sodium, 36 mg Calcium, 1 gm Fiber

DIABETIC: 1 Starch/Carbohydrate, 1 Fat

Pineapple Tarts

■ ■ ■

I was testing these when my ever-growing grandsons were visiting, so of course they asked for a taste. Pineapple lovers both, they voted these a giant hit and asked if I could give the recipe to their mom! For a sweet taste of Hawaii without the trip to the airport, give these lovely treats a try. *Serves 6*

1 (4-serving) package JELL-O sugar-free vanilla cook-and-serve pudding mix
1 (4-serving) package JELL-O sugar-free lemon gelatin
⅔ cup Carnation Nonfat Dry Milk Powder
1 cup (one 8-ounce can) crushed pineapple, packed in fruit juice, undrained

1 cup (one 8-ounce can) pineapple tidbits, packed in fruit juice, drained, and ¼ cup liquid reserved
½ cup Diet Mountain Dew
1 (6-single serve) package Keebler graham cracker crusts
6 tablespoons Cool Whip Lite

In a large saucepan, combine dry pudding mix, dry gelatin, and dry milk powder. Stir in undrained crushed pineapple, reserved pineapple liquid, and Diet Mountain Dew. Cook over medium heat until mixture thickens and starts to boil, stirring constantly. Remove from heat. Reserve 6 pineapple tidbits. Gently stir remaining pineapple tidbits into pudding mixture. Evenly spoon mixture into graham cracker crusts. Refrigerate for at least 1 hour. Just before serving, top each with 1 tablespoon Cool Whip Lite and garnish with 1 pineapple tidbit.

HINT: If you can't find tidbits, use chunk pineapple and coarsely chop.

Each serving equals:
HE: ⅔ Fruit, ½ Bread, ⅓ Skim Milk, 1 Slider
190 Calories, 6 gm Fat, 4 gm Protein, 30 gm Carbohydrate, 273 mg Sodium, 104 mg Calcium, 1 gm Fiber
DIABETIC: 1 Fruit, 1 Starch/Carbohydrate, 1 Fat

Waikiki Lemon Coconut Cream Pie

■ ❊ ■

Maybe it's living so near the beach, but dessert chefs in Hawaii seem to feature light and citrusy flavors like the ones in this beautifully creamy pie! The tartness of the lemon blends so well with the supersweet coconut, so what you get is a terrific balance—and a dessert worth writing home about! *Serves 8*

2 (4-serving) packages JELL-O sugar-free instant vanilla pudding mix
1 (4-serving) package JELL-O sugar-free lemon gelatin
1⅓ cups Carnation Nonfat Dry Milk Powder
2 cups Diet Mountain Dew
½ cup Cool Whip Free

1 teaspoon coconut extract
¼ cup flaked coconut ☆
1 (6-ounce) Keebler graham cracker piecrust
1 tablespoon purchased graham cracker crumbs or 1 (2½-inch) graham cracker made into crumbs

In a large bowl, combine dry pudding mixes, dry gelatin, and dry milk powder. Add Diet Mountain Dew. Mix well using a wire whisk. Blend in Cool Whip Free and coconut extract. Add 2 tablespoons coconut. Mix well to combine. Spread mixture into piecrust. In a small bowl, combine graham cracker crumbs and remaining 2 tablespoons coconut. Evenly sprinkle crumb mixture over top. Refrigerate for at least 1 hour. Cut into 8 servings.

HINT: A self-seal sandwich bag works great for crushing graham cracker.

Each serving equals:
HE: ½ Skim Milk, ½ Bread, 1 Slider, 18 Optional Calories
194 Calories, 6 gm Fat, 5 gm Protein, 30 gm Carbohydrate, 549 mg Sodium, 140 mg Calcium, 1 gm Fiber
DIABETIC: 1½ Starch/Carbohydrate, 1 Fat, ½ Skim Milk

Hawaiian Strawberry Crumb Pie

■ ■ ■

I'd gladly "walk a mile" for a really good strawberry dessert, but when I saw the strawberries they were serving in Maui, I knew I'd travel even farther for the best! This pie is the perfect grand finale for a festive summer supper under the stars, and you'll be setting off some fireworks of your own if you serve it on the Fourth of July!

Serves 8

2 cups sliced fresh strawberries
1 (6-ounce) Keebler graham cracker piecrust
1 (4-serving) package JELL-O sugar-free vanilla cook-and-serve pudding mix
1 (4-serving) package JELL-O sugar-free strawberry gelatin
1 cup (one 8-ounce can) crushed pineapple, packed in fruit juice, undrained

½ cup Diet Mountain Dew
1 teaspoon coconut extract
2 tablespoons flaked coconut
2 tablespoons purchased graham cracker crumbs or 2 (2½-inch) graham cracker squares, made into crumbs
2 tablespoons (½ ounce) chopped pecans

Preheat oven to 350 degrees. Evenly arrange strawberries in piecrust. In a medium saucepan, combine dry pudding mix, dry gelatin, undrained pineapple, and Diet Mountain Dew. Cook over medium heat until mixture thickens and starts to boil, stirring often. Remove from heat. Stir in coconut extract. Spoon mixture evenly over strawberries. In a small bowl, combine coconut, graham cracker crumbs, and pecans. Evenly sprinkle crumb mixture over top. Bake for 30 minutes. Place pie plate on a wire rack and let set for 15 minutes. Refrigerate for 30 minutes. Cut into 8 servings.

HINT: A self-seal sandwich bag works great for crushing graham crackers.

Each serving equals:
HE: ½ Bread, ½ Fruit, ¼ Fat, ¾ Slider, 15 Optional Calories

167 Calories, 7 gm Fat, 2 gm Protein, 24 gm Carbohydrate, 208 mg Sodium, 11 mg Calcium, 2 gm Fiber

DIABETIC: 1½ Starch/Carbohydrate, 1 Fat, ½ Fruit

Maraschino Cherry Spice Cake

■ ❋ ■

I've always liked featuring these pretty pink-red cherries in my desserts, maybe because they're so cheerful and bright! This cake is wonderfully moist (due to a few secret ingredients like the mayonnaise!) and will make a great impression on your dinner guests when you carry it proudly forth from the kitchen. If the day isn't sunny, this cake will provide a glow of its own!   *Serves 8*

⅔ cup **Carnation Nonfat Dry Milk Powder**
¾ cup water
2 teaspoons white vinegar
1½ cups **Bisquick Reduced Fat Baking Mix**
¾ cup pourable **Sugar Twin** or **Sprinkle Sweet**

2 teaspoons apple pie spice
16 maraschino cherries ☆
½ cup **Kraft fat-free mayonnaise**
¼ cup **Land O Lakes no-fat sour cream**
1 teaspoon vanilla extract
½ cup **Cool Whip Lite**

Preheat oven to 350 degrees. Spray a 9-by-9-inch cake pan with butter-flavored cooking spray. In a small bowl, combine dry milk powder, water, and vinegar. Set aside. In a large bowl, combine baking mix, Sugar Twin, and apple pie spice. Coarsely chop 12 maraschino cherries. Stir chopped cherries into baking mix mixture. Add milk mixture, mayonnaise, sour cream, and vanilla extract. Mix gently just to combine. Spread batter evenly into prepared cake pan. Bake for 30 to 35 minutes or until a toothpick inserted in center comes out clean. Place cake pan on a wire rack and allow cake to cool completely. Cut cake into 8 servings. Cut remaining 4 maraschino cherries in half. When serving, top each piece of cake with 1 tablespoon Cool Whip Lite and a cherry half.

Each serving equals:
HE: 1 Bread, ¼ Skim Milk, ½ Slider, 16 Optional Calories
154 Calories, 2 gm Fat, 4 gm Protein, 30 gm Carbohydrate, 407 mg Sodium, 115 mg Calcium, 1 gm Fiber
DIABETIC: 1½ Starch/Carbohydrate

Golden Gate Carrot Cake

■ ❋ ■

It's true that San Francisco is a foggy town, so maybe that's why they painted the Golden Gate Bridge a vivid shade of orange. But maybe the guy mixing the paint had carrot cake on his mind! Here's my recipe to honor that beautiful structure. I can't promise that every time you make it the sun will pop out, but after one taste, you won't mind a cloudy day.   *Serves 8*

1½ cups all-purpose flour
¾ cup pourable Sugar Twin or
  Sprinkle Sweet ☆
1 teaspoon baking soda
1 teaspoon ground cinnamon
¾ cup unsweetened applesauce
1 egg or equivalent in egg substitute
1 teaspoon vanilla extract
2 cups grated carrots

½ cup + 1 tablespoon raisins
¼ cup (1 ounce) chopped
  walnuts
1 (8-ounce) package
  Philadelphia fat-free cream
  cheese
1 tablespoon skim milk
1 teaspoon coconut extract
1 cup Cool Whip Free
2 tablespoons flaked coconut

Preheat oven to 325 degrees. Spray a 9-by-9-inch cake pan with butter-flavored cooking spray. In a large bowl, combine flour, ½ cup Sugar Twin, baking soda, and cinnamon. Add applesauce, egg, and vanilla extract. Mix gently to combine. Stir in carrots, raisins, and walnuts. Spread batter into prepared cake pan. Bake for 30 to 35 minutes or until a toothpick inserted in center comes out clean. Place cake pan on a wire rack and allow to cool completely. In a large bowl, stir cream cheese with a spoon until soft. Stir in skim milk, coconut extract, and remaining ¼ cup Sugar Twin. Add Cool Whip Free. Mix gently to combine. Spread frosting evenly over cooled cake. Evenly sprinkle coconut over top. Cut into 8 servings. Refrigerate leftovers.

Each serving equals:
HE: 1 Bread, ¾ Fruit, ¾ Protein, ½ Vegetable, ¼ Fat, ¼ Slider,
8 Optional Calories

211 Calories, 3 gm Fat, 8 gm Protein, 38 gm Carbohydrate, 323 mg Sodium,
110 mg Calcium, 3 gm Fiber

DIABETIC: 1½ Starch/Carbohydrate, 1 Fruit, 1 Meat, ½ Fat

Date Nut Muffins

■ ❄ ■

There are date palms all over the state of California, and while you can easily buy fresh dates in farmers' markets, this recipe is just as tasty when you use the brand of dates you find packaged in your own grocery store. These freeze beautifully and even seem to deepen a bit in flavor when they are reheated. *Serves 8*

1 cup pitted dates, coarsely
  chopped
¾ cup boiling water
1 teaspoon vanilla extract
1½ cups Bisquick Reduced Fat
  Baking Mix

½ cup pourable Sugar Twin or
  Sprinkle Sweet
½ cup (2 ounces) chopped walnuts
¼ cup Land O Lakes no-fat sour
  cream

Preheat oven to 375 degrees. Spray 8 wells of a 12-hole muffin pan with butter-flavored cooking spray or line with paper liners. In a medium bowl, combine dates, water, and vanilla extract. In a large bowl, combine baking mix, Sugar Twin, and walnuts. Add date mixture and sour cream. Mix just until combined. Evenly spoon batter into prepared muffin wells. Bake for 20 to 25 minutes or until a toothpick inserted in center comes out clean. Immediately remove muffins from pan and place on a wire rack. Serve warm or cold.

Each serving equals:
HE: 1 Bread, 1 Fruit, ½ Fat, ¼ Protein, 14 Optional Calories
193 Calories, 5 gm Fat, 3 gm Protein, 34 gm Carbohydrate, 272 mg Sodium,
46 mg Calcium, 2 gm Fiber
DIABETIC: 1 Starch, 1 Fruit, 1 Fat

Paradise Banana Bread

■ ❋ ■

You may have wondered if every tourist leaving Hawaii was required to carry home a can of macadamia nuts. I'm here to tell you it's not true, but it's still pretty difficult to avoid that classic Hawaiian nut when you're there on vacation! It'll provide a wonderful bit of crunch in this fruitier-than-usual banana bread.

Serves 8 (1 thick or 2 thin slices)

1 cup + 2 tablespoons Bisquick Reduced Fat Baking Mix
6 tablespoons purchased graham cracker crumbs or 6 (2½-inch) graham crackers, made into crumbs
½ cup pourable Sugar Twin or Sprinkle Sweet
¼ cup (1 ounce) chopped macadamias or walnuts

⅔ cup (2 ripe medium) mashed bananas
1 cup (one 8-ounce can) crushed pineapple, packed in fruit juice, drained
2 tablespoons Land O Lakes no-fat sour cream
1 teaspoon rum extract

Preheat oven to 350 degrees. Spray a 9-by-5-inch loaf pan with butter-flavored cooking spray. In a large bowl, combine baking mix, graham cracker crumbs, and Sugar Twin. Stir in macadamia nuts. In a small bowl, combine mashed bananas, pineapple, sour cream, and rum extract. Add banana mixture to baking mix mixture. Mix gently just to combine. Spread batter evenly into prepared loaf pan. Bake for 55 to 65 minutes or until a toothpick inserted in center comes out clean. Place loaf pan on a wire rack and let set for 5 minutes. Remove bread from pan and continue cooling on wire rack. Cut into 8 thick or 16 thin slices.

HINT: A self-seal sandwich bag works great for crushing graham crackers.

Each serving equals:
HE: 1 Bread, ¾ Fruit, ¼ Fat, 17 Optional Calories
140 Calories, 4 gm Fat, 2 gm Protein, 24 gm Carbohydrate, 236 mg Sodium, 31 mg Calcium, 1 gm Fiber
DIABETIC: 1 Starch, 1 Fruit, ½ Fat

Crunchy Trail Mix

■ ■ ■

Hiking is popular all over America, but with so many magnificent national parks in this region, every weekend finds thousands of people walking, running, rock climbing and riding bikes for recreation. Here's a great blend to bring along in a Ziploc bag. You won't run out of energy with this mix!

Serves 8 (full ½ cup)

½ cup (2 ounces) chopped dry-
   roasted peanuts
½ cup raisins

⅔ cup (3 ounces) chopped dried
   apricots
3 cups (4½ ounces) Wheat Chex

In a large bowl, combine peanuts, raisins, and apricots. Stir in Wheat Chex. Store in an airtight container.

HINT: To plump up raisins without "cooking," place in a glass measuring cup and microwave on HIGH for 20 seconds.

Each serving equals:
HE: 1 Fruit, ¾ Bread, ½ Fat, ¼ Protein

152 Calories, 4 gm Fat, 4 gm Protein, 25 gm Carbohydrate, 166 mg Sodium, 18 mg Calcium, 3 gm Fiber

DIABETIC: 1 Fruit, 1 Fat, ½ Starch

Denver Cheese Omelet

■ ■ ■

There's something about gazing out the windshield at the snow-topped Rocky Mountains that encourages Colorado visitors to enjoy a hearty breakfast! This updated version of the classic Denver morning entree simply raises the ante and makes a good thing even better.

Serves 4 (½ cup)

½ cup finely chopped green bell pepper
½ cup finely chopped onion
½ cup (3 ounces) diced Dubuque 97% fat-free ham or any extra-lean ham
4 eggs or equivalent in egg substitute

¼ cup skim milk
⅛ teaspoon black pepper
½ cup + 1 tablespoon (2¼ ounces) shredded Kraft reduced-fat Cheddar cheese

In a large skillet sprayed with butter-flavored cooking spray, sauté green pepper, onion, and ham for 5 minutes. Meanwhile, in a medium bowl, combine eggs, skim milk, and black pepper. Mix well using a wire whisk until fluffy. Pour egg mixture into skillet with vegetables. Mix well to combine. Fold in Cheddar cheese. Lower heat and continue cooking for 3 to 5 minutes or until eggs are set but still moist, gently stirring often.

Each serving equals:
HE: 2¼ Protein (1 limited), ½ Vegetable, 6 Optional Calories

152 Calories, 8 gm Fat, 15 gm Protein, 5 gm Carbohydrate, 385 mg Sodium, 154 mg Calcium, 1 gm Fiber

DIABETIC: 2 Meat, ½ Vegetable

High Country Campers' Breakfast

■ ■ ■

When you crawl from your tent or climb out of your motor home, wondering what breakfast could possibly equal the glorious mountain views all around you, I suggest giving this skillet combo a shot at filling the bill! Just be careful to keep your food locked up between meals so you don't tempt the local bears into joining you!

Serves 6

1 full cup (6 ounces) diced
    Dubuque 97% fat-free ham or
    any extra-lean ham
½ cup chopped onion
½ cup finely chopped celery
2 cups (one 16-ounce can)
    tomatoes, chopped and
    undrained
10 ounces (one 16-ounce can)
    pinto beans, rinsed and
    drained

¼ cup Heinz Light Harvest
    Ketchup or any reduced-
    sodium ketchup
⅛ teaspoon black pepper
6 eggs or equivalent in egg
    substitute

In a large skillet sprayed with butter-flavored cooking spray, sauté ham, onion, and celery for 8 to 10 minutes. Stir in undrained tomatoes. Add pinto beans, ketchup, and black pepper. Mix well to combine. Make 6 indentations in bean mixture. Carefully break 1 egg into each indentation. Lower heat, cover, and cook for 4 to 6 minutes or until eggs are set to desired doneness. Cut into 6 servings. Serve immediately.

Each serving equals:
HE: 2½ Protein (1 limited), 1 Vegetable, 10 Optional Calories

174 Calories, 6 gm Fat, 14 gm Protein, 16 gm Carbohydrate, 571 mg Sodium, 77 mg Calcium, 3 gm Fiber

DIABETIC: 2 Meat, 1 Vegetable, ½ Starch

Olive-Nut Spread

■ ■ ■

Californians seem to live most of their lives outside, so patio parties are a frequent occurrence. Here's a tangy and flavorful spread that's as good on crudités as it is on your favorite cracker or mini bread. Its crunchy-nutty nature really appealed to Cliff.

Serves 6 (¼ cup)

*½ cup (2 ounces) pimiento-
  stuffed green olives*
*½ cup (2 ounces) chopped
  walnuts*

*¾ cup Kraft fat-free
  mayonnaise*

Finely chop olives and walnuts using either a food processor or hand grinder. In a medium bowl, combine olive-and-walnut mixture with mayonnaise. Cover and refrigerate for at least 15 minutes. Gently stir again just before serving.

HINT: Good on crackers or with vegetables.

Each serving equals:
HE: ⅔ Fat, ⅓ Protein, ¼ Slider

95 Calories, 7 gm Fat, 1 gm Protein, 7 gm Carbohydrate, 288 mg Sodium, 14 mg Calcium, 1 gm Fiber

DIABETIC: 1½ Fat

Lanai Sunset Punch

■ ■ ■

There's something about the light in Hawaii that seems entirely different from everywhere else we've traveled. Dawn is just pale and pretty. But sunset is an explosion of visual fireworks—once seen, never forgotten. This refreshing party drink is a true delight, a mini vacation in a glass. *Serves 4 (full 1 cup)*

1 cup (one 8-ounce can) crushed
   pineapple, packed in fruit
   juice, undrained
½ cup Diet Mountain Dew

1 cup unsweetened orange juice
2 cups diet ginger ale
1 cup ice cubes
4 mint sprigs (optional)

In a blender container, combine undrained pineapple and Diet Mountain Dew. Cover and process on BLEND for 15 seconds or until mixture is smooth. Pour mixture into a large bowl. Stir in orange juice and diet ginger ale. Add ice cubes. Mix well to combine. Garnish with mint sprigs. Serve at once.

Each serving equals:

HE: 1 Fruit

44 Calories, 0 gm Fat, 0 gm Protein, 11 gm Carbohydrate, 27 mg Sodium, 14 mg Calcium, 0 gm Fiber

DIABETIC: 1 Fruit

Big Island Piña Colada

■ ■ ■

It's the Miss America of tropical beverages, a star that simply sparkles with the taste of all that sunshine and sand! Here's a version that leaves out the liquor but blends in so much delicious taste, you'll never miss the "kick." *Serves 4*

1 cup cold water
2 cups (two 8-ounce cans)
crushed pineapple, packed in
fruit juice, undrained
2 teaspoons coconut extract

1 teaspoon rum extract
⅔ cup Carnation Nonfat Dry
Milk Powder
2 cups ice cubes ☆

In a blender container, combine cold water, undrained pineapple, coconut extract, and rum extract. Cover and process on BLEND for 10 seconds. Add dry milk powder and 1 cup ice cubes. Re-cover and process on BLEND for 20 seconds. Add remaining 1 cup ice cubes, re-cover, and process on BLEND for 15 seconds or until mixture is smooth. Serve at once.

Each serving equals:
HE: 1 Fruit, ½ Skim Milk

80 Calories, 0 gm Fat, 4 gm Protein, 16 gm Carbohydrate, 63 mg Sodium, 168 mg Calcium, 1 gm Fiber

DIABETIC: 1 Fruit, ½ Skim Milk

THE NORTHWEST

■ ■ ■

We've always celebrated the pioneer spirit in America, considering ourselves a land of rugged individualists, but nowhere was that more true than among the people who headed northwest, to settle in Montana and Idaho, Washington and Oregon, with the most independent and free-spirited among them braving the almost endless journey up to Alaska.

Many thousands of intrepid travelers went west via the Oregon Trail, dreaming of the green and fertile valleys at journey's end. Others took the longer route of ocean passage, rounding Cape Horn in months-long, perilous voyages in order to reach what they envisioned as a kind of promised land.

But where Oregon offered rich farmland to those who survived the trip and staked a claim, other parts of the region were less hospitable. Eastern Montana was rocky and poor for growing crops, though it provided an excellent source of game. Washington was also not particularly welcoming to settlers, covered as it was with acres of dense forest. Idaho and Montana experienced fierce winters that discouraged all but the hardiest pioneers. And Alaska—well, if the ice and snow didn't get to you, the months of darkness were rough going. And then there were the blackflies, and the grizzly bears. . .

But the Northwest was more than the sum of these parts. It was, in its own way, a kind of paradise. From the waters of the Pacific emerged some of the most spectacular fish anyone had ever seen—giant crabs, shrimp, and halibut that weighed hundreds of pounds. From the rivers that crossed the region came salmon, salmon, and more salmon. Yes, it rained often, but the foggy, damp climate produced orchards of fruit trees heavy with huge red apples and luscious pears. There were sweet cherries, all kinds of berries, and nuts that grew in profusion. Even the vegetables were exceptional—and when you ventured north to Alaska, they were extraordinary. The short summers there would normally have discouraged growth, but because summer days lasted as long as twenty hours, farmers were digging up carrots and radishes that weighed more than a pound, and raising cabbages of astonishing size. (I'm told if you visit the Alaska State Fair, you'll see prize-winning cabbages of as much as ninety pounds!)

So for those self-reliant people who dared to make their homes in this region, there were culinary rewards to be enjoyed. And when the cities and towns of the Northwest were further transformed by an influx of immigrants from Asia, especially China and Japan, so too was the cuisine of this beautiful and challenging land.

Everywhere we've traveled in the Northwest, we've found dishes that focused on the region's wonderfully fresh fruits. Those fruits—apples, pears, berries, and cherries—were made into just about everything under the sun, and so I knew my recipes needed to reflect that. Every restaurant featured entrees designed around the abundant fresh seafood that might be only hours out of the ocean when it was served. I also couldn't leave Seattle without tasting the luscious salmon that needed only a light broiling or grilling.

To get an instantaneous sense of the Northwest's bounteous food choices, all you need to do is spend a morning (or a full day!) at Seattle's Pike Place Market. This spectacular farmers' market, founded in 1907, is a magnificent tribute to the Northwest, featuring more than one hundred farmers and fishmongers who display their colorful wares seven days a week, from morning till night.

It was such a feast for the eyes and for all the senses, it made me want to create new recipes right on the spot! The dish I immediately scribbled down was

Pike Place Market Bounty Pie, which is really a meatloaf that I've "frosted" with a bushel basket of fresh veggies.

It's impossible to talk about the Northwest without recognizing the revolution that began there only a few years ago. Of course I'm talking about the gourmet coffee craze, symbolized in large part by the nationwide explosion of Starbucks and other coffee bars! This is the heart of cappuccino country, the land of caffeine, but what began as a regional passion is now a national obsession. For all those of you who love your coffee with the same intensity, I created *Café-au-Lait Chocolate Chip Bars.* I can't wait until you try them!

When you ask about Idaho and food, it seems that just about everyone will answer "Potatoes!" And why not? This state has given its best, its sturdiest and tastiest spuds so that we may enjoy America's favorite side dish. You can boil 'em, bake 'em, dice 'em, or do whatever you like with 'em, but I want to recommend a bowl of my *Idaho Potato Chowder* the next time you race shivering into your house and need to get warm really fast. This is the soup that'll do it for you.

I had a really good time naming the recipes in this section, probably because the place names across the Northwest have a wonderful ring to them. I mean, how can you resist stirring up *Walla Walla Creamed Onion Bake* just for the name alone? If you're an onion lover like me, you'll dig in to this splendidly satisfying dish with gusto.

And just wait until you taste *Willamette Valley Blackberry Cobbler!* There is just no more lush and magnificent farmland for growing sweet fruit than on both shores of the Willamette River. The next time I visit Oregon, I would love to ride the stern-wheeler that cruises along this memorably beautiful spot.

But I confess that the fruit recipe that pleased me most has got to be *Bing Cherry Bread Pudding.* Ever since childhood, I've had a "thing" for this old-fashioned dessert. My grandmother made a wonderful version of it, and so did my mother, who certainly knew the way to her daughter's heart! But with this recipe, even more than all the bread puddings I've created over the years, I think I made it a three-generation five-star event!

I remember learning the words to "America the Beautiful" when I was a little girl. I knew all about those "amber waves of grain" because I lived in Iowa. But as I sang the rest of the song's words, I think the kernel of a dream was born, a dream that echoed across the Northwest when I finally got to see it with my own eyes. Nowhere are the skies more spacious, or the purple mountains more majestic, and as you stand on the coast of this glorious place, you really understand the magnificent meaning of "from sea to shining sea."

THE NORTHWEST RECIPES

Mount Hood Carrot Soup

Idaho Potato Chowder

North Pacific Tuna Chowder

Snow Pea and Chicken Soup

Double Raspberry Salad

Asparagus Almondine

Walla Walla Creamed Onion Bake

Mushroom Strata

Slumgullion

Salmon Newburg with Asparagus

Seattle Shrimp Salad

Northwest Territory Crab au Gratin

Puget Sound Salmon Loaf

Salmon Stroganoff

Salmon Rolls

Baked Chicken in Orange-Almond
  Sauce

Chicken-Broccoli Stir-Fry

Chicken and Pasta in Dijon
  Mustard Sauce

Hazelnut Turkey Bake

Pike Place Market Bounty Pie

Big Sky Stew

Steaks with Blue Cheese Topping

Raspberry-Almond Cream Treats

Northwest Strawberry Rice Pudding

Bing Cherry Bread Pudding

Willamette Valley Blackberry
  Cobbler

Baked Alaska

Fresh Raspberry Pie

Oregon Trail Berry Crumb Pie

Rogue Valley Pear Pie

Filbert Applesauce Cake

Café-au-Lait Chocolate Chip Bars

Orange Sticky Buns

Blueberry Pancakes with Blueberry
  Sauce

Apple Waffles with Cider Syrup

Trail Blazers' Apricot Oatmeal
  Bread

Lemon Scones

Mount Hood Carrot Soup

■ ❄ ■

If you're lucky enough to visit Portland, Oregon, I hope you can fit in a visit to Mount Hood. At the very least, on a clear day, you'll see this magnificent mountain (snow topped even in summer). I was intrigued to discover that the beautifully designed lodge on top was a WPA project built during the Depression.

Serves 4 (1 full cup)

2 cups (one 16-ounce can)
  Healthy Request Chicken
  Broth
1 cup water
3 cups chopped carrots

½ cup diced onion
¼ teaspoon lemon pepper
⅛ teaspoon thyme
⅓ cup (1 ounce) uncooked
  Minute Rice

In a large saucepan, combine chicken broth, water, carrots, onion, lemon pepper, and thyme. Bring mixture to a boil. Lower heat, cover, and simmer for 15 minutes. Add uncooked rice. Mix well to combine. Continue simmering for 15 minutes or until carrots and rice are tender. Pour mixture into a blender container. Cover and process on PUREE for 30 to 45 seconds. Return mixture to saucepan and continue simmering for an additional 10 minutes, stirring occasionally.

Each serving equals:
HE: 1¾ Vegetable, ¼ Bread, 16 Optional Calories
76 Calories, 0 gm Fat, 3 gm Protein, 16 gm Carbohydrate, 280 mg Sodium, 36 mg Calcium, 3 gm Fiber
DIABETIC: 1½ Vegetable, ½ Starch/Carbohydrate

Idaho Potato Chowder

■ ❄ ■

Few foods are identified with their states as completely as the great Idaho spud, and I created this recipe to honor that sturdy and remarkable veggie! If you're not used to leaving the peels on your potatoes, just scrub them well and give it a try: the extra fiber is really good—and good for you.

Serves 4 (1 cup)

3 cups (15 ounces) diced
   unpeeled raw Idaho potatoes
1 cup finely chopped celery
½ cup finely chopped onion
1 cup hot water
1½ cups (one 12-fluid-ounce can)
   Carnation Evaporated Skim
   Milk

2 teaspoons reduced-calorie margarine
1 tablespoon chopped fresh parsley or 1 teaspoon dried parsley
   flakes
⅛ teaspoon black pepper

In a medium saucepan, combine potatoes, celery, onion, and water. Cook over medium heat for 15 to 20 minutes or until vegetables are just tender. Partially mash vegetables using a potato masher. Stir in evaporated skim milk, margarine, parsley, and black pepper. Lower heat and simmer for 6 to 8 minutes or until mixture is heated through, stirring occasionally.

Each serving equals:

HE: ¾ Skim Milk, ¾ Bread, ¾ Vegetable, ¼ Fat

169 Calories, 1 gm Fat, 9 gm Protein, 31 gm Carbohydrate, 161 mg Sodium, 25 mg Calcium, 3 gm Fiber

DIABETIC: 1 Skim Milk, 1 Starch, ½ Vegetable

North Pacific Tuna Chowder

■ ❋ ■

I've never been deep-sea fishing, but I've seen photographs of the fish pulled from the great Pacific Ocean by the men and women who risk their lives at sea every day. Can you imagine trying to reel in a giant tuna or a 300-pound halibut? (That's what won a recent Aleutian Islands fishing derby!) Here's a soup worthy of those heroes! *Serves 4 (1¼ cups)*

¾ cup finely chopped celery
¼ cup finely chopped onion
1 (10¾-ounce) can Healthy
  Request Cream of Mushroom
  Soup
¼ cup (one 2-ounce jar) chopped
  pimiento, undrained
1½ cups (one 12-fluid-ounce can)
  Carnation Evaporated Skim
  Milk

½ teaspoon yellow mustard
1 cup frozen peas, thawed
1½ cups (8 ounces) diced cooked
  potatoes
2 (6-ounce) cans white tuna,
  packed in water, drained and
  flaked
1 teaspoon dried parsley flakes
⅛ teaspoon black pepper

In a medium saucepan sprayed with butter-flavored cooking spray, sauté celery and onion for 6 to 8 minutes. Stir in mushroom soup, undrained pimiento, evaporated skim milk, and mustard. Add peas, potatoes, tuna, parsley flakes, and black pepper. Mix well to combine. Lower heat and simmer for 5 minutes or until mixture is heated through, stirring often.

HINT: Thaw peas by placing in a colander and rinsing under hot water for one minute.

Each serving equals:
HE: 1½ Protein, 1 Bread, ¾ Skim Milk, ½ Vegetable, ½ Slider,
1 Optional Calorie

255 Calories, 3 gm Fat, 21 gm Protein, 36 gm Carbohydrate, 542 mg Sodium,
364 mg Calcium, 5 gm Fiber

DIABETIC: 3 Meat, 1½ Starch/Carbohydrate, ½ Skim Milk, ½ Vegetable

Snow Pea and Chicken Soup

■ ❅ ■

Great numbers of workers from China were instrumental in the building of our transcontinental railroads, though often they did the most menial work, including the cooking. These "chefs" prepared Americanized versions of the foods they were used to eating back home, which is why Chinese restaurants in our country still serve some dishes unknown in China. This Asian-style soup should please palates in both nations, I hope! *Serves 4 (1¼ cups)*

*4 cups (two 16-ounce cans)
   Healthy Request Chicken
   Broth
1 cup (5 ounces) diced cooked
   chicken breast*

*½ cup shredded carrots
¼ cup chopped green onion
1¾ cups snow peas, cut into bite-
   sized pieces
½ teaspoon lemon pepper*

In a large saucepan, combine chicken broth and chicken. Add carrots, green onion, snow peas, and lemon pepper. Bring mixture to a boil. Lower heat and simmer for 15 to 20 minutes or until snow peas are just tender.

HINT: If you don't have leftovers, purchase a chunk of cooked chicken breast from your local deli.

Each serving equals:
HE: 1¼ Protein, 1¼ Vegetable, 8 Optional Calories
97 Calories, 1 gm Fat, 14 gm Protein, 8 gm Carbohydrate, 509 mg Sodium, 37 mg Calcium, 2 gm Fiber
DIABETIC: 1½ Meat, 1 Vegetable

Double Raspberry Salad

■ ■ ■

It's tempting to fill this section with only fresh berry recipes, but I know there are times of the year when we can't get them everywhere or at a reasonable price. This dish uses frozen raspberries, but remember—they're frozen fresh right out of the fields, and they're good in their own way, especially served like this!

Serves 8

2 (4-serving) packages JELL-O sugar-free raspberry gelatin

3 cups boiling water

¼ cup raspberry spreadable fruit

3 cups frozen unsweetened raspberries

½ cup Land O Lakes no-fat sour cream

¼ cup Cool Whip Free

In a large bowl, combine dry gelatin and water. Mix well to dissolve gelatin. Stir in spreadable fruit. Pour 1 cup mixture into a medium bowl and reserve for later use. Add frozen raspberries to remaining gelatin mixture. Mix well until berries are separated and mixture starts to thicken. Pour mixture into an 8-by-8-inch dish. Refrigerate until firm, about 3 hours. Meanwhile, add sour cream and Cool Whip Free to reserved gelatin mixture. Mix well until mixture is smooth, using a wire whisk. Refrigerate until salad is firm. Carefully spread topping mixture over set salad. Cut into 8 servings.

Each serving equals:

HE: 1 Fruit, ¼ Slider, 7 Optional Calories

60 Calories, 0 gm Fat, 1 gm Protein, 14 gm Carbohydrate, 24 mg Sodium, 30 mg Calcium, 3 gm Fiber

DIABETIC: 1 Fruit

Asparagus Almondine

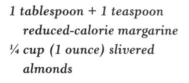

When I was growing up, asparagus was considered a special treat, saved for rare occasions and considered "for company." But now that this extravagantly good vegetable is widely available, you can enjoy it more often. This version lets the asparagus shine, and the slivered almonds make for a lovely contrast in taste and texture.

Serves 4 (½ cup)

1 tablespoon + 1 teaspoon reduced-calorie margarine	3 cups frozen cut asparagus, thawed
¼ cup (1 ounce) slivered almonds	2 teaspoons lemon juice

In a large skillet, melt margarine. Stir in almonds. Sauté almonds for 5 to 6 minutes or until golden. Add asparagus and lemon juice. Mix well to combine. Continue cooking for 6 minutes or until asparagus is heated through, stirring occasionally.

HINT: Thaw asparagus by placing in a colander and rinsing under hot water for one minute.

Each serving equals:
HE: 1½ Vegetable, 1 Fat, ¼ Protein
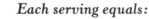
106 Calories, 6 gm Fat, 5 gm Protein, 8 gm Carbohydrate, 52 mg Sodium, 50 mg Calcium, 3 gm Fiber
DIABETIC: 1½ Vegetable, 1 Fat

Walla Walla Creamed Onion Bake

■ ❈ ■

There are some place names that are irresistible, and for me, Walla Walla, Washington, has always been one I loved to say aloud! This part of the country is famous for its especially flavorful onions, so I created this recipe to celebrate them. (If you can't get Walla Walla, you can substitute any sweet onions, like Vidalia.)

Serves 6

6 cups thinly sliced Walla Walla onions
½ cup hot water
1½ cups (one 12-fluid-ounce can) Carnation Evaporated Skim Milk

3 tablespoons all-purpose flour
1 teaspoon dried parsley flakes
⅛ teaspoon black pepper
½ cup + 1 tablespoon (2¼ ounces) dried fine bread crumbs

Preheat oven to 350 degrees. Spray an 8-by-8-inch baking dish with butter-flavored cooking spray. In a large saucepan, combine onions and water. Cook over medium heat for 6 to 8 minutes or until onions are just tender. Drain well. Evenly arrange onions in prepared baking dish. In a covered jar, combine evaporated skim milk and flour. Shake well to blend. Pour mixture into a medium saucepan sprayed with butter-flavored cooking spray. Add parsley flakes and black pepper. Cook over medium heat for 5 to 6 minutes or until mixture thickens, stirring constantly. Pour hot mixture over onions. Evenly sprinkle bread crumbs over top. Lightly spray top with butter-flavored cooking spray. Bake for 25 to 35 minutes. Place baking dish on a wire rack and let set for 5 minutes. Divide into 6 servings.

Each serving equals:
HE: 2 Vegetable, ⅔ Bread, ½ Skim Milk

157 Calories, 1 gm Fat, 7 gm Protein, 30 gm Carbohydrate, 166 mg Sodium, 57 mg Calcium, 3 gm Fiber

DIABETIC: 2 Vegetable, 1 Starch, ½ Skim Milk

Mushroom Strata

■ ❋ ■

This wonderfully cozy mushroom casserole is a terrific choice for those brisk fall or early-spring evenings, when you crave a little extra warmth! Isn't it great that good, fresh mushrooms are easier to find than ever? Just remember to keep them dry in your fridge until you're ready to use them, then scrub well and enjoy! *Serves 6*

6 slices reduced-calorie bread,
    cut into ½-inch cubes ☆
2 cups sliced fresh mushrooms
½ cup finely chopped onion
½ cup finely chopped celery
⅔ cup Carnation Nonfat Dry
    Milk Powder

1 cup water
½ cup Kraft fat-free mayonnaise
2 eggs, beaten, or equivalent in
    egg substitute
½ teaspoon lemon pepper
¾ cup (3 ounces) shredded Kraft
    reduced-fat Cheddar cheese

Preheat oven to 350 degrees. Spray an 8-by-8-inch baking dish with butter-flavored cooking spray. Layer half of bread cubes in prepared baking dish. In a large skillet sprayed with butter-flavored cooking spray, sauté mushrooms for 2 to 3 minutes. Spoon mushrooms evenly over bread in baking dish. In same skillet, sauté onion and celery for 5 minutes. Evenly layer onion mixture over mushrooms. Arrange remaining bread cubes over top. In a medium bowl, combine dry milk powder, water, and mayonnaise. Stir in eggs and lemon pepper. Pour mixture evenly over bread cubes. Evenly sprinkle Cheddar cheese over top. Bake for 35 to 45 minutes. Place baking dish on a wire rack and let set for 5 minutes. Divide into 6 servings.

HINT: Strata can be prepared, covered, and refrigerated for up to 24 hours before baking.

Each serving equals:
HE: 1 Protein (⅓ limited), 1 Vegetable, ½ Bread, ⅓ Skim Milk,
13 Optional Calories

217 Calories, 5 gm Fat, 18 gm Protein, 25 gm Carbohydrate, 579 mg Sodium, 458 mg Calcium, 3 gm Fiber

DIABETIC: 1 Meat, 1 Starch/Carbohydrate, ½ Vegetable

Slumgullion

■ ❋ ■

Don't you just love the name Slumgullion? This dish was made famous by the great American writer Jack London, who described it as a kind of catch-as-catch-can dish eaten by workers in the migratory camps. London, who never really stopped hearing *The Call of the Wild,* probably ate his share of this quick-fix dish.

Serves 6

2 cups (one 16-ounce can) whole-
    kernel corn, rinsed and
    drained
2 cups (one 16-ounce can)
    tomatoes, chopped and
    undrained
1 cup chopped onion

2 eggs or equivalent in egg
    substitute
⅓ cup skim milk
1 teaspoon dried parsley flakes
⅛ teaspoon black pepper
4 slices reduced-calorie bread,
    made into crumbs

Preheat oven to 350 degrees. Spray an 8-by-8-inch baking dish with butter-flavored cooking spray. In a large bowl, combine corn, undrained tomatoes, and onion. Add eggs, skim milk, parsley flakes, and black pepper. Mix well to combine. Stir in bread crumbs. Spread mixture into prepared baking dish. Lightly spray top with butter-flavored cooking spray. Bake for 45 to 50 minutes. Place baking dish on a wire rack and let set for 5 minutes. Divide into 6 servings.

Each serving equals:

HE: 1 Bread, 1 Vegetable, ⅓ Protein (limited), 5 Optional Calories

139 Calories, 3 gm Fat, 6 gm Protein, 22 gm Carbohydrate, 341 mg Sodium, 69 mg Calcium, 4 gm Fiber

DIABETIC: 1 Starch, 1 Vegetable

Salmon Newburg with Asparagus

■ ■ ■

Our Pacific Coast is probably the best place in the world to dine on fresh salmon, but fortunately for those of us who don't live in the region, those places are also home to giant fish canneries who send their gorgeous pink salmon to every supermarket in America! This used to be a kind of glamorous restaurant special, but now you can make it easily—and healthfully—at home!   *Serves 6*

> 1 (10¾-ounce) can Healthy
>   Request Cream of Mushroom
>   Soup
> ⅔ cup Carnation Nonfat Dry
>   Milk Powder
> ½ cup water
> ½ cup Kraft fat-free mayonnaise
> ⅛ teaspoon ground nutmeg
> ⅛ teaspoon black pepper
>
> 1 (14¾-ounce) can pink salmon,
>   drained, boned, and flaked
> 1½ cups frozen cut asparagus,
>   thawed
> 1 teaspoon sherry extract or 1
>   tablespoon sherry (optional)
> 3 cups hot cooked noodles,
>   rinsed and drained

In a large skillet sprayed with butter-flavored cooking spray, combine mushroom soup, dry milk powder, and water. Cook over medium heat for 5 minutes, stirring occasionally. Stir in mayonnaise, nutmeg, and black pepper. Add salmon, asparagus, and sherry extract. Mix well to combine. Lower heat and simmer for 8 to 10 minutes or until mixture is heated through, stirring occasionally. For each serving, place ½ cup noodles on a plate and spoon about ¾ cup salmon mixture over top.

HINT: 1. Thaw asparagus by placing in a colander and rinsing under hot water for one minute.
2. 2⅔ cups uncooked noodles usually cooks to about 3 cups.

Each serving equals:
HE: 2 Protein, 1 Bread, ½ Vegetable, ⅓ Skim Milk, ½ Slider,
1 Optional Calorie

270 Calories, 6 gm Fat, 22 gm Protein, 32 gm Carbohydrate, 897 mg Sodium, 301 mg Calcium, 2 gm Fiber

DIABETIC: 2 Meat, 1½ Starch/Carbohydrate, ½ Vegetable

Seattle Shrimp Salad

■ ■ ■

I suggest preparing this recipe with frozen shrimp; you may be surprised how splendidly firm and fresh these hardy crustaceans taste once they're thawed. The secret? They're flash-frozen moments after they're out of the ocean and shelled, so you get the benefit of living right near the water, even if you don't! I love the pretty color of the shrimp in this festive salad.   *Serves 6 (1 cup)*

¾ cup Kraft fat-free mayonnaise
¼ cup Kraft Fat Free French
  Dressing
¼ cup sweet pickle relish
1 teaspoon dried onion flakes
1 teaspoon dried parsley flakes
⅛ teaspoon black pepper

3 cups cooked shell macaroni,
  rinsed and drained
1 cup finely chopped cauliflower
1 cup sliced celery
1 (6-ounce) package frozen
  cooked shrimp, thawed

In a large bowl, combine mayonnaise, French dressing, pickle relish, onion flakes, parsley flakes, and black pepper. Add macaroni, cauliflower, and celery. Mix well to combine. Fold in shrimp. Cover and refrigerate for at least 30 minutes. Gently stir again just before serving.

HINT: 1. 2 cups uncooked shell macaroni usually cooks to about 3 cups.
     2. Thaw shrimp by placing in a colander and rinsing under hot water for one minute.
     3. Canned shrimp, rinsed and drained, may be substituted for frozen.

Each serving equals:
HE: 1 Protein, 1 Bread, ⅔ Vegetable, ½ Slider, 6 Optional Calories
161 Calories, 1 gm Fat, 9 gm Protein, 29 gm Carbohydrate, 481 mg Sodium, 24 mg Calcium, 1 gm Fiber
DIABETIC: 1½ Starch/Carbohydrate, 1 Meat, ½ Vegetable

Northwest Territory Crab au Gratin

■ ❋ ■

The shellfish that is harvested along our Northwest coast is among the most delicious you'll ever taste. But even if you don't have a visit planned, you can savor this flavor of the region in this rich and cheesy casserole. "Au gratin" is French for baked with cheese, but I'd also translate it as "with pizzazz"!

Serves 6

¾ cup finely chopped onion
1½ cups (one 12-fluid-ounce can) Carnation Evaporated Skim Milk
3 tablespoons all-purpose flour
2 (4.5-ounce drained weight) cans crabmeat, drained
¼ cup (one 2-ounce jar) chopped pimiento, drained

½ cup + 1 tablespoon (2¼ ounces) shredded Kraft reduced-fat Cheddar cheese
1 teaspoon dried parsley flakes
⅛ teaspoon black pepper
4 slices reduced-calorie bread, made into small soft crumbs

Preheat oven to 350 degrees. Spray an 8-by-8-inch baking dish with butter-flavored cooking spray. In a large skillet sprayed with butter-flavored cooking spray, sauté onion for 5 minutes. In a covered jar, combine evaporated skim milk and flour. Shake well to blend. Pour milk mixture into skillet with onion. Continue cooking until mixture thickens, stirring constantly. Add crabmeat, pimiento, Cheddar cheese, parsley flakes, and black pepper. Mix well to combine. Continue cooking until cheese melts, stirring often. Spoon half of crabmeat mixture into prepared baking dish. Cover with half of bread crumbs. Repeat layers. Lightly spray top with butter-flavored cooking spray. Bake for 20 to 25 minutes. Place baking dish on a wire rack and let set for 5 minutes. Divide into 6 servings.

Each serving equals:

HE: 2 Protein, ½ Skim Milk, ½ Bread, ¼ Vegetable

171 Calories, 3 gm Fat, 15 gm Protein, 21 gm Carbohydrate, 307 mg Sodium, 108 mg Calcium, 2 gm Fiber

DIABETIC: 2 Meat, ½ Skim Milk, ½ Starch

Puget Sound Salmon Loaf

■ ❋ ■

No wonder the whales keep coming back to Washington's beautiful Puget Sound—the peaceful waters and lush forests are almost like a dreamworld at dawn or sunset. It must be lovely living amid such beauties of nature, but even if I can't visit there often, I can dine on the region's rich salmon and taste its glories.

Serves 6

1 (14¾-ounce) can pink salmon, drained and flaked
½ cup finely chopped onion
1 cup fresh spinach leaves, stems discarded and finely shredded

30 Ritz Reduced Fat Crackers, made into crumbs
¼ cup Land O Lakes no-fat sour cream
⅔ cup skim milk
1½ teaspoons dried dill weed

Preheat oven to 350 degrees. Spray an 8-by-8-inch baking dish with butter-flavored cooking spray. Remove skin and bones from salmon, if desired. In a large bowl, combine salmon, onion, spinach, and cracker crumbs. Add sour cream, skim milk, and dill weed. Mix well to combine. Pat mixture into prepared loaf pan. Bake for 55 to 60 minutes. Place loaf pan on a wire rack and let set for 5 minutes. Cut into 6 servings.

HINT: A self-seal sandwich bag works great for crushing crackers.

Each serving equals:
HE: 2 Protein, 1 Bread, ½ Vegetable, ¼ Slider
185 Calories, 5 gm Fat, 16 gm Protein, 19 gm Carbohydrate, 397 mg Sodium, 184 mg Calcium, 1 gm Fiber
DIABETIC: 2½ Meat, 1 Starch, ½ Vegetable

Salmon Stroganoff

■ ■ ■

If you've got a can of salmon on your pantry shelf (and a few other little things), you won't need to call the takeout place tonight! This creamy dish tastes really luxurious, and you're eating healthy, nourishing fish most likely canned along our spectacular Pacific Coast. Don't omit the dried dill weed—it makes a flavorful dish a dazzler!

Serves 6

¼ cup thinly sliced green onion

¾ cup Dannon plain fat-free yogurt

⅔ cup Carnation Nonfat Dry Milk Powder

1 teaspoon cornstarch

½ teaspoon dried dill weed

½ cup water

½ cup (one 2.5-ounce jar) sliced mushrooms, drained

1 (14¾-ounce) can pink salmon, drained, boned, and flaked

3 cups hot cooked noodles, rinsed and drained

In a large skillet sprayed with butter-flavored cooking spray, sauté onion for 5 minutes or until tender. In a medium bowl, combine yogurt, dry milk powder, cornstarch, dill weed, and water. Add yogurt mixture to onion. Mix well to combine. Stir in mushrooms and salmon. Lower heat and simmer for 6 to 8 minutes, or until mixture is heated through, stirring often. For each serving, place ½ cup noodles on a plate and spoon about ½ cup salmon mixture over top.

HINT: 2⅔ cups uncooked noodles usually cooks to about 3 cups.

Each serving equals:
HE: 2 Protein, 1 Bread, ½ Skim Milk, ¼ Vegetable

223 Calories, 3 gm Fat, 21 gm Protein, 28 gm Carbohydrate, 468 mg Sodium, 261 mg Calcium, 2 gm Fiber

DIABETIC: 2 Meat, 1 Starch, ½ Skim Milk

Salmon Rolls

■ ❋ ■

Salmon was for years considered a luxury food, saved by the British upper crust for very special occasions. But now that so much superb salmon is harvested from our Northwestern waters, it's possible to enjoy this rich and nutritious fish as often as you like. This recipe looks as if a skilled caterer had been working in your kitchen!

Serves 8

1 (8-ounce) package Philadelphia fat-free cream cheese

1 (14¾-ounce) can pink salmon, drained, boned, and flaked

¾ cup finely chopped celery

¼ cup finely chopped onion

2 teaspoons lemon juice

½ teaspoon dill weed

1 (8-ounce) can Pillsbury Reduced Fat Crescent Rolls

½ cup Land O Lakes no-fat sour cream

Preheat oven to 350 degrees. In a large bowl, stir cream cheese with a spoon until soft. Stir in salmon, celery, onion, lemon juice, and dill weed. Set aside. Place crescent rolls on a large baking sheet sprayed with butter-flavored cooking spray. Pat into a 14-by-9-inch rectangle, being sure to seal perforations. Evenly spread salmon mixture over top. Roll up as for a jelly roll, starting with the long side. Seal edge well. Cut into 8 (1-inch) rolls and arrange on baking sheet. Bake for 25 to 30 minutes or until rolls are golden brown. For each serving, place 1 salmon roll on a plate and top with 1 tablespoon sour cream.

Each serving equals:

HE: 2 Protein, 1 Bread, ¼ Vegetable, 15 Optional Calories

186 Calories, 6 gm Fat, 16 gm Protein, 17 gm Carbohydrate, 691 mg Sodium, 96 mg Calcium, 0 gm Fiber

DIABETIC: 2½ Meat, 1 Starch/Carbohydrate

Baked Chicken in Orange-Almond Sauce

■ ❈ ■

Here's a sweet way to serve chicken that makes your everyday poultry seem like a special treat. Usually, it's more pricey birds like duck that get a special fruited glaze, but I figured, Why not use a few handy ingredients to let the sunshine in just anytime at all?   *Serves 4*

16 ounces skinned and boned uncooked chicken breasts, cut into 4 pieces
½ cup unsweetened orange juice
3 tablespoons orange marmalade spreadable fruit

2 teaspoons reduced-calorie margarine
½ teaspoon almond extract
1 tablespoon dried parsley flakes
1 teaspoon dried onion flakes
2 tablespoons (½ ounce) chopped almonds

Preheat oven to 350 degrees. Spray an 8-by-8-inch baking dish with butter-flavored cooking spray. Evenly arrange chicken pieces in prepared baking dish. In a small bowl, combine orange juice, spreadable fruit, margarine, almond extract, parsley flakes, and onion flakes. Drizzle orange mixture evenly over chicken. Evenly sprinkle almonds over top. Bake for 30 to 40 minutes. Place baking dish on a wire rack and let set for 5 minutes. Divide into 4 servings.

Each serving equals:
HE: 3 Protein, 1 Fruit, ½ Fat, 8 Optional Calories
189 Calories, 5 gm Fat, 24 gm Protein, 12 gm Carbohydrate, 80 mg Sodium, 26 mg Calcium, 0 gm Fiber
DIABETIC: 3 Meat, 1 Fruit, ½ Fat

Chicken-Broccoli Stir-Fry

■ ❈ ■

Most of the time, we take Chinese food for granted, rarely recalling the hard-working immigrant Chinese laborers who helped build our transcontinental railroads—and who brought their cooking techniques with them. Many of these people settled in the Northwest, and I think they'd be pleased to know how many Americans enjoy a tasty stir-fry! *Serves 4 (scant 1 cup)*

16 ounces skinned and boned uncooked chicken breasts, cut into 24 pieces
3 cups chopped fresh broccoli
½ cup chopped onion
¼ cup plum or grape spreadable fruit
1 tablespoon water
¼ teaspoon ground ginger

In a large skillet sprayed with butter-flavored cooking spray, sauté chicken, broccoli, and onion for 8 to 10 minutes. In a small bowl, combine spreadable fruit, water, and ginger. Add spreadable fruit mixture to chicken mixture. Mix well to combine. Lower heat and simmer for 5 minutes or until mixture is heated through, stirring occasionally.

Each serving equals:
HE: 3 Protein, 1¾ Vegetable, 1 Fruit
183 Calories, 3 gm Fat, 25 gm Protein, 14 gm Carbohydrate, 70 mg Sodium, 41 mg Calcium, 2 gm Fiber
DIABETIC: 3 Meat, 1 Vegetable, 1 Fruit

Chicken and Pasta in Dijon Mustard Sauce

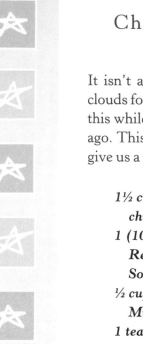

■ ❊ ■

It isn't always easy keeping your spirits up when the sun hides behind the clouds for days at a time, as it can do in Washington State. Cliff and I discovered this while filming our PBS TV show over several weeks there a couple of years ago. This is just the kind of spicy, sunny, tummy-soothing supper that would give us a real lift! *Serves 4 (1 full cup)*

1½ cups (8 ounces) diced cooked chicken breast

1 (10¾-ounce) can Healthy Request Cream of Mushroom Soup

½ cup Dijon Country Style Mustard

1 teaspoon dried onion flakes

2 teaspoons dried parsley flakes

½ cup (one 2.5-ounce jar) sliced mushrooms, drained

½ cup (two 2-ounce jars) chopped pimiento, drained

2 cups cooked rotini or penne pasta, rinsed and drained

In a large skillet sprayed with butter-flavored cooking spray, sauté chicken for 3 to 4 minutes. Stir in mushroom soup, mustard, onion flakes, and parsley flakes. Add mushrooms, pimiento, and rotini pasta. Mix well to combine. Lower heat and simmer for 8 to 10 minutes or until mixture is heated through, stirring occasionally.

HINT: 1. If you don't have leftovers, purchase a chunk of cooked chicken breast from your local deli.
2. 1½ cups uncooked rotini pasta usually cooks to about 2 cups.

Each serving equals:
HE: 2 Protein, 1 Bread, ¼ Vegetable, ½ Slider, 1 Optional Calorie
264 Calories, 4 gm Fat, 25 gm Protein, 32 gm Carbohydrate, 1150 mg Sodium, 71 mg Calcium, 2 gm Fiber
DIABETIC: 2 Meat, 1½ Starch/Carbohydrate, ½ Vegetable

Hazelnut Turkey Bake

■ ❋ ■

It's the Northwest's most common nut, and a delectable source of uncommon flavor for familiar recipes! It doesn't take more than a bit of chopped hazelnut to give this creamy turkey feast an extra measure of crunch and tangy taste.

Serves 6

¼ cup (1 ounce) chopped hazel-
    nuts
¾ cup diced green bell pepper
1 (10¾-ounce) can Healthy
    Request Cream of Celery Soup
½ cup skim milk
¼ cup (one 2-ounce jar) chopped
    pimiento, undrained

1½ cups (8 ounces) diced cooked
    turkey breast
3 cups hot cooked noodles,
    rinsed and drained
1 teaspoon dried parsley flakes

Preheat oven to 350 degrees. Spray an 8-by-8-inch baking dish with butter-flavored cooking spray. In a large skillet sprayed with butter-flavored cooking spray, sauté hazelnuts and green pepper for 5 minutes. Stir in celery soup, skim milk, and undrained pimiento. Add turkey, noodles, and parsley flakes. Mix well to combine. Spread mixture into prepared baking dish. Bake for 30 minutes. Place baking dish on a wire rack and let set for 5 minutes. Divide into 6 servings.

HINT: If you don't have leftovers, purchase a chunk of cooked turkey breast from your local deli.

Each serving equals:
HE: 1½ Protein, 1 Bread, ⅓ Fat, ¼ Vegetable, ¼ Slider, 15 Optional Calories
221 Calories, 5 gm Fat, 17 gm Protein, 27 gm Carbohydrate, 234 mg Sodium, 112 mg Calcium, 2 gm Fiber
DIABETIC: 1½ Starch/Carbohydrate, 1 Meat

Pike Place Market Bounty Pie

■ ❋ ■

Seattle's Pike Place Market is a feast for the senses, a home for the best our farmers and fishermen bring home for our tables. Most restaurant chefs don't decide what they'll be serving for dinner until they visit the market in the early morning and see what looks good. When I was creating this recipe, it *all* looked good to me!

Serves 6

1 tablespoon all-purpose flour
16 ounces ground 90% lean turkey or beef
¾ cup (3 ounces) dried fine bread crumbs
½ cup Land O Lakes no-fat sour cream
½ cup finely chopped onion
½ teaspoon dried basil

1 cup chopped fresh broccoli
½ cup chopped red bell pepper
¾ cup grated carrots
¾ cup chopped unpeeled zucchini
1 cup peeled and chopped fresh tomatoes
½ cup + 1 tablespoon (2¼ ounces) shredded Kraft reduced-fat Cheddar cheese

Preheat oven to 350 degrees. Spray a 9-inch pie plate with butter-flavored cooking spray. Evenly sprinkle flour into prepared pie plate. In a large bowl, combine meat, bread crumbs, sour cream, onion, and basil. Mix well to combine. Pat meat mixture into pie plate to cover bottom and up the sides to form a "crust." Bake for 30 minutes. Place pie plate on a wire rack. Meanwhile, in a large skillet sprayed with butter-flavored cooking spray, sauté broccoli, red bell pepper, carrots, zucchini, and tomatoes for 5 minutes. Evenly spoon vegetables into partially baked crust. Sprinkle Cheddar cheese evenly over top. Continue baking for 15 minutes. Place pie plate on a wire rack and let set for 5 minutes. Divide into 6 servings.

Each serving equals:

HE: 2½ Protein, 1½ Vegetable, ¾ Bread, ¼ Slider

261 Calories, 9 gm Fat, 21 gm Protein, 24 gm Carbohydrate, 323 mg Sodium, 274 mg Calcium, 4 gm Fiber

DIABETIC: 2½ Meat, 1 Vegetable, 1 Starch

Big Sky Stew

■ ❋ ■

Until you've actually seen the endless blue sky over Montana, you just have to take it on faith that it's glorious country out there! It's also a land to inspire hearty appetites, so here's a simple, substantial stew that would sustain a bunkhouse of cowboys—or a tableful of teenagers!

Serves 6 (1 cup)

16 ounces lean round steak, cut into 24 pieces
1 cup sliced celery
1 cup sliced carrots
½ cup chopped onion
2 cups (10 ounces) diced unpeeled potatoes

2 cups (one 16-ounce can) tomatoes, chopped and undrained
1 (10¾-ounce) can Healthy Request Mushroom Soup
2 teaspoons dried parsley flakes

In a large skillet sprayed with butter-flavored cooking spray, lightly brown steak. Stir in celery, carrots, onion, and potatoes. In a small bowl, combine undrained tomatoes, mushroom soup, and parsley flakes. Add tomato mixture to meat mixture. Mix well to combine. Lower heat, cover, and simmer for 30 minutes or until meat and vegetables are tender, stirring occasionally.

Each serving equals:
HE: 2 Protein, 1½ Vegetable, ⅓ Bread, ¼ Slider, 8 Optional Calories
237 Calories, 5 gm Fat, 27 gm Protein, 21 gm Carbohydrate, 399 mg Sodium, 93 mg Calcium, 3 gm Fiber
DIABETIC: 2 Meat, 1 Vegetable, 1 Starch

Steaks with Blue Cheese Topping

■ ❄ ■

Even if you're a fan of blue cheese salad dressing, you may never have imagined serving it with steak, as they often do in Oregon. The state is renowned for producing delicious blue cheese, so it makes perfect sense they'd invent other uses besides salad dressing for this tangy item. This recipe was a big hit with Cliff.

Serves 4

4 (3-ounce) lean tenderized minute or cube steaks
¼ cup Kraft Fat Free Blue Cheese Dressing

3 tablespoons (¾ ounce) crumbled blue cheese
½ teaspoon dried minced garlic
1 teaspoon dried parsley flakes

In a large skillet sprayed with butter-flavored cooking spray, brown steaks for 3 to 4 minutes on each side. In a small bowl, combine blue cheese dressing, blue cheese, garlic, and parsley flakes. Drizzle blue cheese mixture evenly over steaks. Lower heat, cover, and simmer for 5 minutes.

Each serving equals:

HE: 2½ Protein, ¼ Slider, 5 Optional Calories

140 Calories, 4 gm Fat, 20 gm Protein, 6 gm Carbohydrate, 208 mg Sodium, 5 mg Calcium, 0 gm Fiber

DIABETIC: 2½ Meat

Raspberry-Almond Cream Treats

■ ■ ■

Are the berries picked in the lush, green Willamette Valley really bigger than those grown anywhere else in the country, or do they just seem grander in scale because they're so sweet and juicy? I think if I lived out there, I'd be dining on berry desserts as often as possible, and these would be among my absolute favorites!

Serves 6

1 (4-serving) package JELL-O sugar-free instant vanilla pudding mix

⅔ cups Carnation Nonfat Dry Milk Powder

1½ cups water

¾ cup Dannon plain fat-free yogurt

1 teaspoon almond extract

1½ cups fresh raspberries

6 tablespoons Cool Whip Lite

2 tablespoons (½ ounce) slivered almonds

In a medium bowl, combine dry pudding mix, dry milk powder, and water. Mix well using a wire whisk. Blend in yogurt and almond extract. Add raspberries. Mix gently to combine. Evenly spoon mixture into 6 dessert dishes. Top each dish with 1 tablespoon Cool Whip Lite and garnish with 1 teaspoon almonds. Refrigerate for at least 30 minutes.

Each serving equals:

HE: ½ Skim Milk, ⅓ Fruit, ¼ Slider, 16 Optional Calories

105 Calories, 1 gm Fat, 8 gm Protein, 16 gm Carbohydrate, 383 mg Sodium, 173 mg Calcium, 1 gm Fiber

DIABETIC: ½ Skim Milk, ½ Starch/Carbohydrate

Northwest Strawberry Rice Pudding

■ ■ ■

I'm the strawberry nut in our household, so when we travel, I'm always looking to see what strawberry-themed dishes appear on regional menus. I loved the idea of stirring my favorite fruit into a wonderfully cozy rice pudding, and I even tweaked it a bit by adding the zip of orange juice and a bit of Diet Dew. Mmm-mm!

Serves 6

2 cups whole fresh
  strawberries ☆
1 (4-serving) package JELL-O
  sugar-free instant vanilla pudding mix
⅔ cup Carnation Nonfat Dry
  Milk Powder

½ cup unsweetened orange
  juice
1 cup Diet Mountain Dew
⅓ cup Cool Whip Free
1½ cups cold cooked rice

Reserve 6 whole strawberries. Coarsely chop remaining strawberries. In a large bowl, combine dry pudding mix, dry milk powder, orange juice, and Diet Mountain Dew. Mix well using a wire whisk. Blend in Cool Whip Free. Add rice and chopped strawberries. Mix gently to combine. Evenly spoon mixture into 6 dessert dishes and top each with 1 whole strawberry.

HINT: 1 cup uncooked instant rice usually cooks to about 1½ cups.

Each serving equals:

HE: ½ Bread, ½ Fruit, ⅓ Skim Milk, ¼ Slider, 3 Optional Calories

96 Calories, 0 gm Fat, 3 gm Protein, 21 gm Carbohydrate, 268 mg Sodium, 102 mg Calcium, 1 gm Fiber

DIABETIC: 1 Starch/Carbohydrate, ½ Fruit

Bing Cherry Bread Pudding

■ ❋ ■

A good friend was driving along Montana's Flathead Lake when she spotted a sign that said CHERRIES. She pulled the car over and bought three whole pounds! "I nibbled them constantly for the next few days," she told me. This bread pudding was inspired by just such terrific fruit—and I'm sure my cherry-loving son, James, would approve!

Serves 6

⅔ cup Carnation Nonfat Dry
 Milk Powder
¼ cup pourable Sugar Twin or
 Sprinkle Sweet
1 cup water
6 slices reduced-calorie Italian
 bread, toasted and cubed

2 cups halved and pitted Bing
 cherries
¼ cup (1 ounce) sliced
 almonds ☆
6 tablespoons Land O Lakes
 no-fat sour cream

Preheat oven to 350 degrees. Spray an 8-by-8-inch baking dish with butter-flavored cooking spray. In a large bowl, combine dry milk powder, Sugar Twin, and water. Stir toasted bread pieces into milk mixture. Add Bing cherries and 2 tablespoons almonds. Mix well to combine. Spread mixture into prepared baking dish. Evenly sprinkle remaining 2 tablespoons almonds over top. Bake for 35 to 45 minutes. Place baking dish on a wire rack and let set for 5 minutes. Divide into 6 servings. When serving, top each with 1 tablespoon sour cream.

Each serving equals:
HE: ⅔ Fruit, ½ Bread, ⅓ Skim Milk, ⅓ Fat, ¼ Slider, 9 Optional Calories
151 Calories, 3 gm Fat, 7 gm Protein, 24 gm Carbohydrate, 177 mg Sodium,
156 mg Calcium, 4 gm Fiber
DIABETIC: 1 Starch/Carbohydrate, ½ Fruit, ½ Fat

Willamette Valley Blackberry Cobbler

■ ❋ ■

It's one of the most beautiful valleys in all of America—lush, green, and perfect for growing the sweetest fruit around. This recipe takes a lot of blackberries, but the finished product is definitely worth it! If buying the best fruit seems extravagant, remind yourself that living healthy is worth it—and so are you!

Serves 6

4½ cups fresh blackberries
¾ cup pourable Sugar Twin or
   Sprinkle Sweet ☆
1 tablespoon cornstarch
1 tablespoon water
1 teaspoon lemon juice

1 cup + 2 tablespoons Bisquick
   Reduced Fat Baking Mix
2 tablespoons Land O Lakes
   no-fat sour cream
⅓ cup skim milk

Preheat oven to 375 degrees. Spray an 8-by-8-inch baking dish with butter-flavored cooking spray. In a large bowl, combine blackberries, ½ cup Sugar Twin, cornstarch, water, and lemon juice. Evenly spread blackberry mixture into prepared baking dish. In a medium bowl, combine baking mix, 2 tablespoons Sugar Twin, sour cream, and skim milk. Carefully spread batter over blackberry mixture. Lightly spray top with butter-flavored cooking spray. Evenly sprinkle remaining 2 tablespoons Sugar Twin over top. Bake for 18 to 20 minutes or until the filling is bubbly and the topping is golden brown. Place baking dish on a wire rack and let set for at least 5 minutes. Divide into 6 servings.

Each serving equals:
HE: 1 Bread, 1 Fruit, ¼ Slider, 7 Optional Calories
158 Calories, 2 gm Fat, 3 gm Protein, 32 gm Carbohydrate, 275 mg Sodium, 80 mg Calcium, 6 gm Fiber
DIABETIC: 1 Starch, 1 Fruit

Baked Alaska

■　■　■

When the United States bought Alaska from Russia back in the 1860s, everyone wanted to know all about the far-off territory that was now part of our country. Delmonico's restaurant in New York City even created a recipe to celebrate the region's snow-topped mountains, calling it Baked Alaska. This magnificent dessert requires some extra effort on the part of the cook, but the end result is truly luscious!

Serves 8

2 eggs or equivalent in egg substitute
2 teaspoons vanilla extract ☆
½ cup skim milk
1 tablespoon + 1 teaspoon reduced-calorie margarine
1 cup all-purpose flour
1 cup + 2 tablespoons pourable Sugar Twin or Sprinkle Sweet ☆

1 teaspoon baking powder
6 egg whites
¼ teaspoon cream of tartar
4 cups Wells' Blue Bunny sugar-and fat-free strawberry ice cream or any sugar- and fat-free ice cream

Preheat oven to 350 degrees. Spray a 9-by-9-inch cake pan with butter-flavored cooking spray. In a large bowl, combine eggs and 1 teaspoon vanilla extract. Stir in skim milk and margarine. Add flour, ¾ cup Sugar Twin, and baking powder. Mix just to combine. Pour batter into prepared cake pan. (Batter will be thin.) Bake for 22 to 26 minutes or until a toothpick inserted in center comes out clean. Remove cake from pan and allow to cool on a wire rack. Increase oven temperature to 500 degrees. Meanwhile, in a large bowl, beat egg whites with an electric mixer until soft peaks form. Add remaining 6 tablespoons Sugar Twin, remaining 1 teaspoon vanilla extract, and cream of tartar. Continue beating until stiff peaks form. To assemble, place a piece of brown paper on a baking sheet, arrange partially cooled cake on paper, place ice cream in a mound on cake, and cover cake and ice cream evenly with meringue mixture. Bake for 3 to 5 minutes or just until the meringue browns. Remove from oven, cut into 8 servings and serve immediately.

HINT: 1. Egg whites beat best at room temperature.
2. Meringue cuts easily if you dip a sharp knife in warm water before cutting.

Each serving equals:

HE: ⅔ Bread, ½ Protein (¼ limited), ¼ Fat, 1 Slider, 10 Optional Calories

178 Calories, 2 gm Fat, 10 gm Protein, 30 gm Carbohydrate, 213 mg Sodium, 168 mg Calcium, 1 gm Fiber

DIABETIC: 2 Starch/Carbohydrate, ½ Meat

Fresh Raspberry Pie

■ ❋ ■

The rumors of frequent rainfall in the Pacific Northwest are true, but all that moisture seems to encourage the region's raspberries to grow bigger and rosier than any you've ever seen! This pie is one of the prettiest I've ever seen—perfect for an engagement party or bridal shower.

Serves 8

1 Pillsbury refrigerated unbaked
  9-inch piecrust
1 (4-serving) package
  JELL-O sugar-free vanilla
  cook-and-serve pudding
  mix

1 (4-serving) package JELL-O
  sugar-free raspberry gelatin
1⅓ cups water
4½ cups fresh raspberries
1 tablespoon pourable Sugar
  Twin or Sprinkle Sweet

Let piecrust set at room temperature for 10 minutes. Meanwhile, in a medium saucepan, combine dry pudding mix, dry gelatin, and water. Cook over medium heat until mixture starts to boil, stirring often. Remove from heat. Stir in raspberries. Place saucepan on a wire rack and let set for at least 5 minutes. Cut the piecrust in half on the folded line. Gently roll each half into a ball. Wipe counter with a wet cloth and place a sheet of waxed paper over damp spot. Place one of the balls on the waxed paper. Cover with another piece of waxed paper and roll out into a 9-inch circle, with rolling pin. Carefully remove waxed paper from one side and place crust into an 8-inch pie plate. Remove other piece of waxed paper. Evenly spoon raspberry mixture into piecrust. Repeat process of rolling out remaining piecrust half. Place second crust over top of pie and flute edges. Lightly spray top of crust with butter-flavored cooking spray. Evenly sprinkle Sugar Twin over top. Make about 8 slashes with a knife to allow steam to escape. Bake at 450 degrees for 10 minutes. Reduce heat to 350 degrees and continue baking for 40 to 45 minutes. Place pie plate on a wire rack and allow to cool completely. Cut into 8 servings.

HINT: Place piece of uncooked elbow macaroni upright in center of pie to keep filling from cooking out of crust.

Each serving equals:
HE: ¾ Fruit, ½ Bread, ¾ Slider, 6 Optional Calories
159 Calories, 7 gm Fat, 1 gm Protein, 23 gm Carbohydrate, 159 mg Sodium, 15 mg Calcium, 5 gm Fiber
DIABETIC: 1 Fruit, 1 Starch/Carbohydrate, 1 Fat

Oregon Trail Berry Crumb Pie

■ ❋ ■

As we drove through Oregon, I couldn't help thinking about the long, hard ride the pioneers endured to reach this new land. They deserved a real reward at the end of that trail ride, and I invented this dessert in their honor. The blend of blueberries and raspberries seems to make each berry's flavor more distinctive.

Serves 8

1 (4-serving) package JELL-O sugar-free vanilla cook-and-serve pudding mix
1 (4-serving) package JELL-O sugar-free lemon gelatin
1¼ cups water
1½ cups fresh blueberries
1½ cups fresh raspberries
1 (6-ounce) Keebler graham cracker piecrust

2 tablespoons purchased graham cracker crumbs or 2 (2½-inch) graham cracker squares, made into crumbs
1 tablespoon (¼ ounce) chopped walnuts
2 tablespoons pourable Sugar Twin or Sprinkle Sweet

Preheat oven to 350 degrees. In a medium saucepan, combine dry pudding mix, dry gelatin, and water. Cook over medium heat until mixture thickens and starts to boil, stirring often. Remove from heat. Gently stir in blueberries and raspberries. Evenly spoon hot mixture into piecrust. In a small bowl, combine graham cracker crumbs, walnuts, and Sugar Twin. Sprinkle crumb mixture evenly over fruit filling. Bake for 30 minutes. Place pie plate on a wire rack and let set for 30 minutes. Refrigerate for at least 1 hour. Cut into 8 servings.

HINT: A self-seal sandwich bag works great for crushing graham crackers.

Each serving equals:
HE: ½ Bread, ½ Fruit, ¾ Slider, 18 Optional Calories
158 Calories, 6 gm Fat, 2 gm Protein, 24 gm Carbohydrate, 207 mg Sodium, 8 mg Calcium, 3 gm Fiber
DIABETIC: 1 Starch/Carbohydrate, 1 Fat, ½ Fruit

Rogue Valley Pear Pie

■ ✳ ■

The Rogue River runs more than 200 miles through Oregon before it hits the Pacific Ocean, and the orchards that line its banks are famous for their lush, juicy pears. Pick the very best fruit you can find, make sure it's ripe, and serve this scrumptious dessert with all the hoopla it deserves!   *Serves 8*

*3 cups (6 medium) peeled and
   sliced pears*
*1 (6-ounce) Keebler graham
   cracker piecrust*
*1 (4-serving) package JELL-O
   sugar-free vanilla cook-and-
   serve pudding mix*
*⅔ cup Carnation Nonfat Dry
   Milk Powder*
1⅓ cups water

1 teaspoon vanilla extract
½ teaspoon ground cinnamon
*2 tablespoons purchased graham
   cracker crumbs or 2 (2½-inch)
   graham cracker squares, made
   into crumbs*
*1 tablespoon Brown Sugar
   Twin*
*2 tablespoons (½ ounce) chopped
   hazelnuts or pecans*

Preheat oven to 375 degrees. Evenly arrange pear slices in piecrust. In a medium saucepan, combine dry pudding mix, dry milk powder, and water. Cook over medium heat until mixture thickens and starts to boil, stirring constantly. Remove from heat. Stir in vanilla extract and cinnamon. Evenly spoon mixture over pears. In a small bowl, combine graham cracker crumbs, Brown Sugar Twin, and hazelnuts. Evenly sprinkle crumb mixture over top. Bake for 30 to 35 minutes. Place pie plate on a wire rack and let set for 35 to 45 minutes. Refrigerate for at least 1 hour. Cut into 8 servings.

HINT: A self-seal sandwich bag works great for crushing graham crackers.

Each serving equals:
HE: ¾ Fruit, ½ Bread, ¼ Skim Milk, ¼ Fat, ¾ Slider, 17 Optional Calories
231 Calories, 7 gm Fat, 9 gm Protein, 33 gm Carbohydrate, 253 mg Sodium,
262 mg Calcium, 2 gm Fiber
DIABETIC: 1½ Starch/Carbohydrate, 1 Fruit, 1 Fat

Filbert Applesauce Cake

Here, I've blended two Pacific Northwest standouts into one spectacular cake. You've got one, two, three sources of apple-y goodness coupled with the wonderful crunch of the favorite local nut, for a cake that will win you applause at your next card party or Sunday brunch.

Serves 8

¼ cup reduced-calorie margarine

⅓ cup pourable Sugar Twin or Sprinkle Sweet

1 egg or equivalent in egg substitute

1 cup unsweetened applesauce

⅓ cup unsweetened apple juice

1½ cups Bisquick Reduced Fat Baking Mix

1½ teaspoons apple pie spice

¼ cup (1 ounce) chopped filberts or hazelnuts

Preheat oven to 350 degrees. Spray a 9-by-9-inch cake pan with butter-flavored cooking spray. In a large bowl, cream margarine and Sugar Twin. Stir in egg, applesauce, and apple juice. Add baking mix and apple pie spice. Mix gently to combine. Fold in filberts. Spread batter into prepared cake pan. Bake for 40 to 50 minutes or until a toothpick inserted in center comes out clean. Place cake pan on a wire rack and allow to cool completely. Cut into 8 servings.

Each serving equals:

HE: 1 Bread, 1 Fat, ⅓ Fruit, ¼ Protein, 4 Optional Calories

159 Calories, 7 gm Fat, 3 gm Protein, 21 gm Carbohydrate, 338 mg Sodium, 40 mg Calcium, 1 gm Fiber

DIABETIC: 1½ Starch/Carbohydrate, 1 Fat

Café-au-Lait Chocolate Chip Bars

■ ❋ ■

Inspired by the region that helped make really good coffee a national obsession, here's maybe the most delicious bar cookie recipe I've created in a long time! You can vary the flavor of these depending on the coffee blend you prefer. Even I was surprised by how luscious these tasted! *Serves 8 (2 each)*

¼ cup reduced-calorie margarine
¼ cup Land O Lakes no-fat sour cream
1 egg or equivalent in egg substitute
½ cup cold coffee
½ cup pourable Sugar Twin or Sprinkle Sweet
1 cup + 2 tablespoons all-purpose flour

1 teaspoon baking powder
½ teaspoon baking soda
½ teaspoon ground cinnamon
¼ cup (1 ounce) mini chocolate chips
¼ cup (1 ounce) chopped walnuts

Preheat oven to 350 degrees. Spray a 9-by-9-inch cake pan with butter-flavored cooking spray. In a large bowl, combine margarine, sour cream, and egg. Stir in coffee and Sugar Twin. Add flour, baking powder, baking soda, and cinnamon. Mix gently just to combine. Fold in chocolate chips and walnuts. Spread batter into prepared cake pan. Bake for 20 to 22 minutes. Place cake pan on a wire rack and allow to cool completely. Cut into 16 bars.

Each serving equals:

HE: 1 Fat, ¾ Bread, ¼ Protein, ¼ Slider, 12 Optional Calories

142 Calories, 6 gm Fat, 4 gm Protein, 18 gm Carbohydrate, 229 mg Sodium, 60 mg Calcium, 1 gm Fiber

DIABETIC: 1 Fat, 1 Starch

Orange Sticky Buns

■ ❄ ■

Here's another example of how easily you can dazzle your family and friends with just a bit of effort. What a perfect way to end a festive birthday breakfast or welcome new neighbors over coffee! The tangy orange flavor and the citrusy sweetness bring out something special in a batch of basic rolls. *Serves 8*

8 Rhodes frozen yeast dinner
 rolls
⅓ cup orange marmalade spreadable fruit

2 tablespoons unsweetened
 orange juice
¼ cup (1 ounce) chopped hazelnuts or pecans

Spray a 9-by-9-inch cake pan with butter-flavored cooking spray. Evenly arrange rolls in prepared pan. Cover with cloth and let rolls thaw and rise. In a medium bowl, combine spreadable fruit and orange juice. Drizzle orange mixture evenly over rolls. Evenly sprinkle hazelnuts over top. Bake at 375 degrees for 15 to 20 minutes. Place cake pan on a wire rack and let set for at least 15 minutes. Divide into 8 servings.

Each serving equals:
HE: 1 Bread, ⅔ Fruit, ½ Fat

127 Calories, 3 gm Fat, 3 gm Protein, 22 gm Carbohydrate, 100 mg Sodium, 8 mg Calcium, 1 gm Fiber

DIABETIC: 1 Starch, 1 Fruit, ½ Fat

Blueberry Pancakes with Blueberry Sauce

■ ❄ ■

Some days the steady rain and frequent fog make for poor morale among those who live in the Northwest, but recipes like this make it all worthwhile. The next time skies are gray and you don't feel like getting out of bed, stir up a batch of the best berry pancakes ever! *Serves 6*

2¼ cups fresh blueberries ☆
1 cup water
1 (4-serving) package JELL-O sugar-free vanilla cook-and-serve pudding mix
1½ cups Bisquick Reduced Fat Baking Mix

2 tablespoons pourable Sugar Twin or Sprinkle Sweet
¼ cup Land O Lakes no-fat sour cream
¾ cup skim milk
1 teaspoon vanilla extract

Reserve ½ cup blueberries. Mash remaining blueberries with a fork. In a medium saucepan, combine mashed blueberries, water, and dry pudding mix. Cook over medium heat until mixture thickens and starts to boil, stirring often. Lower heat and simmer while preparing pancakes. In a medium bowl, combine baking mix, Sugar Twin, sour cream, skim milk, and vanilla extract. Gently fold in reserved blueberries. Using a ⅓-cup measuring cup as a guide, pour batter onto a hot griddle or skillet sprayed with butter-flavored cooking spray to form 6 pancakes. Lightly brown on both sides. For each serving, place 1 pancake on a plate and spoon about ¼ cup blueberry sauce over top.

Each serving equals:
HE: 1⅓ Bread, ½ Fruit, ¼ Slider, 17 Optional Calories
174 Calories, 2 gm Fat, 4 gm Protein, 35 gm Carbohydrate, 457 mg Sodium, 85 mg Calcium, 2 gm Fiber
DIABETIC: 1½ Starch/Carbohydrate, ½ Fruit

Apple Waffles with Cider Syrup

■ ❋ ■

Washington State apples are among the best in the country, so it makes sense to cook them up and stir them into fresh waffle batter. If you've never made your own syrup, you've got a real treat in store. Why not serve these for a birthday morning breakfast and start the gift giving with these waffles?   *Serves 8*

> 1 (4-serving) package JELL-O sugar-free vanilla cook-and-serve pudding mix
> 2 cups unsweetened apple cider or juice
> 1 teaspoon apple pie spice
> 1½ cups Bisquick Reduced Fat Baking Mix
>
> ⅓ cup pourable Sugar Twin or Sprinkle Sweet
> 1 cup (2 small) cored, peeled, and chopped cooking apples
> 1 cup skim milk
> 2 tablespoons Land O Lakes no-fat sour cream

In a medium saucepan, combine dry pudding mix, apple cider and apple pie spice. Cook over medium-low heat until mixture thickens and starts to boil, stirring occasionally. Meanwhile, in a large bowl, combine baking mix, Sugar Twin, and apples. Add skim milk and sour cream. Mix gently to combine. Using a full ¼-cup measuring cup of batter per serving, bake waffles according to waffle manufacturer's directions. For each serving, place 1 waffle-iron on a plate and spoon about ¼ cup cider syrup over top. Serve at once.

Each serving equals:

HE: 1 Bread, ¾ Fruit, ¼ Slider, 9 Optional Calories

142 Calories, 2 gm Fat, 2 gm Protein, 29 gm Carbohydrate, 336 mg Sodium, 61 mg Calcium, 1 gm Fiber

DIABETIC: 1 Starch/Carbohydrate, 1 Fruit

Trail Blazers' Apricot Oatmeal Bread

■ ❋ ■

They say that an army travels on its stomach, and I'm sure the same was true for those great trail blazers of more than a century ago who headed West in search of the Columbia and Missouri Rivers. Here's a fruited quick bread that's more than sturdy enough to travel well, but even if it only travels from the kitchen to the dining table, you'll feel like blazing your own trail after just one piece!

Serves 8 (1 thick or 2 thin slices)

1⅓ cups Bisquick Reduced Fat
    Baking Mix
¼ cup (¾ ounce) quick oats
½ cup pourable Sugar Twin or
    Sprinkle Sweet
1 teaspoon ground cinnamon
⅓ cup Land O Lakes no-fat sour
    cream

⅔ cup skim milk
2 teaspoons vanilla extract
⅔ cup (3 ounces) chopped dried
    apricots
¼ cup (1 ounce) chopped
    walnuts

Preheat oven to 350 degrees. Spray a 9-by-5-inch loaf pan with butter-flavored cooking spray. In a large bowl, combine baking mix, oats, Sugar Twin, and cinnamon. Add sour cream, skim milk, and vanilla extract. Mix gently just to combine. Fold in apricots and walnuts. Spread batter into prepared loaf pan. Bake for 40 to 50 minutes or until a toothpick inserted in center comes out clean. Place loaf pan on a wire rack and let set for 10 minutes. Remove bread from pan and continue cooling on wire rack. Cut into 8 thick or 16 thin slices.

Each serving equals:

HE: 1 Bread, ½ Fruit, ¼ Fat, ¼ Slider, 11 Optional Calories

184 Calories, 4 gm Fat, 5 gm Protein, 32 gm Carbohydrate, 190 mg Sodium, 53 mg Calcium, 4 gm Fiber

DIABETIC: 1½ Starch, ½ Fruit, ½ Fat

Lemon Scones

■ ❋ ■

Most people feel that a cup of coffee or tea is just way too lonely without a piece of fresh baked pastry, so here's my candidate for a perfect "go-with"! Scones are a sweet mainstay when afternoon tea is served in England, but in this country we've made them welcome everywhere too.

Serves 8

2¼ cups Bisquick Reduced Fat Baking Mix
1 (4-serving) package JELL-O sugar-free lemon gelatin
¼ cup Land O Lakes no-fat sour cream

½ cup Diet Mountain Dew
1 tablespoon + 1 teaspoon pourable Sugar Twin or Sprinkle Sweet

Preheat oven to 400 degrees. Spray a baking sheet with butter-flavored cooking spray. In a large bowl, combine baking mix and dry gelatin. Add sour cream and Diet Mountain Dew. Mix gently just to combine. Place dough on a piece of waxed paper and pat into a 9-inch circle. Cut into 8 wedges. Place wedges on prepared baking sheet. Lightly spray with butter-flavored cooking spray. Evenly sprinkle ½ teaspoon Sugar Twin over top of each. Bake for 12 to 14 minutes. Place baking sheet on a wire rack and let set for at least 5 minutes. Good warm or cold. Especially good with blueberry spreadable fruit.

Each serving equals:
HE: 1½ Bread, 14 Optional Calories

130 Calories, 2 gm Fat, 3 gm Protein, 25 gm Carbohydrate, 405 mg Sodium, 44 mg Calcium, 1 gm Fiber

DIABETIC: 1½ Starch

THE HEARTLAND

■ ■ ■

Even if my beloved Midwest wasn't also known as America's Heartland, it would be my name for this part of the country. It's been home to my heart all my life, and it's the source for me of all that is best about our country. This is a region of unashamed, old-fashioned virtues, where neighbors know they can rely on their neighbors, and where the American dream is alive and well.

Beginning many generations ago, here is where so many immigrants chose to put down stakes, to devote themselves to rearing families and raising crops to supply our nation's tables. The Great Plains offered endless miles of fertile farmland, the ideal setting for the hardworking men and women from Germany, Scandinavia, and all over Europe who arrived here, determined to build their new country from the ground up. Dairy farms thrived, and cattle roamed the prairie. Fields of grain flourished in the rich soil, and in my home state of Iowa (and across the region), corn grew high and proud, providing sustenance to millions of Americans everywhere.

Out of these conditions developed a cooking style that combined the best of Old World traditions with the imagination and innovation that would shape a nation's future. Fish were plentiful in the region's rivers and lakes. Vegetable gardens and fruit orchards flourished under the loving care of farm wives while their husbands joined with their neighbors in harvesting crops that seemed to increase with every year. Cliff and I were both raised in that tradition, and it has truly shaped our characters and views of the world. He remembers: "We raised corn and hay and cattle. We always had our big Sunday meals at noon, except when we were baling hay. Neighbors worked together in the late summer months, and the farmers pulled together to get all the work done. Then we'd all have lunch at three P.M. All the farm wives were good cooks. They were used to feeding great crowds of people, and no one left the table hungry."

The Midwest is a region where potlucks and church suppers, family reunions and picnics by the river provide wonderful opportunities for young and old to visit together, to share the foods we learned to prepare at our grandmothers' knees, and to strengthen the bonds of friendship that sustain small-town life in America. It's a place where food brings us together and reminds us that what we share is more important than the ways in which we may disagree.

And each of those foods actually tells a story of the people who settled this land. As I began selecting recipes for this section, I felt my ties to my ancestors and their ancestors renewed as I considered the origins and flavors of each memorable dish.

You'll see that my Heartland recipes emphasize the kinds of comfort foods found at potluck suppers all over this region. From northern Minnesota and Wisconsin to the Ozark Mountains of Missouri, you'll always see tangy relishes and crunchy slaws, fresh salads and vegetable dishes that are as well-loved today as they were a century ago. I grew up eating these foods, and you would have thought that I'd be satisfied that my home-grown versions were the only classics a cook would ever need.

But as I have traveled around the country, poring over all kinds of regional, church, and community cookbooks, I've always been amazed at the diversity. You think there are only six ways to fix anything, and you find out there are six million ways! I kept finding, as Cliff and I toured different parts of the country, that there were new ways to do things.

So what is the true taste of the Heartland, when the foods we treasure originated in so many different places? For an answer, I'll nominate some of our best-loved ingredients:

CORN—This beautiful yellow grain sustained the Native Americans for centuries, and even today it is at the core of so many traditional Midwestern foods. No supper plate seems complete without a serving of that savory, creamy delight, *Squaw Corn,* or a colorful scoop of *Iowa Corn Relish,* such a vivid advertisement for the fresh vegetables harvested all across our great state. Corn is the mother lode, nourishing Midwesterners across the generations.

BEEF—Midwestern men are meat-and-potatoes men, and not even a commitment to living healthy can change what's been bred in the bone. So I consider it a pleasurable duty to create meaty recipes that all members of the family can enjoy without concern. Oh, I might "sneak" in some vegetables along with the meat (*Ground Beef–Stuffed Acorn Squash*), but my dishes deliver plenty of hearty beef taste. You can serve my *Swedish Meatballs or Heartland Shepherd's Pie* and know without a doubt that your family is eating well—and getting the nourishment they need.

RHUBARB—I know that we Heartland bakers don't have a monopoly on wonderful rhubarb recipes, but I think you'll agree that we've truly given this luscious fruit our best shot in salads, compotes, and of course pies! Ever since I was a child, I've looked forward to the first rhubarb dessert of the season, and this year I made it *Covered Wagon Rhubarb Pie.* It's my way of recognizing the courage and steadfastness of those men and women who crossed an ocean and then miles of unfamiliar territory to find their way home—and who settled here.

Whether you're planning a family reunion, organizing a potluck, or just want to savor foods that reinforce our ties to our past as a nation, I hope you'll find what you're looking for in these recipes of the heart.

THE HEARTLAND RECIPES

Prairie Beef-Vegetable Soup

Home-Style Beef-Barley Soup

Milwaukee Beer Soup

Cincinnati Five-Way Chili

Church Social Gelatin Salad

Iowa Corn Relish

Sweet-and-Sour Slaw

Wilted-Lettuce Salad

Marinated Bean Salad

Red Cabbage with Apples

Middle America German Potato Salad

Creamy Carrots and Onions

Midwest Succotash

Squaw Corn

Potato Pancakes

Sour Cream Twice-Baked Potatoes

Chicago-Style Deep-Dish Pizza

Cabbage-Tomato-Rice Casserole

Door County Fish Boil

Chicken-Broccoli-Corn Casserole

Heartland Shepherd's Pie

Swedish Meatballs

Ground Beef–Stuffed Acorn Squash

Cheeseburger Macaroni

Special Swiss Steak

Simmered Steak and Celery

Pork Loins with Cider Sauce

Braised Pork and Cabbage

Pork and Peas in Cream Sauce

Spiced Baked Apples

Brownie Pudding Cake

Scrumptious Strawberry Shortcake

Quick Apple Dumplings

Fruit Kolaches

Schaum Torte

Covered Wagon Rhubarb Pie

Sour Cream Walnut Coffee Cake

Prairie Beef-Vegetable Soup

■ ❄ ■

Even when times were hard, a heavy iron pot of soup likely simmered on the stoves of every farmhouse across the Great Plains. Somehow, everyone would be fed and sustained. This recipe recalls those times of stirring a little bit of a lot of ingredients into a sturdy, soothing, heartwarming soup!   *Serves 6 (1½ cups)*

1¾ cups (one 14½-ounce can) Swanson Beef Broth

1 cup water

2 cups (one 16-ounce can) tomatoes, chopped and undrained

½ cup chopped onion

1½ cups frozen cut green beans, thawed

1½ cups frozen sliced carrots, thawed

2 cups (10 ounces) diced raw potatoes

1½ cups (8 ounces) diced lean cooked roast beef

2 cups chopped cabbage

1 teaspoon dried parsley flakes

⅛ teaspoon black pepper

In a large saucepan, combine beef broth, water, and undrained tomatoes. Stir in onion, green beans, carrots, and potatoes. Bring mixture to a boil. Add roast beef, cabbage, parsley flakes, and black pepper. Mix well to combine. Lower heat, cover, and simmer for 20 minutes or until vegetables are tender, stirring occasionally.

HINT: 1. Thaw green beans and carrots by placing in a colander and rinsing under hot water for one minute.

2. If you don't have leftovers, purchase a chunk of lean cooked roast beef from your local deli or use Healthy Choice Deli slices.

Each serving equals:
HE: 2½ Vegetable, 1⅓ Protein, ½ Bread, 6 Optional Calories
179 Calories, 3 gm Fat, 18 gm Protein, 20 gm Carbohydrate, 415 mg Sodium, 70 mg Calcium, 4 gm Fiber
DIABETIC: 2 Vegetable, 1 Meat, ½ Starch

Home-Style Beef-Barley Soup

When those brisk winds blow off the Great Lakes and deliver what's known as "lake-effect snow," nothing tastes better than a cozy-warm bowl of beef-barley soup! With each spoonful, it'll warm your body and give your soul a little hug. If you've never cooked with barley before, you'll be amazed at how it "fills out" when stirred into the soup.

Serves 6 (1⅓ cups)

½ cup (3 ounces) pearl barley
1¾ cups (one 14½-ounce can)
  Swanson Beef Broth
4 cups water ☆
2 full cups (12 ounces) diced lean
  cooked roast beef

1½ cups diced carrots
1 cup diced celery
½ cup chopped onion
1 teaspoon dried parsley
  flakes
⅛ teaspoon black pepper

In a large saucepan, combine barley, beef broth, and ¼ cup water. Cook for 5 minutes or until barley is tender, stirring occasionally. Add remaining 3¾ cups water, roast beef, carrots, celery, and onion. Mix well to combine. Stir in parsley flakes and black pepper. Bring mixture to a boil. Lower heat, cover, and simmer for 15 minutes or until vegetables are tender.

HINT: If you don't have leftovers, purchase a chunk of lean cooked roast beef from your local deli or use Healthy Choice Deli slices

Each serving equals:
HE: 2 Protein, 1 Vegetable, ⅔ Bread, 6 Optional Calories
180 Calories, 4 gm Fat, 19 gm Protein, 17 gm Carbohydrate, 319 mg Sodium, 30 mg Calcium, 4 gm Fiber
DIABETIC: 2 Meat, 1 Vegetable, ½ Starch

Milwaukee Beer Soup

■ ■ ■

Even if you're not a drinker, you may be surprised how much pizzazz a simple can of lite beer adds to this hearty potato-cheese soup! The alcohol vanishes during cooking, but the flavor stays and stays. It's a great choice for a Super Bowl party or autumn supper after a day of raking leaves.   *Serves 4 (1 cup)*

1 cup shredded carrots
½ cup chopped onion
2 cups (one 16-ounce can) Healthy Request Chicken Broth
⅔ cup Carnation Nonfat Dry Milk Powder
3 tablespoons all-purpose flour
1 cup (8 ounces) lite beer or water

1 teaspoon Dijon mustard
1 teaspoon dried parsley flakes
1½ cups (8 ounces) diced cooked potatoes
1½ cups (6 ounces) shredded Kraft reduced-fat Cheddar cheese

In a large saucepan sprayed with butter-flavored cooking spray, sauté carrots and onion for 5 minutes. In a covered jar, combine chicken broth, dry milk powder, and flour. Shake well to blend. Pour broth mixture into saucepan. Add beer. Mix well to combine. Continue cooking until mixture thickens, stirring often. Stir in Dijon mustard, parsley flakes, potatoes, and Cheddar cheese. Lower heat and simmer until cheese melts and mixture is heated through, stirring often.

Each serving equals:
HE: 2 Protein, ¾ Bread, ¾ Vegetable, ½ Skim Milk, ¼ Slider,
4 Optional Calories
251 Calories, 7 gm Fat, 19 gm Protein, 28 gm Carbohydrate, 690 mg Sodium,
448 mg Calcium, 2 gm Fiber
DIABETIC: 1½ Meat, 1 Starch, 1 Vegetable, ½ Skim Milk

Cincinnati Five-Way Chili

■ ✳ ■

Chili is another one of those regional favorites that is prepared differently depending on the town you're in at the time! In Cincinnati, Ohio, they make their chili with cocoa and cinnamon, add spaghetti, and serve it over oyster crackers. Even if you're a chili purist, I hope you'll give this unique and surprisingly tasty preparation a try.

Serves 6

8 ounces ground 90% lean turkey or beef
1½ cups chopped onion ☆
½ teaspoon dried minced garlic
1 cup (one 8-ounce can) Hunt's Tomato Sauce
1¾ cups (one 14½-ounce can) Swanson Beef Broth
¾ cup water
1 tablespoon cider vinegar
1 tablespoon chili seasoning

½ teaspoon unsweetened cocoa
½ teaspoon ground cinnamon
⅛ teaspoon black pepper
3 cups hot cooked spaghetti, rinsed and drained
6 ounces (one 8-ounce can) red kidney beans, rinsed and drained
¾ cup (3 ounces) shredded Kraft reduced-fat Cheddar cheese
6 tablespoons oyster crackers

In a large saucepan sprayed with butter-flavored cooking spray, brown meat and ¾ cup onion. Stir in garlic, tomato sauce, beef broth, water, and vinegar. Add chili seasoning, cocoa, cinnamon, and black pepper. Mix well to combine. Bring mixture to a boil. Lower heat, cover, and simmer for 15 minutes. For each serving, place ½ cup spaghetti on a plate, ladle scant 1 cup chili over spaghetti, and sprinkle 2 tablespoons kidney beans, 2 tablespoons Cheddar cheese, 2 tablespoons onion, and 1 tablespoon oyster crackers over top.

HINT: 2½ cups broken uncooked spaghetti usually cooks to about 3 cups.

Each serving equals:
HE: 2 Protein, 1 Bread, 1 Vegetable, ½ Slider, 5 Optional Calories
299 Calories, 7 gm Fat, 20 gm Protein, 39 gm Carbohydrate, 711 mg Sodium, 120 mg Calcium, 7 gm Fiber
DIABETIC: 2 Meat, 1½ Starch, 1 Vegetable

Church Social Gelatin Salad

■ ■ ■

I used to wish that every church in America produced its own cookbook because I so enjoyed every one I ever read! What an ideal dish this is for any gathering of friends, but I thought it would be especially sweet and pretty to offer at your next fund-raising supper. A salad this tasty will surely produce an overflowing collection plate! It's just heavenly! *Serves 6*

1 (4-serving) package JELL-O sugar-free raspberry gelatin
1 cup boiling water
¼ cup cold water
1½ cups frozen unsweetened red raspberries
1 (4-serving) package JELL-O sugar-free instant vanilla pudding mix

1 (4-serving) package JELL-O sugar-free lemon gelatin
⅔ cup Carnation Nonfat Dry Milk Powder
1 cup Diet Mountain Dew
¾ cup Cool Whip Free

In a large bowl, combine dry raspberry gelatin and boiling water. Mix well to dissolve gelatin. Stir in cold water and frozen raspberries. Pour mixture into an 8-by-8-inch dish. Refrigerate until firm, about 3 hours. In a medium bowl, combine dry pudding mix, dry lemon gelatin, and dry milk powder. Add Diet Mountain Dew. Mix well using a wire whisk. Blend in Cool Whip Free. Evenly spread pudding mixture over set gelatin. Refrigerate for at least 15 minutes. Divide into 6 servings.

Each serving equals:
HE: ⅓ Skim Milk, ⅓ Fruit, ½ Slider, 5 Optional Calories
84 Calories, 0 gm Fat, 5 gm Protein, 16 gm Carbohydrate, 343 mg Sodium, 99 mg Calcium, 1 gm Fiber
DIABETIC: 1 Starch/Carbohydrate

Iowa Corn Relish

■ ❄ ■

You didn't think I'd let you go without supplying a traditional corn relish from my home state, did you? After all, corn is served at just about every meal in our truck stops, blended into casseroles, baked into side dishes. This is corn country, and we're proud of it.

Serves 6 (½ cup)

2 cups (one 16-ounce can) whole-kernel corn, rinsed and drained
1 cup finely chopped celery
¼ cup finely chopped green bell pepper
¼ cup finely chopped onion

⅓ cup sweet pickle relish
¼ cup (one 2-ounce jar) chopped pimiento, drained
½ cup Kraft Fat Free French Dressing
⅛ teaspoon black pepper

In a large bowl, combine corn, celery, green pepper, and onion. Stir in pickle relish and pimiento. Add French dressing and black pepper. Mix well to combine. Cover and refrigerate for at least 2 hours. Gently stir again just before serving.

Each serving equals:
HE: ⅔ Bread, ½ Vegetable, ½ Slider, 7 Optional Calories

108 Calories, 0 gm Fat, 2 gm Protein, 25 gm Carbohydrate, 445 mg Sodium, 14 mg Calcium, 2 gm Fiber

DIABETIC: 1 Starch/Carbohydrate, ½ Vegetable

Sweet-and-Sour Slaw

■ ■ ■

The immigrants who settled the Midwest brought with them the comfort foods of home, and this crunchy salad sparkles with the blend of sweet and sour flavors that are so beloved across Eastern Europe. This recipe requires *cider* vinegar, so please don't try to substitute some other kind—it won't be as good.

Serves 6 (1 cup)

⅔ cup Carnation Nonfat Dry
   Milk Powder
½ cup water
¼ cup pourable Sugar Twin or
   Sprinkle Sweet

2 tablespoons cider vinegar
1 teaspoon dried onion flakes
⅛ teaspoon black pepper
6 cups shredded cabbage

In a large bowl, combine dry milk powder and water. Stir in Sugar Twin, vinegar, onion flakes, and black pepper. Add cabbage. Mix well to combine. Cover and refrigerate for at least 30 minutes. Gently stir again just before serving.

Each serving equals:
HE: 2 Vegetable ¼ Skim Milk, 4 Optional Calories

48 Calories, 0 gm Fat, 4 gm Protein, 8 gm Carbohydrate, 54 mg Sodium, 134 mg Calcium, 2 gm Fiber

DIABETIC: 1 Vegetable

Wilted-Lettuce Salad

■ ■ ■

Now, don't get me wrong, I'm not suggesting a recipe to use when all you have in your fridge is a brown-edged, dried-up head of lettuce. In this dish, "wilted" is something wonderful that happens to leaf lettuce when it's tossed with a special hot dressing. It's a real winner.   *Serves 4 (1 cup)*

½ cup finely chopped onion   *4 cups leaf lettuce, torn into*
¼ cup cider vinegar   *   small pieces*
¼ cup Hormel Bacon Bits   *2 hard-boiled eggs, chopped*

In a large skillet sprayed with butter-flavored cooking spray, sauté onion for 5 minutes. Add vinegar and bacon bits. Mix well to combine. Bring mixture to a boil. Lower heat and simmer for 5 minutes, stirring occasionally. In a large bowl, combine lettuce and chopped eggs. Drizzle hot vinegar mixture over top. Toss lightly to coat. Serve at once.

HINT: If you want the look and feel of egg without the cholesterol, toss out the yolk and dice the white.

Each serving equals:
HE: 1¼ Vegetable, ½ Protein (limited), ¼ Slider, 5 Optional Calories
92 Calories, 4 gm Fat, 7 gm Protein, 7 gm Carbohydrate, 289 mg Sodium, 74 mg Calcium, 2 gm Fiber
DIABETIC: 1 Vegetable, 1 Meat

Marinated Bean Salad

■ ■ ■

When my friend Barbara first came to visit with Cliff and me in DeWitt, we took her to a fish fry at the Knights of Columbus—just to give her a taste of life in a small Midwestern town. Besides the crispy fish fillets, potatoes, and applesauce, the buffet table featured just this kind of colorful and tangy bean salad.

Serves 6 (⅔ cup)

10 ounces (one 16-ounce can) red kidney beans, rinsed and drained

2 cups (one 16-ounce can) cut green beans, rinsed and drained

1 cup chopped red onion

¼ cup (one 2-ounce jar) chopped pimiento, drained

¾ cup (3 ounces) shredded Kraft reduced-fat Cheddar cheese

¾ cup Kraft Fat Free French Dressing

1 teaspoon dried parsley flakes

In a medium bowl, combine kidney beans, green beans, and onion. Stir in pimiento and Cheddar cheese. Add French dressing and parsley flakes. Mix well to combine. Cover and refrigerate for at least 30 minutes. Gently stir again just before serving.

Each serving equals:
HE: 1½ Protein, 1 Vegetable, ½ Slider, 10 Optional Calories
162 Calories, 2 gm Fat, 8 gm Protein, 28 gm Carbohydrate, 586 mg Sodium, 116 mg Calcium, 6 gm Fiber
DIABETIC: 1½ Starch/Carbohydrate, 1 Vegetable, ½ Meat

Red Cabbage with Apples

■ ■ ■

Cabbage is cooked and served in dozens of ways across the Midwest, with most of these old-time recipes handed down over the years from mother to daughter. My mother used to serve a scrumptious dish of red cabbage with apples when I was living at home, and I wanted to celebrate her Bohemian heritage.

Serves 4 (1 cup)

4 cups shredded red cabbage
2 cups (4 small) cored, peeled,
*   and chopped cooking apples*
¼ cup cider vinegar
¼ cup water
2 tablespoons pourable Sugar
*   Twin or Sprinkle Sweet*

2 tablespoons Brown Sugar Twin
2 tablespoons Hormel Bacon
*   Bits*
½ teaspoon caraway seed
⅛ teaspoon black pepper

In a large skillet sprayed with butter-flavored cooking spray, combine cabbage, apples, vinegar, water, Sugar Twin, and Brown Sugar Twin. Stir in bacon bits, caraway seed, and black pepper. Cover and simmer for 15 minutes or until cabbage and apples are tender, stirring occasionally.

Each serving equals:
HE: 2 Vegetable, 1 Fruit, 19 Optional Calories

77 Calories, 1 gm Fat, 2 gm Protein, 15 gm Carbohydrate, 136 mg Sodium, 48 mg Calcium, 3 gm Fiber

DIABETIC: 1 Vegetable, 1 Fruit

Middle America German Potato Salad

■ ❊ ■

If you've only ever eaten the good old American traditional style of potato salad, which is served cold and with a mayo-based dressing, let me entice you into trying something very special: a hot potato salad brought here from Germany, with a super-delicious dressing that's both sweet and vinegary. What a welcome "immigrant" this dish has always been!   *Serves 6 (1 cup)*

1½ cups chopped onion
½ cup cider vinegar
½ cup water
1 tablespoon all-purpose flour
½ cup Hormel Bacon Bits
1 tablespoon pourable Sugar
   Twin or Sprinkle Sweet

1 teaspoon dried parsley flakes
⅛ teaspoon black pepper
5 cups (30 ounces) diced cooked
   potatoes

In a large skillet sprayed with butter-flavored cooking spray, sauté onion for 5 minutes. In a covered jar, combine vinegar, water, and flour, Shake well to blend. Pour vinegar mixture into skillet with onion. Add bacon bits, Sugar Twin, parsley flakes, and black pepper. Mix well to combine. Lower heat and continue cooking until mixture starts to thicken, stirring often. Stir in potatoes. Simmer for 5 minutes or until potatoes are heated through, stirring often.

Each serving equals:
HE: 1 Bread, ½ Vegetable, ¼ Slider, 19 Optional Calories
162 Calories, 2 gm Fat, 7 gm Protein, 29 gm Carbohydrate, 342 mg Sodium, 19 mg Calcium, 3 gm Fiber
DIABETIC: 1½ Starch/Carbohydrate, ½ Vegetable

Creamy Carrots and Onions

■ ■ ■

If creamed veggies bring back wonderful childhood memories for you, you're not alone! Cozy dishes like this were a mainstay on the table of many family farms in the Midwest when I was growing up, and I still want to enjoy that luscious flavor—but in a healthy way. Cliff gobbled these down with a big smile on his face, and I bet your family will, too!   *Serves 6 (¾ cup)*

4 cups frozen sliced carrots
2 cups sliced onion
¼ cup water
1 (10¾-ounce) can Healthy
   Request Cream of Chicken
   Soup

1 teaspoon dried parsley flakes
⅛ teaspoon black pepper

In an 8-cup glass measuring bowl, combine carrots, onion, and water. Microwave on HIGH (100% power) for 8 to 9 minutes, stirring after 4 minutes. Stir in chicken soup, parsley flakes, and black pepper. Continue to microwave on HIGH for 1 to 2 minutes or until mixture is heated through. Gently stir again just before serving.

HINT: Great with grilled or baked chicken or roast turkey.

Each serving equals:
HE: 2 Vegetable, ¼ Slider, 10 Optional Calories

89 Calories, 1 gm Fat, 2 gm Protein, 18 gm Carbohydrate, 259 mg Sodium, 39 mg Calcium, 4 gm Fiber

DIABETIC: 2 Vegetable

Midwest Succotash

■ ❊ ■

True, "official" succotash usually includes lima beans, but when you're married to a green bean kind of guy, you want to stir up veggie dishes that tickle his tastebuds. This recipe was created with Cliff in mind, and I'm happy to report that he gave it two thumbs up!

Serves 4 (1 cup)

½ cup finely chopped onion

2 cups (one 16-ounce can) whole-kernel corn, rinsed and drained

2 cups (one 16-ounce can) cut green beans, rinsed and drained

½ cup (3 ounces) finely diced Dubuque 97% fat-free ham or any extra-lean ham

⅓ cup Carnation Nonfat Dry Milk Powder

½ cup water

1 teaspoon dried parsley flakes

⅛ teaspoon black pepper

In a large skillet sprayed with butter-flavored cooking spray, sauté onion for 5 minutes. Stir in corn, green beans, and ham. In a small bowl, combine dry milk powder and water. Add milk mixture, parsley flakes, and black pepper to vegetable mixture. Mix well to combine. Lower heat and simmer for 6 to 8 minutes, stirring occasionally.

Each serving equals:

HE: 1¼ Vegetable, 1 Bread, ½ Protein, ¼ Skim Milk

146 Calories, 2 gm Fat, 8 gm Protein, 24 gm Carbohydrate, 588 mg Sodium, 109 mg Calcium, 3 gm Fiber

DIABETIC: 1 Vegetable, 1 Starch, ½ Meat

Squaw Corn

■ ❈ ■

Some of the simple recipes we serve in this region come from the rustic kitchens of men who worked outdoors, away from home for weeks at a time. This dish originated in the Wisconsin and Minnesota camps of lumberjacks, who cooked with staples like dried corn, which they always had on hand. We'll use frozen because we can.

Serves 6 (½ cup)

¾ cup finely chopped onion
3 cups frozen whole-kernel corn, thawed
2 teaspoons pourable Sugar Twin or Sprinkle Sweet
1 teaspoon dried parsley flakes
⅛ teaspoon black pepper
6 tablespoons Land O Lakes no-fat sour cream
¼ cup Hormel Bacon Bits

In a large skillet sprayed with butter-flavored cooking spray, sauté onion for 6 to 8 minutes or until tender. Stir in corn, Sugar Twin, parsley flakes, and black pepper. Add sour cream and bacon bits. Mix well to combine. Lower heat and simmer for 5 minutes or until mixture is heated through, stirring often.

HINT: Thaw corn by placing in a colander and rinsing under hot water for one minute.

Each serving equals:
HE: 1 Bread, ¼ Vegetable, ¼ Slider, 12 Optional Calories
92 Calories, 0 gm Fat, 3 gm Protein, 20 gm Carbohydrate, 30 mg Sodium, 36 mg Calcium, 2 gm Fiber
DIABETIC: 1½ Starch/Carbohydrate

Potato Pancakes

■ ■ ■

Here's one of my favorite ways to serve potatoes, and it doesn't take much more time than the plain old boiled kind! Just a little dab of no-fat sour cream helps these turn out moist and rich tasting. When it's harvest time and you're busier than ever, mix up a batch of these for dinner and enjoy the pleasure on your family's faces.

Serves 4 (2 each)

3 cups (10 ounces) shredded loose-packed frozen potatoes

½ cup finely chopped onion

1 tablespoon all-purpose flour

2 eggs or equivalent in egg substitute

1 tablespoon Land O Lakes no-fat sour cream

1 teaspoon dried parsley flakes

⅛ teaspoon black pepper

In a large bowl, combine potatoes and onion. Add flour, egg, sour cream, parsley flakes, and black pepper. Mix well to combine. Using a ⅓-cup measuring cup as a guide, drop mixture onto a hot griddle or 2 large skillets sprayed with butter-flavored cooking spray, to form 8 pancakes. Flatten pancakes with a spatula. Cook over medium heat for 3 to 4 minutes or until well browned and crisp on bottom. Turn pancakes and continue cooking for 2 to 3 minutes or until browned on second side. Serve hot.

Each serving equals:

HE: ½ Bread, ¼ Protein (limited), ¼ Vegetable, 11 Optional Calories

106 Calories, 2 gm Fat, 5 gm Protein, 17 gm Carbohydrate, 37 mg Sodium, 29 mg Calcium, 2 gm Fiber

DIABETIC: 1 Starch, ½ Meat

Sour Cream Twice-Baked Potatoes

■ ❄ ■

I wonder who the first clever cook was who decided to scoop out baked potato halves, blend the cooked potato with sour cream, cheese, and spices, then spoon the mixture back into the shells and bake it again! (I bet she was a Plainswoman . . . !) I'd like to give that person a blue ribbon for ingenuity. This is a favorite of all my kids.

Serves 4 (2 halves)

4 medium-sized (5 ounces each) baking potatoes

¼ cup Land O Lakes no-fat sour cream

¼ cup (¾ ounce) grated Kraft fat-free Parmesan cheese

1 teaspoon dried onion flakes

1 teaspoon dried parsley flakes

Paprika

Preheat oven to 425 degrees. Place potatoes on a baking sheet and bake for 45 to 60 minutes or until tender. Cut each potato in half lengthwise. Scoop potato pulp into a large bowl, reserving shells. Mash potato pulp with a potato masher or fork. Stir in sour cream, Parmesan cheese, onion flakes, and parsley flakes. Evenly spoon mixture into reserved potato shells. Lightly sprinkle paprika over top. Arrange potato halves on a baking sheet and bake for 10 minutes or until tops are lightly browned.

Each serving equals:

HE: 1 Bread, ¼ Protein, 15 Optional Calories

132 Calories, 0 gm Fat, 4 gm Protein, 29 gm Carbohydrate, 104 mg Sodium, 41 mg Calcium, 3 gm Fiber

DIABETIC: 1½ Starch/Carbohydrate

Chicago-Style Deep-Dish Pizza

■ ■ ■

New York is justly proud of its thin-crusted pizzas, and California is where all those unusual gourmet topping combos came from, but true pizza fans head for Chicago when they want the heartiest pizza anywhere! Toppings are piled on, the crust is substantial, and the hungriest appetite is satisfied. Now you can skip a trip to the Windy City and make this favorite at home.   *Serves 8*

1 (11-ounce) can Pillsbury refrigerated French loaf

1 cup finely chopped onion

1¾ cups (one 15-ounce can) Hunt's Tomato Sauce

½ teaspoon dried minced garlic

2 teaspoons pourable Sugar Twin or Sprinkle Sweet

2 teaspoons Italian seasoning

1 cup (one 4-ounce can) sliced mushrooms, drained

½ cup chopped green bell pepper

1½ cups (6 ounces) shredded Kraft reduced-fat Cheddar cheese

¾ cup (3 ounces) shredded Kraft reduced-fat mozzarella cheese

Preheat oven to 400 degrees. Spray a 9-by-13-inch baking dish with olive oil–flavored cooking spray. Unroll French loaf and arrange in prepared baking dish, patting dough up sides of baking dish. In a large skillet sprayed with olive oil–flavored cooking spray, sauté onion for 5 minutes. Stir in tomato sauce, garlic, Sugar Twin, and Italian seasoning. Bring mixture to a boil. Lower heat and simmer for 6 to 8 minutes. Spread sauce mixture evenly over crust. Evenly sprinkle mushrooms and green pepper over sauce. Sprinkle Cheddar and mozzarella cheeses evenly over top. Let set for 5 minutes. Bake for 18 to 22 minutes. Place baking dish on a wire rack and let set for 5 minutes. Cut into 8 servings.

Each serving equals:

HE: 1½ Protein, 1½ Vegetable, 1 Bread, 1 Optional Calorie

210 Calories, 6 gm Fat, 14 gm Protein, 25 gm Carbohydrate, 826 mg Sodium, 223 mg Calcium, 2 gm Fiber

DIABETIC: 1½ Vegetable, 1 Meat, 1 Starch

Cabbage-Tomato-Rice Casserole

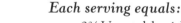

I've heard it said that America's heartland is casserole country, and I would agree. Cooks here are always creating smart and thrifty blends of ingredients that bake up beautifully together. Prepared from simple foods on hand, these dishes form the sturdy backbone of our Midwestern menus—and make living on a careful budget a pleasure instead of a pain! *Serves 4*

3 cups shredded cabbage	2 teaspoons pourable Sugar Twin
½ cup finely chopped onion	or Sprinkle Sweet
2 cups (one 16-ounce can)	⅛ teaspoon black pepper
tomatoes, chopped and	2 cups cooked rice
undrained	¾ cup (3 ounces) shredded Kraft
1 teaspoon yellow mustard	reduced-fat Cheddar cheese ☆

Preheat oven to 350 degrees. Spray an 8-by-8-inch baking dish with butter-flavored cooking spray. In a large skillet sprayed with butter-flavored cooking spray, sauté cabbage and onion for 5 minutes. Stir in undrained tomatoes, mustard, Sugar Twin, and black pepper. Add rice and ½ cup Cheddar cheese. Mix well to combine. Spread mixture into prepared baking dish. Evenly sprinkle remaining ¼ cup Cheddar cheese over top. Bake for 30 minutes. Place baking dish on a wire rack and let set for 5 minutes. Divide into 4 servings.

HINT: 1⅓ cups uncooked instant rice usually cooks to about 2 cups.

Each serving equals:

HE: 2¾ Vegetable, 1 Bread, 1 Protein, 1 Optional Calorie

188 Calories, 4 gm Fat, 10 gm Protein, 28 gm Carbohydrate, 206 mg Sodium, 244 mg Calcium, 3 gm Fiber

DIABETIC: 2 Vegetable, 1 Starch, 1 Meat

Door County Fish Boil

■ ■ ■

In Door County, Wisconsin, there's only one way to serve the traditional fish boil—by setting huge iron kettles to cook outdoors! I've created a scaled-down version of this regional classic, especially for those apartment dwellers who might not have a chance to make dinner outside.   *Serves 6*

3 cups (15 ounces) chopped
  unpeeled red-skinned potatoes
1½ cups chopped onion
4 cups water
1 teaspoon lemon pepper
3½ cups coarsely chopped cabbage
16 ounces white fish, cut into 8
  pieces

1 cup (one 8-ounce can) small
  whole beets, drained
½ cup Land O Lakes no-fat sour
  cream
1 tablespoon prepared horseradish sauce
1 teaspoon dried parsley flakes

In a large saucepan, combine potatoes, onion, water, and lemon pepper. Bring mixture to a boil. Stir in cabbage. Lower heat, cover, and simmer for 10 minutes. Add fish. Mix well to combine. Re-cover and continue simmering for 5 to 6 minutes or until fish is tender. Remove fish and vegetables with a slotted spoon and arrange on a platter. Cover to keep warm. Stir beets into remaining water. Cook for 3 to 5 minutes or until hot. Drain and arrange beets evenly on platter. In a small bowl, combine sour cream, horseradish sauce, and parsley flakes. Drizzle mixture evenly over top. Divide into 6 servings.

Each serving equals:
HE: 2 Vegetable, 1 Protein, ½ Bread, ¼ Slider, 3 Optional Calories
165 Calories, 1 gm Fat, 14 gm Protein, 25 gm Carbohydrate, 243 mg Sodium, 91 mg Calcium, 3 gm Fiber
DIABETIC: 2 Meat, 1½ Vegetable, 1 Starch

Chicken-Broccoli-Corn Casserole

■ ❋ ■

There's nothing that pleases a Heartland husband more than the sight of a bubbling casserole being carried to the supper table! Unfortunately, Cliff wasn't very happy with this one, since it contains his least favorite vegetable, broccoli. But since most men I know like it just fine, you're likely to get the smile and thanks you so richly deserve!   *Serves 6*

*3 cups frozen cut broccoli,
    thawed*
*1 cup frozen whole-kernel corn,
    thawed*
*2 full cups (12 ounces) diced
    cooked chicken breast*
*1 (10¾-ounce) can Healthy
    Request Cream of Chicken
    Soup*

*1 cup (one 8-ounce can) cream-
    style corn*
*1 teaspoon dried onion
    flakes*
*1 teaspoon dried parsley
    flakes*
⅛ teaspoon black pepper
*10 Ritz Reduced Fat Crackers,
    made into crumbs*

Preheat oven to 350 degrees. Spray an 8-by-8-inch baking dish with butter-flavored cooking spray. In a large bowl, combine broccoli, whole-kernel corn, and chicken. Add chicken soup, cream-style corn, onion flakes, parsley flakes, and black pepper. Mix well to combine. Spread mixture into prepared baking dish. Evenly sprinkle cracker crumbs over top. Lightly spray top with butter-flavored cooking spray. Bake for 35 to 40 minutes. Place baking dish on a wire rack and let set for 5 minutes. Divide into 6 servings.

HINT: 1. Thaw broccoli and whole-kernel corn by placing in a colander and rinsing under hot water for one minute.
2. If you don't have leftovers, purchase a chunk of cooked chicken breast from your local deli.
3. A self-seal sandwich bag works great for crushing crackers.

Each serving equals:
HE: 2 Protein, 1 Bread, 1 Vegetable, ¼ Slider, 10 Optional Calories

232 Calories, 4 gm Fat, 23 gm Protein, 26 gm Carbohydrate, 428 mg Sodium, 64 mg Calcium, 4 gm Fiber

DIABETIC: 2 Meat, 1½ Starch/Carbohydrate, 1 Vegetable

Heartland Shepherd's Pie

■ ❄ ■

Easy casseroles that deliver meat and potatoes in one hearty dish are a great idea, especially in the middle of farm country, where chores keep everyone busy from dawn to bedtime! This version smells so good as it bubbles in your oven, you'll be absolutely *ravenous* when it's time for dinner. *Serves 6*

16 ounces ground 90% lean
 turkey or beef
1 cup finely chopped onion
2 cups (one 16-ounce can) cut
 green beans, rinsed and
 drained
1 (10¾-ounce) can Healthy
 Request Tomato Soup

2⅓ cups hot water
2 cups (4½ ounces) instant
 potato flakes
2 tablespoons Land O Lakes no-
 fat sour cream
1 teaspoon dried parsley
 flakes
Paprika

Preheat oven to 350 degrees. Spray an 8-by-8-inch baking dish with butter-flavored cooking spray. In a large skillet sprayed with butter-flavored cooking spray brown meat and onion. Add green beans and tomato soup. Mix well to combine. Spread mixture into prepared baking dish. In a large bowl, combine hot water and potato flakes. Mix well using a fork. Stir in sour cream and parsley flakes. Spread potato mixture over meat mixture. Lightly sprinkle paprika over top. Bake for 30 minutes. Place baking dish on a wire rack and let set for 5 minutes. Divide into 6 servings.

Each serving equals:
HE: 2 Protein, 1 Bread, 1 Vegetable, ¼ Slider, 15 Optional Calories
247 Calories, 7 gm Fat, 17 gm Protein, 29 gm Carbohydrate, 262 mg Sodium, 47 mg Calcium, 3 gm Fiber
DIABETIC: 2 Meat, 1 Starch, 1 Vegetable

Swedish Meatballs

■ ❆ ■

It's the spices that make the magic in this classic recipe, brought over to this country by the many settlers who left Scandinavia to make their homes out here. This is a great dish for festive buffets, the recipe can easily be doubled or tripled for large gatherings, and the meatballs reheat beautifully.   *Serves 6*

16 ounces ground 90% lean turkey or beef

½ cup + 1 tablespoon (2¼ ounces) dried fine bread crumbs

1½ cups (one 12-fluid-ounce can) Carnation Evaporated Skim Milk ☆

1 tablespoon dried onion flakes

½ teaspoon ground allspice

½ teaspoon ground nutmeg

1 (10¾-ounce) can Healthy Request Cream of Mushroom Soup

1 teaspoon dried parsley flakes

⅛ teaspoon black pepper

In a large bowl, combine meat, bread crumbs, ½ cup evaporated skim milk, onion flakes, allspice, and nutmeg. Mix well to combine. Form into 24 (1-inch) meatballs. Place meatballs in a large skillet sprayed with butter-flavored cooking spray and brown on all sides. In a small bowl, combine mushroom soup, remaining 1 cup evaporated skim milk, parsley flakes, and black pepper. Spoon soup mixture evenly over meatballs. Lower heat, cover, and simmer for 15 to 20 minutes. For each serving, place 4 meatballs on a plate and spoon ¼ cup sauce mixture over top.

Each serving equals:

HE: 2 Protein, ½ Skim Milk, ½ Bread, ¼ Slider, 8 Optional Calories

211 Calories, 7 gm Fat, 19 gm Protein, 18 gm Carbohydrate, 616 mg Sodium, 55 mg Calcium, 1 gm Fiber

DIABETIC: 2 Meat, 1 Starch, 1 Skim Milk

Ground Beef–Stuffed Acorn Squash

■ ❋ ■

Something wonderful happens to squash when it's baked slowly in the oven, then stuffed with a savory blend of meat and spices that remarkably masquerade as "sausage"! The fruit and oats make a fantastically filling dish even more of a feast. Even if your home is far from the nation's Heartland, you will feel a culinary link with the Midwest after just one bite.   *Serves 4*

2 small (about 16 ounces each) acorn squash	¼ teaspoon poultry seasoning
⅓ cup water	¼ cup (¾ ounce) quick oats
8 ounces ground 90% lean turkey or beef	½ cup (1 small) cored, peeled, and finely chopped cooking apple
⅛ teaspoon black pepper	2 teaspoons dried onion flakes
¼ teaspoon ground sage	1 teaspoon dried parsley flakes
¼ teaspoon garlic powder	¼ cup skim milk

Preheat oven to 350 degrees. Cut each squash in half. Scoop out and discard seeds and membrane. Place squash halves, cut side down, in a 9-by-13-inch baking dish. Pour water into pan. Bake for 30 minutes. Meanwhile, in a large skillet sprayed with butter-flavored cooking spray, brown meat. Stir in black pepper, sage, garlic powder, and poultry seasoning. Add oats, apple, onion flakes, parsley flakes, and skim milk. Mix well to combine. Turn squash up and evenly spoon mixture into squash cavities. Continue baking for 25 to 30 minutes or until squash is tender.

Each serving equals:

HE: 1½ Bread, 1½ Protein, ¼ Fruit, 6 Optional Calories

222 Calories, 6 gm Fat, 14 gm Protein, 28 gm Carbohydrate, 71 mg Sodium, 137 mg Calcium, 8 gm Fiber

DIABETIC: 1½ Starch, 1½ Meat

Cheeseburger Macaroni

■ ❋ ■

I always have my son Tommy in mind when I'm creating cheeseburger recipes, but he lives in Arizona now with his wife, Angie, and daughter, Cheyanne. I don't want him ever to forget the true taste of the Heartland, so now I simply e-mail him any new recipes that he inspired! *Serves 4 (1 cup)*

8 ounces ground 90% lean turkey or beef
¼ cup chopped onion
1¾ cups (one 14½-ounce can) stewed tomatoes, coarsely chopped, and undrained
¼ cup Heinz Light Harvest Ketchup or any reduced-sodium ketchup

1 teaspoon chili seasoning
2 cups hot cooked elbow macaroni, rinsed and drained
¾ cup (3 ounces) shredded Kraft reduced-fat Cheddar cheese

In a large skillet sprayed with butter-flavored cooking spray, brown meat and onion. Stir in undrained stewed tomatoes, ketchup, and chili seasoning. Add macaroni and Cheddar cheese. Mix well to combine. Lower heat and simmer for 6 minutes or until cheese melts and mixture is heated through, stirring occasionally.

HINT: 1⅓ cups uncooked elbow macaroni usually cooks to about 2 cups.

Each serving equals:
HE: 2½ Protein, 1 Bread, 1 Vegetable, 15 Optional Calories
285 Calories, 9 gm Fat, 20 gm Protein, 31 gm Carbohydrate, 551 mg Sodium, 205 mg Calcium, 2 gm Fiber
DIABETIC: 2 Meat, 1½ Starch, 1 Vegetable

Special Swiss Steak

■ ❋ ■

Midwestern men are raised to think meat, meat, meat, when it comes to meals, and so I've made a point of stirring up recipes that deliver what they enjoy most—in the healthiest form I can! These little steaks are great to keep in the freezer and serve just about anytime, and this "saucy" recipe sneaks in a couple of vegetable servings they won't even notice. *Serves 4*

3 tablespoons all-purpose flour
1 teaspoon dried parsley flakes
⅛ teaspoon black pepper
4 (4-ounce) lean tenderized minute or cube steaks
1 (10¾-ounce) can Healthy Request Tomato Soup

2 cups (one 16-ounce can) tomatoes, chopped and undrained
1 teaspoon Worcestershire sauce
½ cup chopped onion
1 cup finely chopped celery

In a saucer, combine flour, parsley flakes, and black pepper. Coat steaks on both sides in flour mixture. Evenly arrange coated steaks in a large skillet sprayed with butter-flavored cooking spray. Brown steaks for 3 minutes on each side. In a large bowl, combine tomato soup, undrained tomatoes, Worcestershire sauce, and any remaining flour mixture. Stir in onion and celery. Spoon mixture evenly over steaks. Lower heat, cover, and simmer for 30 minutes or until steaks are tender. For each serving, place 1 piece of steak on a plate and spoon about ⅔ cup tomato mixture over top.

Each serving equals:
HE: 3 Protein, 1¾ Vegetable, ¼ Bread, ½ Slider, 5 Optional Calories
253 Calories, 5 gm Fat, 30 gm Protein, 22 gm Carbohydrate, 486 mg Sodium, 68 mg Calcium, 3 gm Fiber
DIABETIC: 3 Meat, 1½ Vegetable, 1 Starch

Simmered Steak and Celery

■ ❋ ■

Because the Midwest is cattle country, a cookbook author wouldn't be very popular out there if she suggested eliminating all beef products from the menu. The good news is, I don't have to. Lean beef is a healthy choice, in moderation, and it's also a great morale-builder for a family that's been trying to cut down on junk food.

Serves 4

16 ounces lean minute steak, cut
    into 32 pieces
1½ cups diced celery
½ cup chopped onion
1 teaspoon dried parsley flakes

1 (10¾-ounce) can Healthy
    Request Cream of Celery Soup
½ cup water
2 cups hot cooked noodles,
    rinsed and drained

In a large skillet sprayed with butter-flavored cooking spray, sauté meat for 10 minutes. Add celery, onion, and parsley flakes. Mix well to combine. In a medium bowl, combine celery soup and water. Stir soup mixture into meat mixture. Lower heat, cover, and simmer for 20 minutes or until meat and vegetables are tender, stirring occasionally. For each serving, place ½ cup noodles on a plate and spoon about ¾ cup meat sauce over top.

HINT: Full 1¾ cups uncooked noodles usually cooks to about 2 cups.

Each serving equals:
HE: 3 Protein, 1 Bread, 1 Vegetable, ½ Slider, 1 Optional Calorie

291 Calories, 7 gm Fat, 27 gm Protein, 30 gm Carbohydrate, 388 mg Sodium, 81 mg Calcium, 2 gm Fiber

DIABETIC: 3 Meat, 1½ Starch/Carbohydrate, 1 Vegetable

Pork Loins with Cider Sauce

■ ❋ ■

Even before the rest of the country was informed of the healthy possibilities of "the other white meat," we in the Midwest knew that pork prepared in low-fat ways was good for us! The sauce for this dish smells so incredibly good, you may be tempted to keep "tasting" as it simmers away. *Serves 4*

4 (4-ounce) lean pork tenderloins or cutlets
1 (4-serving) package JELL-O sugar-free vanilla cook-and-serve pudding mix
1½ cups unsweetened apple cider or juice
¼ teaspoon apple pie spice
2 teaspoons dried onion flakes
2 teaspoons dried parsley flakes

In a large skillet sprayed with butter-flavored cooking spray, brown pork for 3 to 4 minutes on each side. Meanwhile, in a medium saucepan, combine dry pudding mix and apple cider. Stir in apple pie spice, onion flakes, and parsley flakes. Cook over medium heat until mixture thickens, stirring often. Spoon cider sauce evenly over browned pork. Lower heat, cover, and simmer for 15 to 20 minutes or until pork is tender. When serving, place 1 tenderloin on a plate and spoon about ⅓ cup cider sauce over top.

Each serving equals:
HE: 3 Protein, ¾ Fruit, ¼ Slider
200 Calories, 4 gm Fat, 24 gm Protein, 17 gm Carbohydrate, 175 mg Sodium, 20 mg Calcium, 0 gm Fiber
DIABETIC: 3 Meat, 1 Fruit

Braised Pork and Cabbage

■ ■ ■

This is the kind of easy skillet supper served in small towns all over the Midwest. It celebrates an important agricultural product of our region (hogs), stirs in inexpensive local vegetables (onions and cabbage), and delivers a rich, down-home taste with the simplest flavorings.   *Serves 4 (1 cup)*

½ cup finely chopped onion
3 cups coarsely chopped
*   cabbage*
1 cup unsweetened apple juice

2 tablespoons Brown Sugar Twin
1 teaspoon dried parsley flakes
2 full cups (12 ounces) diced lean
*   cooked roast pork*

In a large skillet sprayed with butter-flavored cooking spray, sauté onion and cabbage for 5 minutes. Stir in apple juice, Brown Sugar Twin, and parsley flakes. Add roast pork. Mix well to combine. Lower heat, cover, and simmer for 15 minutes or until cabbage is tender, stirring occasionally.

HINT: If you don't have leftovers, purchase a chunk of lean cooked roast pork from your local deli.

Each serving equals:

HE: 3 Protein, 1¾ Vegetable, ½ Fruit, 2 Optional Calories

214 Calories, 6 gm Fat, 27 gm Protein, 13 gm Carbohydrate, 56 mg Sodium, 50 mg Calcium, 2 gm Fiber

DIABETIC: 3 Meat, 1 Vegetable, ½ Fruit

Pork and Peas in Cream Sauce

■ ■ ■

My kids, like most children brought up in the Heartland, were members of the 4-H Club. They and their friends raised farm animals—calves, pigs, and lambs among them—with the goal of selling them for meat. We're not sentimental about eating what we produce out here, no matter how cute the animals were growing up. So—you can still love the movie Babe and enjoy this hearty skillet supper!

Serves 4

4 (4 ounce) lean pork tenderloins
  or cutlets
1 (10¾-ounce) can Healthy
  Request Cream of Mushroom
  Soup

2 tablespoons skim milk
½ cup finely chopped onion
2 cups frozen peas, thawed
⅛ teaspoon black pepper

Preheat oven to 350 degrees. Spray an 8-by-8-inch baking dish with butter-flavored cooking spray. Evenly arrange meat in prepared baking dish. In a medium bowl, combine mushroom soup, skim milk, onion, peas, and black pepper. Spoon soup mixture evenly over meat. Cover and bake for 50 minutes. Uncover and continue baking for 10 minutes. Place baking dish on a wire rack and let set for 5 minutes. Divide into 4 servings.

HINT: Thaw peas by placing in a colander and rinsing under hot water for one minute.

Each serving equals:
HE: 3 Protein, 1 Bread, ¼ Vegetable, ½ Slider, 7 Optional Calories
255 Calories, 7 gm Fat, 30 gm Protein, 18 gm Carbohydrate, 387 mg Sodium, 115 mg Calcium, 4 gm Fiber
DIABETIC: 3 Meat, 1½ Starch/Carbohydrate

Spiced Baked Apples

■ ■ ■

When I was a professional dieter, I would snack on plain raw apples and never feel truly satisfied. Now that I'm committed to living healthy the rest of my life, I decided to turn those apples into a treat worthy of the name! Amazing, isn't it, how less than an hour in the oven can transform a simple piece of fruit?

Serves 4

4 small unpeeled baking apples
6 tablespoons purchased graham cracker crumbs or 6 (2½-inch) graham cracker squares, made into crumbs
½ cup pourable Sugar Twin or Sprinkle Sweet ☆

2 tablespoons (½ ounce) chopped pecans
2 teaspoons reduced-calorie margarine
⅔ cup boiling water

Preheat oven to 350 degrees. Core apples, then pare each ¼ of the way down. Place apples in an 8-by-8-inch baking dish. In a small bowl, combine graham cracker crumbs, ¼ cup Sugar Twin, and pecans. Evenly stuff mixture into center of apples. Stir remaining ¼ cup Sugar Twin and margarine into boiling water. Pour evenly over apples. Bake for 30 to 45 minutes or until apples are tender, basting with liquid every 15 minutes. Serve warm.

HINT: A self-seal sandwich bag works great for crushing graham crackers.

Each serving equals:
HE: 1 Fruit, ¾ Fat, ½ Bread, 18 Optional Calories

144 Calories, 4 gm Fat, 1 gm Protein, 26 gm Carbohydrate, 91 mg Sodium, 12 mg Calcium, 3 gm Fiber

DIABETIC: 1 Fruit, 1 Fat, ½ Starch

Brownie Pudding Cake

■ ❋ ■

I always like to say that the Midwest is pie country, but it's cake country too! Everyone enjoys sharing their favorite baked goods at potluck suppers, so they keep a file of sweet successes good for all occasions. This chocoholic's dream dessert is very rich, so a modest-sized piece will still be satisfying.　　*Serves 8*

*⅔ cup Carnation Nonfat Dry
　Milk Powder*
2 cups water ☆
1 cup all-purpose flour
*6 tablespoons unsweetened
　cocoa ☆*
*⅔ cup pourable Sugar Twin or
　Sprinkle Sweet*
2 teaspoons baking powder

½ teaspoon baking soda
*2 tablespoons Land O Lakes
　no-fat sour cream*
1 teaspoon vanilla extract
*¼ cup (1 ounce) mini chocolate
　chips*
*¼ cup (1 ounce) chopped
　walnuts*
¼ cup Brown Sugar Twin

Preheat oven to 350 degrees. Spray an 8-by-8-inch baking dish with butter-flavored cooking spray. In a small bowl, combine dry milk powder and ¾ cup water. In a large bowl, combine flour, ¼ cup cocoa, Sugar Twin, baking powder, and baking soda. Add milk mixture, sour cream, and vanilla extract. Mix gently to combine. Spread batter into prepared baking dish. Evenly sprinkle chocolate chips and walnuts over top. In a medium saucepan, combine remaining 2 tablespoons cocoa, Brown Sugar Twin, and remaining 1¼ cups water. Bring mixture to a boil, stirring often. Spoon hot mixture evenly over cake batter. DO NOT stir. Bake for 30 to 35 minutes or until a toothpick inserted near center comes out clean. Place baking dish on a wire rack and let set for at least 15 minutes. Divide into 8 servings. Serve warm or cold.

Each serving equals:
HE: ⅔ Bread, ¼ Skim Milk, ¼ Fat, ¾ Slider

140 Calories, 4 gm Fat, 5 gm Protein, 21 gm Carbohydrate, 314 mg Sodium, 160 mg Calcium, 2 gm Fiber

DIABETIC: 1½ Starch/Carbohydrate, ½ Fat

Scrumptious Strawberry Shortcake

■ ■ ■

As long as I've had a tiny patch of green to call my own, I've grown strawberries. How else to satisfy my passion for this sweet jewel of a fruit? For me, the only true version of this popular dessert is served on a fresh-baked biscuit, so here's a way to enjoy this delight both healthy and homemade!   *Serves 4*

4 cups sliced ripe strawberries ☆
2 tablespoons Diet Mountain
    Dew
½ cup pourable Sugar Twin or
    Sprinkle Sweet ☆
¾ cup Bisquick Reduced Fat
    Baking Mix

⅓ cup Carnation Nonfat Dry
    Milk Powder
¼ cup water
2 tablespoons Land O Lakes
    no-fat sour cream
½ cup Cool Whip Lite

Preheat oven to 425 degrees. Reserve 4 strawberry slices for garnish. In a blender container, combine 1 cup strawberries, Diet Mountain Dew, and ¼ cup Sugar Twin. Cover and process on HIGH for 15 seconds. Pour mixture into a large bowl. Stir in remaining 3 cups strawberries. Refrigerate. Meanwhile, in a medium bowl, combine baking mix, dry milk powder, and remaining ¼ cup Sugar Twin. Add water and sour cream. Mix well to combine. Drop by spoonful onto an ungreased baking sheet to form 4 shortcakes. Bake for 8 to 12 minutes or until golden brown. Cut each shortcake in half. For each serving, place a shortcake bottom on a dessert plate, spoon ¾ cup strawberry sauce over, arrange shortcake top over sauce, top with 2 tablespoons Cool Whip Lite, and garnish with a reserved strawberry slice.

Each serving equals:
HE: 1 Bread, 1 Fruit, ¼ Skim Milk, ¼ Slider, 19 Optional Calories

179 Calories, 3 gm Fat, 5 gm Protein, 33 gm Carbohydrate, 304 mg Sodium, 130 mg Calcium, 4 gm Fiber

DIABETIC: 1 Starch/Carbohydrate, 1 Fruit

Quick Apple Dumplings

■ ❋ ■

Here's a perfect case where an old-fashioned recipe brought here by the pioneers can be reimagined using the most modern and convenient ingredients! These sweet and fruity confections deliver that comfort-food flavor that reminds us of home and family.

Serves 8

1 (8-ounce) package Pillsbury
   Reduced Fat Crescent Rolls
2 cups (4 small) cored, peeled,
   and finely diced cooking apples
1 cup pourable Sugar Twin or
   Sprinkle Sweet ☆

1 teaspoon apple pie spice
¼ cup (1 ounce) chopped
   walnuts
½ cup water

Preheat oven to 425 degrees. Unroll crescent rolls and pat into an 8-by-12-inch rectangle. In a medium bowl, combine apples, ¼ cup Sugar Twin, apple pie spice, and walnuts. Spread mixture evenly over dough. Roll up jelly-roll style. Cut into 8 (1-inch) slices. In a small saucepan, combine remaining ¾ cup Sugar Twin and water. Bring mixture to a boil. Pour mixture into an 8-by-12-inch baking dish. Evenly arrange apple rolls over "syrup." Bake for 15 to 20 minutes. Place baking dish on a wire rack and let set for at least 5 minutes. Serve warm or cold.

Each serving equals:
HE: 1 Bread, ½ Fruit, ¼ Fat, 19 Optional Calories

139 Calories, 7 gm Fat, 2 gm Protein, 17 gm Carbohydrate, 233 mg Sodium, 9 mg Calcium, 1 gm Fiber

DIABETIC: 1 Starch, 1 Fat, ½ Fruit

Fruit Kolaches

■ ❄ ■

I've made many versions of these fruit-filled rolls over the years, honoring the memory of my mother and grandmother who taught me how to cook and bake. My son James is the cherry fanatic among my kids, and he thinks these are "pretty good, Mom!"

Serves 16

16 Rhodes frozen yeast dinner
  rolls
1 (4-serving) package JELL-O
  sugar-free vanilla cook-and-
  serve pudding mix
1 (4-serving) package JELL-O
  sugar-free cherry gelatin

2 cups (one 16-ounce can) tart
  red cherries, packed in water,
  drained, and ½ cup liquid
  reserved
½ teaspoon almond extract

Preheat oven to 400 degrees. Spray two large baking sheets with butter-flavored cooking spray. Evenly space frozen rolls on prepared baking sheets. Cover each sheet with a cloth and let rolls thaw and rise. In a large saucepan, combine dry pudding mix, dry gelatin, and reserved cherry liquid. Stir in cherries. Cook over medium heat until mixture thickens and starts to boil, stirring often, being careful not to crush cherries. Remove from heat. Stir in almond extract. Make an indentation in the center of each roll. Spoon a full 1 tablespoon of filling mixture into center of each roll. Cover with cloths again and let rolls rest for 10 minutes. Bake for 12 to 15 minutes or until golden brown. Lightly spray rolls with butter-flavored cooking spray. Place baking sheets on a wire rack and let set for 5 minutes. Remove rolls from baking sheets and continue cooling on wire rack.

HINT: Use any complementary fruit, gelatin, and extract of your choice.

Each serving equals:
HE: 1 Bread, ¼ Fruit, 7 Optional Calories

93 Calories, 1 gm Fat, 3 gm Protein, 18 gm Carbohydrate, 132 mg Sodium, 3 mg Calcium, 1 gm Fiber

DIABETIC: 1 Starch

Schaum Torte

■ ■ ■

This spectacular dessert came to America via the sweet shops of Europe, where a dish that included both whipped cream and meringue was never considered "too much of a good thing"! This luscious extravaganza looks so gorgeous, you'll want an audience to appreciate your culinary talents. (*Schaum* is the German word for foam or lather!)   *Serves 12*

4 cups sliced fresh strawberries
1½ cups pourable Sugar Twin or
    Sprinkle Sweet ☆
9 egg whites
1 teaspoon white vinegar
1 tablespoon vanilla
    extract ☆
2 (4-serving) packages JELL-O
    sugar-free vanilla cook-and-
    serve pudding mix

1⅔ cups Carnation Nonfat Dry
    Milk Powder ☆
3 cups water
¾ cup Dannon plain fat-free
    yogurt
1½ cups Cool Whip Free

Preheat oven to 250 degrees. Spray a 9-by-13-inch baking dish with butter-flavored cooking spray. In a large bowl, combine strawberries and ¼ cup Sugar Twin. Cover and refrigerate. Meanwhile, in another large bowl, beat egg whites with an electric mixer until soft peaks form. Add vinegar, 1½ teaspoons vanilla extract, and 1 cup Sugar Twin. Continue beating until stiff peaks form. Spread meringue mixture into prepared baking dish. Bake for 1 hour or until top is firm. Place baking dish on a wire rack and allow to cool completely. Meanwhile, in a large saucepan, combine dry pudding mixes, 1⅓ cups dry milk powder, and water. Cook over medium heat until mixture thickens and starts to boil, stirring constantly. Place saucepan on a wire rack and allow to cool completely, stirring occasionally. Meanwhile, in a medium bowl, combine yogurt and remaining ⅓ cup dry milk powder. Add remaining 1½ teaspoons vanilla extract and remaining ¼ cup Sugar Twin. Mix well to combine. Fold in Cool Whip Free. Cover and refrigerate until meringue and filling have cooled completely. To assemble, spread cooled pudding mixture over cooled meringue crust and top with Cool Whip Free mixture. Cover and refrigerate for at least 2 hours. Just before serving, evenly arrange strawberry slices over top. Cut into 12 servings.

HINT: 1. Egg whites beat best at room temperature.
2. Meringue pie cuts easily if you dip a sharp knife in warm water before slicing.

Each serving equals:

HE: ½ Skim Milk, ⅓ Fruit, ¼ Protein, ¼ Slider, 14 Optional Calories

100 Calories, 0 gm Fat, 7 gm Protein, 18 gm Carbohydrate, 184 mg Sodium, 154 mg Calcium, 1 gm Fiber

DIABETIC: 1 Starch/Carbohydrate, ½ Skim Milk

Covered Wagon Rhubarb Pie

■ ❋ ■

The first stalks of rhubarb peeking out must have been the same encouraging harbinger of spring for the pioneers who settled our country's heartland as they are for us. I seem to count the days each year until it's time for the first rhubarb pie of the season, and just one bite makes me sigh with pleasure at the return of the sun!

Serves 8

1 Pillsbury refrigerated unbaked
  9-inch piecrust
4 cups coarsely chopped fresh
  rhubarb
½ cup water

1 (4-serving) package JELL-O
  sugar-free vanilla cook-and-
  serve pudding mix
1 (4-serving) package JELL-O
  sugar-free strawberry gelatin

Let piecrust set at room temperature for 10 minutes. Meanwhile, in a medium saucepan, combine rhubarb and water. Cover and cook over medium heat for 5 minutes or until rhubarb is just tender. Remove from heat. Add dry pudding mix and dry gelatin. Mix well to combine. Place saucepan on a wire rack and let set for at least 10 minutes. Cut the piecrust in half on the folded line. Gently roll each half into a ball. Wipe counter with a wet cloth and place a sheet of waxed paper over damp spot. Place one of the balls on the waxed paper. Cover with another piece of waxed paper and roll out into a 9-inch circle, with rolling pin. Carefully remove waxed paper from one side and place crust into an 8-inch pie plate. Remove other piece of waxed paper. Evenly spoon rhubarb mixture into piecrust. Repeat process of rolling out remaining piecrust half. Place second crust over top of pie and flute edges. Make about 8 slashes with a knife to allow steam to escape. Bake at 425 degrees for 15 minutes. Reduce heat to 350 degrees and continue baking for 30 minutes. Place pie plate on a wire rack and allow to cool completely. Cut into 8 servings.

HINT: Place piece of uncooked elbow macaroni upright in center of pie to keep filling from cooking out of crust.

Each serving equals:
HE: 1 Vegetable, ½ Bread, ¾ Slider, 5 Optional Calories

143 Calories, 7 gm Fat, 1 gm Protein, 19 gm Carbohydrate, 162 mg Sodium, 52 mg Calcium, 1 gm Fiber

DIABETIC: 1 Starch/Carbohydrate, 1 Fat

Sour Cream Walnut Coffee Cake

■ ❋ ■

We Midwesterners don't have a monopoly on neighborliness, but I think you'll find that in farm country we really cherish our neighbors. We depend on one another to get through tough times, so we try not to wait for special occasions to have people over for coffee and dessert. Here's a fast and flavorful coffeecake that can be ready in less than an hour start-to-finish, so invite your neighbors over today!

Serves 8 (2 each)

1½ cups Bisquick Reduced Fat
  Baking Mix
¾ cup pourable Sugar Twin or
  Sprinkle Sweet ☆
½ cup Land O Lakes no-fat sour
  cream

½ cup skim milk
1 teaspoon vanilla extract
1 teaspoon ground cinnamon
½ cup (2 ounces) chopped
  walnuts

Preheat oven to 375 degrees. Spray an 8-by-8-inch baking dish with butter-flavored cooking spray. In a large bowl, combine baking mix, ½ cup Sugar Twin, sour cream, skim milk, and vanilla extract. Spread half of batter into prepared baking dish. In a small bowl, combine remaining ¼ cup Sugar Twin, cinnamon, and walnuts. Sprinkle half of mixture over batter. Carefully spread remaining batter over nut mixture. Evenly sprinkle remaining nut mixture over top. Bake for 20 to 25 minutes or until a toothpick inserted near center comes out clean. Place baking dish on a wire rack and let set for at least 10 minutes. Cut into 16 pieces. Good warm or cold.

Each serving equals:
HE: 1 Bread, ½ Fat, ¼ Protein, ¼ Slider, 9 Optional Calories
146 Calories, 6 gm Fat, 3 gm Protein, 20 gm Carbohydrate, 286 mg Sodium, 62 mg Calcium, 1 gm Fiber
DIABETIC: 1 Starch, 1 Fat

ALL-AMERICAN CLASSICS

■ ■ ■

Baseball . . . Marching bands . . . Thanksgiving parades . . . Fourth of July fireworks . . . Mom's apple pie . . .

If this were a game show and you had to identify why this list of items belongs together, you'd probably shout out, "They're all-American classics"—and you'd win big bucks, because you're right.

It's been more than two hundred years since our nation was born, and over that time we Americans have created many wonderful traditions and celebrations, ways of bringing people together and making them feel a part of something greater than themselves—a part of the land we call America. Most of our ancestors came to these shores from other countries, but we all shared a dream of freedom and opportunity. As we built our homes and our towns and lives side by side with our neighbors, we joined in a sort of nationwide sewing circle

or quilting bee, helping to weave our many cultures together into a beautiful tapestry: the United States.

I always felt especially touched by the symbol of America as a melting pot, since so many of our most beloved and heartfelt traditions involve preparing and sharing the foods that bring us comfort and make us feel most at home. Stirred into that pot are wonderfully nourishing ingredients raised on our farms and canned in our factories, fished in our coastal waters and plucked from gardens in backyards all across the nation.

When visitors come to see our great country, they all want to eat "American food," even if they've already visited a McDonald's or other American-style restaurant in their own cities abroad. I think that what they want to know and see and taste is the food that Americans eat at home, the dishes that we prepare for graduation picnics and family potlucks, the special recipes handed down from generation to generation and shared among friends.

When you travel across America, following the interstates from coast to coast, you can't help but notice the regional specialties on restaurant menus and truck-stop buffets. But everywhere you go, you're also sure to find the "old reliables," those dishes that all of us think of when we're feeling a little bit homesick, or we just want a taste of the kinds of foods our mothers and grandmothers served when we were children. I'm sure that if I started to list some of the recipes included in this section, I'd hear sighs of contentment and see smiles of anticipation that would surely warm the cockles of any mom's heart!

These "All-American Classics" are my gift to every young bride (or slightly older bride who never learned to cook these great traditional foods). They're perfect for college students, male or female, about to face the challenge of cooking for themselves for the very first time. They provide a wonderful "blast from the past" for people who've gotten out of the habit of cooking because of their busy lives or maybe in reaction to an "empty nest." Best of all, they will help everyone put healthy versions of favorite comfort foods back on the menu.

Why "best of all"? So many of the men and women I've visited with while traveling around the country have told me how much they've missed the foods they love best, usually because they're trying to lose weight or recover from heart disease, lower their cholesterol or cope with a midlife diagnosis of diabetes. While all my Healthy Exchanges recipes are designed to please those with any or all these concerns, I suspect that these recipes will be especially welcome!

Just think how easy it will be to plan your next family gathering or just an easy Sunday supper when you've got recipes like *Mom's Baked Macaroni and Cheese* and *The Best Mashed Potatoes*, *Classic Chicken Noodle Soup* and *Old*

Glory Potato Salad. I had such a good time testing the recipes in this group, since they are all longtime favorites of mine and Cliff's.

I've often mentioned that my worst diet downfall was cake doughnuts, but I am ready to confess that *Hot Fudge Sundaes* ran a close second when it came to favorite splurges! I am a true traditionalist when it comes to this all-American dessert: I like it with vanilla ice cream, topped with pecans (my nut of choice) and a little whipped cream—*mmmmm!* My friend Barbara says that she'd like it better with mint chocolate chip, and of course it's up to you to choose what flavor you prefer. I'm really happy to see how many companies are offering more and more flavors of sugar- and fat-free ice creams so that we can enjoy what we love without any of the guilt.

Another recipe I know you'll love as much as I did is one I call *Grandma's Cinnamon Rolls*. My grandmother had a fabulous recipe for these, and I can remember coming down to breakfast when I was visiting her and knowing before I entered the kitchen that I'd be feasting on her fresh-baked and wonderfully aromatic rolls. Even though the recipe I created uses totally different ingredients than hers did, I think she would be as pleased as I was with the results!

You'll find everything in here, from down-home soups (*Cream of Tomato*—yum) to everybody's best-loved entrees (*Sloppy Joes, Mainstay Meatloaf*), classic salads (*Creamy Coleslaw, Mom's Jelled Fruit Salad*), and the kind of sensational side dishes that won't take a backseat to anything on the table (*Just Plain Good Green Bean Bake, Potluck Baked Beans*). Whether you're dreaming of tuna noodle casserole or a great chocolate cake, cheeseburgers or brownies, here's the answer you long to hear: *It's all in here!*

When I was working on these recipes, Cliff talked about his favorite foods growing up. He mentioned meatloaf, of course, and his grandmother's peanut butter cookies. Then he added, "You know, my mom always made a terrific scalloped potatoes and ham," so I decided to honor my mother-in-law with my own Healthy Exchanges version. She trained my husband's tastebuds and helped give him just enough of an adventurous appetite to enjoy being my everyday, forever-on-call, good-humored, number-one taste-tester!

I guess you could say that Cliff's *my* "All-American Classic."

ALL-AMERICAN CLASSICS RECIPES

Cream of Tomato Soup

Classic Chicken Noodle Soup

Granny's Vegetable Soup

Nana's Broccoli-Cauliflower Soup

Perfection Salad

Mom's Jelled Fruit Salad

Carrot-Celery Salad

Creamy Coleslaw

Old Glory Potato Salad

Everyone's Favorite Macaroni Salad

Creamy Tuna Twist Salad

Just Plain Good Green Bean Bake

Creamy Scalloped Corn

Potluck Baked Beans

The Best Mashed Potatoes

Mom's Baked Macaroni and Cheese

Noodles Romanoff Bake

Time-Honored Tuna-Noodle
    Casserole

Grandma's Turkey Pot Pie

Cheeseburger Deluxe

All-Star Melody Casserole

Mainstay Meatloaf

All-American Spaghetti with Meat
    Sauce

Sloppy Joes

Broccoli-Ham Casserole

No-Fuss Scalloped Potatoes and
    Ham

Superb Ham Loaf

Chocolate Chip Munch Cookies

Peanut Butter Cookies

Chewy Walnut Brownies

Banana Nut Bread

The Ultimate Banana Split Dessert

As American As Apple Pie

Chocolate Cake with Chocolate
    Frosting

Potluck Deviled Eggs

Hot Fudge Sundae

Grandma's Cinnamon Rolls

Chocolate Milkshake

Cream of Tomato Soup

■ ✳ ■

Whether you spent your childhood in a big Eastern city or in a small Texas town, your mom likely offered you that favorite rainy-day lunch that goes so perfectly with a sandwich—a soothing bowl of rich and flavorful tomato soup! Here's a version to please your palate now, and to bring back lots of happy memories.   *Serves 4 (1 cup)*

2 cups (one 16-ounce can) toma-
*   toes, undrained*
2 teaspoons pourable Sugar Twin
*   or Sprinkle Sweet*
1 teaspoon dried parsley flakes

2 cups skim milk
3 tablespoons all-purpose flour
¼ teaspoon baking soda
2 teaspoons reduced-calorie
*   margarine*

In a blender container, combine undrained tomatoes, Sugar Twin, and parsley flakes. Cover and process on BLEND for 30 seconds or until mixture is smooth. In a covered jar, combine skim milk and flour. Shake well to blend. Pour mixture into a large saucepan sprayed with butter-flavored cooking spray. Cook over medium heat until mixture thickens and starts to boil, stirring often. Remove from heat. Stir in tomato mixture and baking soda. Return saucepan to stove. Continue cooking over medium heat until mixture thickens and is heated through, stirring often. Remove from heat. Add margarine. Mix well to combine.

Each serving equals:
HE: 1 Vegetable, ½ Skim Milk, ¼ Bread, ¼ Fat, 1 Optional Calorie
97 Calories, 1 gm Fat, 6 gm Protein, 16 gm Carbohydrate, 342 mg Sodium, 189 mg Calcium, 1 gm Fiber
DIABETIC: 1 Vegetable, ½ Skim Milk, ½ Starch

Classic Chicken Noodle Soup

■ ❋ ■

So many people associate this wonderfully cozy concoction with getting over a bad cold or the flu, but promise me you won't save it just for those days when you're not feeling well! It looks and tastes as if someone spent hours in the kitchen stirring the pot, but you can relish this satisfying soup in only minutes.

Serves 4 (1½ cups)

8 ounces skinned and boned uncooked chicken breasts, cut into 24 pieces
2 cups (one 16-ounce can) Healthy Request Chicken Broth
2 cups water

1 cup finely chopped celery
1 cup finely sliced carrots
½ cup finely chopped onion
1¼ cups (2¼ ounces) uncooked noodles
2 teaspoons dried parsley flakes
1 teaspoon lemon pepper

In a large saucepan, combine chicken, chicken broth, and water. Stir in celery, carrots, and onion. Bring mixture to a boil. Add uncooked noodles, parsley flakes, and lemon pepper. Mix well to combine. Lower heat, cover, and simmer for 15 minutes or until vegetables and noodles are tender, stirring occasionally.

Each serving equals:
HE: 1½ Protein, 1¼ Vegetable, ¾ Bread, 8 Optional Calories
150 Calories, 2 gm Fat, 16 gm Protein, 17 gm Carbohydrate, 307 mg Sodium, 39 mg Calcium, 2 gm Fiber
DIABETIC: 1½ Meat, 1 Vegetable, 1 Starch

Granny's Vegetable Soup

■ ❋ ■

In kitchens across America, a thick, chunky vegetable soup often appears on family menus—and just as often delights everyone from two to ninety-two! Each time you dip in your spoon, you don't know what surprise will turn up: a chunk of potato, a bright yellow kernel of corn, peas or carrots or green beans— all your favorites! You don't have to be a grandma to serve soup this good . . . but if you are, it'll definitely win the hearts of your grandbabies!

Serves 4 (full 1½ cups)

2 cups **Healthy Request** tomato juice or any reduced-sodium tomato juice

¾ cup water

1 cup (5 ounces) diced raw potatoes

1 cup frozen cut green beans, thawed

1 cup frozen sliced carrots, thawed

½ cup finely chopped onion

2 cups chopped cabbage

¾ cup frozen peas, thawed

¾ cup frozen whole-kernel corn, thawed

1 teaspoon dried parsley flakes

1 teaspoon lemon pepper

In a large saucepan, combine tomato juice and water. Stir in potatoes, green beans, carrots, and onion. Bring mixture to a boil. Add cabbage, peas, corn, parsley flakes, and lemon pepper. Mix well to combine. Lower heat, cover, and simmer for 15 to 20 minutes or until vegetables are tender, stirring occasionally.

HINT: Thaw frozen vegetables by placing in a colander and rinsing under hot water for about two minutes.

Each serving equals:

HE: 3¾ Vegetable, 1 Bread

152 Calories, 0 gm Fat, 5 gm Protein, 33 gm Carbohydrate, 400 mg Sodium, 75 mg Calcium, 7 gm Fiber

DIABETIC: 2½ Vegetable, 1 Starch

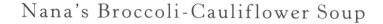

Nana's Broccoli-Cauliflower Soup

■ ❋ ■

This is one of those "inspiration-in-an-instant" dishes that becomes an instant classsic because it's as delicious as it is easy to fix! I got the idea from an old-fashioned soup a good friend's grandmother (Nana Rose) used to stir up when we were young.

Serves 4 (1½ cups)

1½ cups chopped fresh cauli-
    flower
1½ cups chopped fresh broccoli
½ cup chopped onion
2 cups (one 16-ounce can)
    Healthy Request Chicken
    Broth
½ cup water
1 full cup (6 ounces) diced
    Dubuque 97% fat-free ham or
    any extra-lean ham

1 (10¾-ounce) can Healthy
    Request Cream of Mushroom
    Soup
¾ cup (3 ounces) shredded Kraft
    reduced-fat Cheddar cheese
⅓ cup Carnation Nonfat Dry
    Milk Powder
⅓ cup (1 ounce) uncooked
    Minute Rice

In a large saucepan, combine cauliflower, broccoli, onion, chicken broth, and water. Bring mixture to a boil. Stir in ham. Lower heat, cover, and simmer for 10 minutes. Add mushroom soup, Cheddar cheese, and dry milk powder. Mix well to combine. Stir in uncooked rice. Re-cover and continue simmering for 5 minutes or until cheese melts and rice is tender, stirring occasionally.

Each serving equals:
HE: 2 Protein, 1¾ Vegetable, ¼ Skim Milk, ¼ Bread, ½ Slider,
9 Optional Calories

202 Calories, 6 gm Fat, 18 gm Protein, 19 gm Carbohydrate, 930 mg Sodium,
288 mg Calcium, 2 gm Fiber

DIABETIC: 2 Meat, 1 Vegetable, 1 Starch/Carbohydrate

Perfection Salad

■ ■ ■

Here's a dish that regularly turned up on tables across the nation during the 1950s, when the idea of a gelatin vegetable salad seemed delightfully modern and fresh! What was innovative half a century ago has earned the title of classic, and this festive recipe offers a delicately pretty accompaniment to all kinds of entrees.

Serves 6

1 (4-serving) package JELL-O
  sugar-free lemon gelatin
1 cup boiling water
¾ cup cold water
¼ cup white vinegar

1½ cups finely shredded cabbage
1½ cups finely chopped celery
¼ cup (one 2-ounce jar) chopped
  pimiento, drained

In a large bowl, combine dry gelatin and boiling water. Mix well to dissolve gelatin. Stir in cold water and vinegar. Add cabbage, celery, and pimiento. Mix well to combine. Pour mixture into an 8-by-8-inch dish. Refrigerate until firm, about 3 hours. Cut into 6 servings.

Each serving equals:
HE: 1 Vegetable, 7 Optional Calories
16 Calories, 0 gm Fat, 1 gm Protein, 3 gm Carbohydrate, 66 mg Sodium, 20 mg Calcium, 0 gm Fiber
DIABETIC: 1 Free Food

Mom's Jelled Fruit Salad

■ ■ ■

It's said that the foods we learn to love as children will please us all our lives, and I can verify that with this fun and fruity concoction! My mother knew how much we adored finding bits of banana and strawberry and pineapple in our bright and bouncy red JELL-O, so she usually kept little dishes of this tasty treat in the refrigerator for us. The trick of making this turn out just right is using a bit less liquid than the package calls for, since the pineapple is *very* juicy!

Serves 6

2 (4-serving) packages JELL-O sugar-free strawberry gelatin
2 cups boiling water
1 cup cold water
1 cup (one 8-ounce can) crushed pineapple, packed in fruit juice, undrained

2 cups frozen unsweetened strawberries
1 cup (1 medium) diced banana

In a large bowl, combine dry gelatin and boiling water. Mix well to dissolve gelatin. Add cold water and undrained pineapple. Mix well to combine. Stir in strawberries and banana. Pour mixture into an 8-by-8-inch dish. Refrigerate until firm, about 3 hours. Cut into 6 servings.

HINT: To prevent banana from turning brown, mix with 1 teaspoon lemon juice or sprinkle with Fruit Fresh.

Each serving equals:
HE: 1 Fruit, 13 Optional Calories

68 Calories, 0 gm Fat, 2 gm Protein, 15 gm Carbohydrate, 74 mg Sodium, 16 mg Calcium, 2 gm Fiber

DIABETIC: 1 Fruit

Carrot-Celery Salad

■ ■ ■

Every family reunion needs lots of side dishes, and once you've gotten past coleslaw and potato salad, what's everyone's next favorite choice? In our house, it's carrot salad, and in this recipe, the blend of carrots and celery made it a regular on the table. Why not start your own tradition tonight?   *Serves 6 (⅔ cup)*

*4 cups (two 16-ounce cans) sliced
   carrots, rinsed and drained
1 cup finely chopped celery
½ cup chopped onion*

*½ cup chopped green bell pepper
¾ cup Kraft Fat Free French
   Dressing
1 teaspoon dried parsley flakes*

In a large bowl, combine carrots, celery, onion, and green pepper. Add French dressing and parsley flakes. Mix well to combine. Cover and refrigerate for at least 30 minutes. Gently stir again just before serving.

Each serving equals:
HE: 2 Vegetable, ½ Slider, 10 Optional Calories
84 Calories, 0 gm Fat, 1 gm Protein, 20 gm Carbohydrate, 553 mg Sodium,
36 mg Calcium, 3 gm Fiber
DIABETIC: 1½ Vegetable, ½ Starch/Carbohydrate

Creamy Coleslaw

■ ■ ■

You just can't have a picnic without it, whether you're partying on the shores of Lake Erie or sitting on the beach in southern California! Here's my healthy version of this all-American favorite, a dish that is just so easy to prepare, and just as satisfying as the high-fat kind you can spot in any deli in America. Make sure to keep it cold until serving, and you'll have the kind of down-home culinary fireworks your family will love.

Serves 4 (¾ cup)

½ cup Kraft fat-free mayonnaise
2 tablespoons Land O Lakes no-fat sour cream
1 tablespoon white vinegar
Sugar substitute to equal 1 tablespoon sugar

1 teaspoon dried onion flakes
1 teaspoon dried parsley flakes
3 cups purchased coleslaw mix

In a large bowl, combine mayonnaise, sour cream, vinegar, and sugar substitute. Stir in onion flakes and parsley flakes. Add coleslaw mix. Mix well to combine. Cover and refrigerate for at least 30 minutes. Gently stir again just before serving.

HINT: 2½ cups shredded cabbage and ½ cup shredded carrots may be used in place of purchased coleslaw mix.

Each serving equals:
HE: 1½ Vegetable, ¼ Slider, 9 Optional Calories

44 Calories, 0 gm Fat, 1 gm Protein, 10 gm Carbohydrate, 230 mg Sodium, 40 mg Calcium, 1 gm Fiber

DIABETIC: 1 Vegetable, ½ Starch/Carbohydrate

Old Glory Potato Salad

■ ■ ■

Just as our "grand old flag" symbolizes what is best about our country, so too will this tasty salad remind you of the "good old days" that are still with us—and that we hope always will be! This creamy dish is welcomed everywhere, from coast to coast and in all the towns in between. I took out the fat and stirred in lots of flavor, not to mention lots of love! *Serves 6 (1 cup)*

1 cup Kraft fat-free mayonnaise
¼ cup sweet pickle relish
⅛ teaspoon black pepper
4 cups (20 ounces) diced cooked
   potatoes

1¼ cups finely chopped celery
¼ cup finely chopped onion
2 hard-boiled eggs, chopped

In a large bowl, combine mayonnaise, pickle relish, and black pepper. Add potatoes, celery, and onion. Mix well to combine. Fold in chopped eggs. Cover and refrigerate for at least 30 minutes. Gently stir again just before serving.

HINT: If you want the look and feel of egg without the cholesterol, toss out the yolk and dice the whites.

Each serving equals:
HE: ⅔ Bread, ½ Vegetable, ⅓ Protein (limited), ¼ Slider, 17 Optional Calories
154 Calories, 2 gm Fat, 4 gm Protein, 30 gm Carbohydrate, 409 mg Sodium, 25 mg Calcium, 2 gm Fiber
DIABETIC: 1½ Starch/Carbohydrate, ½ Vegetable

Everyone's Favorite Macaroni Salad

■ ■ ■

I like to think of them as the big three of traditional party salads—coleslaw, potato salad, and macaroni salad. No family reunion seems complete without pretty bowls of all three in the center of the table. I've tried so many different recipes for this delectable classic, and I think this one is my "old reliable"! I'd be proud to serve it for a card party or ladies' luncheon, but it's hearty enough to satisfy the men in my family, too.

Serves 4 (½ cup)

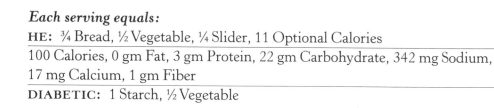

¾ cup Kraft fat-free mayonnaise
1 teaspoon lemon juice
Sugar substitute to equal 1 teaspoon sugar
1 tablespoon finely chopped onion

1 tablespoon finely chopped fresh parsley or 1 teaspoon dried parsley flakes
1½ cups cold cooked elbow macaroni, rinsed and drained
1 cup finely chopped celery

In a large bowl, combine mayonnaise, lemon juice, and sugar substitute. Stir in onion and parsley. Add macaroni and celery. Mix well to combine. Cover and refrigerate for at least 30 minutes. Gently stir again just before serving.

HINT: 1⅓ cups uncooked elbow macaroni usually cooks to about 1½ cups.

Each serving equals:
HE: ¾ Bread, ½ Vegetable, ¼ Slider, 11 Optional Calories

100 Calories, 0 gm Fat, 3 gm Protein, 22 gm Carbohydrate, 342 mg Sodium, 17 mg Calcium, 1 gm Fiber

DIABETIC: 1 Starch, ½ Vegetable

Creamy Tuna Twist Salad

■ ■ ■

Here's a perfect, old-fashioned tuna salad that is great served on its own but would also be attractive stuffed in a big fresh tomato from your garden. What makes this a classic is the color and crunch, turning a tasty dish into a downright irresistible treat!

Serves 6 (1 cup)

¾ cup Kraft fat-free mayonnaise
1 tablespoon cider vinegar
1½ teaspoons dill weed
2½ cups cold cooked rotini pasta, rinsed and drained
½ cup frozen peas, thawed

1½ cups finely chopped celery
½ cup chopped red onion
2 (6-ounce) cans white tuna, packed in water, drained and flaked

In a large bowl, combine mayonnaise, vinegar, and dill weed. Add rotini pasta, peas, celery, and onion. Mix well to combine. Stir in tuna. Cover and refrigerate for at least 30 minutes. Gently stir again just before serving.

HINT: 1. Full 2 cups uncooked rotini pasta usually cooks to about 2½ cups.
2. Thaw peas by placing in a colander and rinsing under hot water for one minute.

Each serving equals:
HE: 1 Bread, 1 Protein, ⅔ Vegetable, ¼ Slider
182 Calories, 2 gm Fat, 17 gm Protein, 24 gm Carbohydrate, 465 mg Sodium, 33 mg Calcium, 2 gm Fiber
DIABETIC: 2 Meat, 1 Starch, ½ Vegetable

Just Plain Good Green Bean Bake

■ ❋ ■

At our family gatherings, this is always the first dish to be completely gobbled down and gone! It must be those tangy, crunchy onion-y bits, or maybe it's the creamy, cheesy sauce that envelops Cliff's favorite veggie. . . . Did you think you'd never again taste those yummy onions-in-a-can because you've chosen to eat healthy? Well, I believe in enjoying what you love in *moderation,* so go for it!

Serves 6

1 (10¾-ounce) can Healthy Request Cream of Mushroom Soup

2 tablespoons Land O Lakes no-fat sour cream

½ teaspoon Worcestershire sauce

½ cup + 1 tablespoon (2¼ ounces) shredded Kraft reduced-fat Cheddar cheese

¾ cup (2⅛ ounces) coarsely crushed Durkee's onion rings ☆

4 cups (two 16-ounce cans) cut green beans, rinsed and drained

½ cup finely chopped onion

Preheat oven to 350 degrees. Spray an 8-by-8-inch baking dish with butter-flavored cooking spray. In a large bowl, combine mushroom soup, sour cream, and Worcestershire sauce. Stir in Cheddar cheese and ¼ cup crushed onion rings. Add green beans and chopped onion. Mix well to combine. Spread mixture into prepared baking dish. Evenly sprinkle remaining ½ cup crushed onion rings over top. Bake for 30 to 35 minutes. Place baking dish on a wire rack and let set for 5 minutes. Divide into 6 servings.

Each serving equals:

HE: 1½ Vegetable, ½ Bread, ½ Protein, ¼ Slider, 13 Optional Calories

95 Calories, 3 gm Fat, 5 gm Protein, 12 gm Carbohydrate, 265 mg Sodium, 187 mg Calcium, 2 gm Fiber

DIABETIC: 1½ Vegetable, ½ Starch/Carbohydrate, ½ Fat

Creamy Scalloped Corn

■ ❋ ■

Before manufacturers figured out how to can Iowa's "favorite son" vegetable, I bet recipes like this one were only a fantasy for people who didn't live near a cornfield! Now, though, you can travel from one end of the land to the other, and you can always feast on corn. It's our gift to the nation, and one we're always happy to share!

Serves 8

*4 cups (two 16-ounce cans)
  cream-style corn*
1 cup finely chopped onion
⅓ cup skim milk
*14 small fat-free saltine crackers,
  made into crumbs*

*1 tablespoon pourable Sugar
  Twin or Sprinkle Sweet*
⅛ teaspoon black pepper

Preheat oven to 375 degrees. Spray an 8-by-8-inch baking dish with butter-flavored cooking spray. In a large bowl, combine cream-style corn, onion, and skim milk. Add cracker crumbs, Sugar Twin, and black pepper. Mix well to combine. Spread mixture into prepared baking dish. Bake for 30 minutes. Place baking dish on a wire rack and let set for 5 minutes. Divide into 8 servings.

HINT: A self-seal sandwich bag works great for crushing crackers.

Each serving equals:
HE: 1¼ Bread, ¼ Vegetable, 4 Optional Calories
136 Calories, 0 gm Fat, 3 gm Protein, 31 gm Carbohydrate, 426 mg Sodium, 22 mg Calcium, 2 gm Fiber
DIABETIC: 1½ Starch/Carbohydrate

Potluck Baked Beans

■ ❋ ■

When you think about it, the very first Thanksgiving that was shared by the Pilgrims and the Native Americans was also our first potluck dinner! A gathering of friends and family to revel in the foods we love best is one of our oldest traditions—and a perfect occasion to offer the people you care for most a healthy and delicious way to please their tastebuds. *Serves 6*

1 cup finely chopped onion
1 cup (one 8-ounce can) Hunt's
    Tomato Sauce
1 tablespoon white vinegar
1 teaspoon yellow mustard
¼ cup Brown Sugar Twin

⅛ teaspoon black pepper
6 tablespoons Hormel Bacon
    Bits
20 ounces (two 16-ounce cans)
    great northern beans, rinsed
    and drained

Preheat oven to 350 degrees. Spray an 8-by-8-inch baking dish with butter-flavored cooking spray. In a large skillet sprayed with butter-flavored cooking spray, sauté onion for 5 minutes. Stir in tomato sauce, vinegar, mustard, Brown Sugar Twin, and black pepper. Bring mixture to a boil. Add bacon bits and great northern beans. Mix well to combine. Lower heat and simmer for 5 minutes, stirring occasionally. Spread hot mixture into prepared baking dish. Bake for 30 minutes. Place baking dish on a wire rack and let set for 5 minutes. Divide into 6 servings.

Each serving equals:

HE: 1⅔ Protein, 1 Vegetable, ¼ Slider, 8 Optional Calories

120 Calories, 2 gm Fat, 9 gm Protein, 19 gm Carbohydrate, 560 mg Sodium, 22 mg Calcium, 6 gm Fiber

DIABETIC: 1½ Starch, 1 Vegetable, ½ Protein

The Best Mashed Potatoes

■ ■ ■

Some people smother them in gravy, while others can't imagine munching mashed potatoes without a big dollop of ketchup. In the South, they cuddle up to pieces of fried chicken, while in downtown Chicago they're blended with garlic for a big-city taste. The only sure thing about mashed potatoes is that everyone, everywhere, loves their creamy goodness!   *Serves 4 (1 full cup)*

4 cups (20 ounces) peeled and
  chopped raw potatoes
1½ cups water
⅓ cup Carnation Nonfat Dry
  Milk Powder

2 tablespoons Land O Lakes
  no-fat sour cream
⅛ teaspoon black pepper

In a medium saucepan, combine potatoes and water. Bring mixture to a boil. Lower heat, cover, and simmer for 10 to 12 minutes or until potatoes are tender. Drain potatoes and reserve ½ cup liquid. Return potatoes to saucepan. Add reserved liquid and dry milk powder. Using an electric mixer on HIGH, whip potatoes until light and fluffy. Stir in sour cream, and black pepper.

Each serving equals:
HE: 1 Bread, ¼ Skim Milk, 8 Optional Calories

136 Calories, 0 gm Fat, 5 gm Protein, 29 gm Carbohydrate, 47 mg Sodium, 24 mg Calcium, 2 gm Fiber

DIABETIC: 1½ Starch

Mom's Baked Macaroni and Cheese

■ ✳ ■

It's a menu mainstay, from the hills of West Virginia to the chilliest reaches of northern Alaska, and mothers all over the country just love to see the smiling faces of their husbands and kids when they carry a bubbling casserole crusty with cheese to the table! I've discovered that stirring in more than one kind of cheese can make all the difference in flavor, but because I'm using the best low-fat and fat-free cheeses on the market, all those you love can dig in without worrying about sacrificing health for taste (or vice versa!).   *Serves 6*

1 (10¾-ounce) can Healthy
    Request Cream of Mushroom
    Soup
⅓ cup skim milk
¼ cup (¾ ounce) grated Kraft
    fat-free Parmesan cheese
1 teaspoon yellow mustard
1 teaspoon dried onion flakes

⅛ teaspoon black pepper
1½ cups (6 ounces) shredded
    Kraft reduced-fat Cheddar
    cheese
2½ cups hot cooked elbow maca-
    roni, rinsed and drained
3 tablespoons (¾ ounce) dried
    fine bread crumbs

Preheat oven to 350 degrees. Spray an 8-by-8-inch baking dish with butter-flavored cooking spray. In a large skillet sprayed with butter-flavored cooking spray, combine mushroom soup, skim milk, Parmesan cheese, mustard, onion flakes, and black pepper. Stir in Cheddar cheese. Cook over medium heat for 5 minutes or until cheese melts, stirring occasionally. Add macaroni. Mix well to combine. Spread mixture into prepared baking dish. Evenly sprinkle bread crumbs over top. Lightly spray crumbs with butter-flavored cooking spray. Bake for 30 to 35 minutes. Place baking dish on a wire rack and let set for 5 minutes. Divide into 6 servings.

HINT: 1⅔ cups uncooked elbow macaroni usually cooks to about 2½ cups.

Each serving equals:
HE: 1½ Protein, 1 Bread, ¼ Slider, 13 Optional Calories

218 Calories, 6 gm Fat, 14 gm Protein, 27 gm Carbohydrate, 398 mg Sodium, 317 mg Calcium, 1 gm Fiber

DIABETIC: 1½ Starch/Carbohydrate, 1 Meat

Noodles Romanoff Bake

■ ❄ ■

Whether they arrived here at the turn of the century from Russia or flew in only a few years ago from Asia, just about every ethnic group brought a favorite noodle dish with them! This cheesy, creamy baked casserole has a bit of an Eastern European flair, but the ingredients are all-American—and oh-say-can-you-see delicious! *Serves 6*

⅓ cup Land O Lakes no-fat sour cream
1 cup fat-free cottage cheese
1 teaspoon Worcestershire sauce
¼ teaspoon dried minced garlic
2 teaspoons dried onion flakes
1 teaspoon dried parsley flakes
⅛ teaspoon black pepper
3 cups hot cooked noodles, rinsed and drained
¾ cup (3 ounces) shredded Kraft reduced-fat Cheddar cheese

Preheat oven to 350 degrees. Spray an 8-by-8-inch baking dish with butter-flavored cooking spray. In a large bowl, combine sour cream, cottage cheese, Worcestershire sauce, garlic, onion flakes, parsley flakes, and black pepper. Stir in noodles. Evenly spread mixture into prepared baking dish. Cover and bake for 20 minutes. Uncover and sprinkle Cheddar cheese evenly over top. Continue baking, uncovered, for 10 to 15 minutes. Place baking dish on a wire rack and let set for 5 minutes. Divide into 6 servings.

HINT: 2½ cups uncooked noodles usually cooks to about 3 cups.

Each serving equals:
HE: 1 Bread, 1 Protein, ¼ Slider, 13 Optional Calories
175 Calories, 3 gm Fat, 13 gm Protein, 24 gm Carbohydrate, 292 mg Sodium, 137 mg Calcium, 1 gm Fiber
DIABETIC: 1½ Starch/Carbohydrate, 1 Meat

Time-Honored Tuna-Noodle Casserole

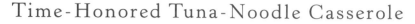

It's thrifty, it's cozy and comforting, and it's on just about everyone's "Top Ten" list of beloved foods. Best of all, tuna casserole brings back those childhood feelings of warmth and Mom's love! Here's a wonderfully rich version of this popular dish, and I think you'll agree it delivers lots of tangy taste along with that satisfying crunchy top.

Serves 4

1 (10¾-ounce) can Healthy Request Cream of Mushroom Soup

2 tablespoons Land O Lakes no-fat sour cream

¼ cup (one 2-ounce jar) chopped pimiento, undrained

1 teaspoon dried onion flakes

⅛ teaspoon black pepper

2 (6-ounce) cans white tuna, packed in water, drained and flaked

1½ cups cooked noodles, rinsed and drained

⅓ cup (¾ ounce) crushed WOW potato chips

Preheat oven to 350 degrees. Spray an 8-by-8-inch baking dish with butter-flavored cooking spray. In a large bowl, combine mushroom soup, sour cream, undrained pimiento, onion flakes, and black pepper. Add tuna. Mix well to combine. Stir in noodles. Spread mixture into prepared baking dish. Evenly sprinkle potato chip crumbs over top. Bake for 30 minutes. Place baking dish on a wire rack and let set for 5 minutes. Divide into 4 servings.

HINT: A self-seal sandwich bag works great for crushing crackers.

Each serving equals:

HE: 1½ Protein, 1 Bread, ½ Slider, 9 Optional Calories

179 Calories, 3 gm Fat, 15 gm Protein, 23 gm Carbohydrate, 452 mg Sodium, 89 mg Calcium, 1 gm Fiber

DIABETIC: 3 Meat, 1½ Starch/Carbohydrate

Grandma's Turkey Pot Pie

■ ❄ ■

Remember when grandmas everywhere across our nation spent hours in the kitchen cooking and baking our favorite foods? Well, these days, Grandma might be too busy running a business or shopping on the Internet to stir up a cozy pot pie for you. But in honor of those good old days, here's a quick and easy way to fix your own! Invite Grandma for dinner, and see what she thinks!

Serves 8

3 full cups (18 ounces) diced
   cooked turkey breast
1 (10¾-ounce) can Healthy
   Request Cream of Celery
   Soup
2 cups (one 16-ounce can)
   Healthy Request Chicken
   Broth ☆
2 cups (one 16-ounce can) cut
   green beans, rinsed and
   drained

2 cups (one 16-ounce can) sliced
   carrots, rinsed and drained
1½ cups Bisquick Reduced Fat
   Baking Mix
⅔ cup Carnation Nonfat Dry
   Milk Powder
2 teaspoons dried onion flakes
2 teaspoons dried parsley flakes
2 tablespoons Land O Lakes
   no-fat sour cream
½ cup water

Preheat oven to 350 degrees. Spray a 9-by-13-inch baking dish with butter-flavored cooking spray. In a large bowl, combine turkey, celery soup, and 1 cup chicken broth. Stir in green beans and carrots. Spread mixture into prepared baking dish. In a medium bowl, combine baking mix, dry milk powder, onion flakes, and parsley flakes. Add remaining 1 cup chicken broth, sour cream, and water. Mix gently to combine. Pour batter evenly over turkey mixture. Bake for 55 to 60 minutes. Lightly spray top with butter-flavored cooking spray. Place baking dish on a wire rack and let set for 5 minutes. Divide into 8 servings.

HINT: If you don't have leftovers, purchase a chunk of cooked turkey breast
   from your local deli.

Each serving equals:

HE: 2¼ Protein, 1 Bread, 1 Vegetable, ¼ Skim Milk, ¼ Slider, 8 Optional Calories

234 Calories, 2 gm Fat, 25 gm Protein, 29 gm Carbohydrate, 886 mg Sodium, 191 mg Calcium, 2 gm Fiber

DIABETIC: 2 Meat, 1½ Starch/Carbohydrate, 1 Vegetable

Cheeseburger Deluxe

■ ❋ ■

My son Tommy is the cheeseburger expert in our family, and he pronounced this recipe "awesome"! He told me that these were incredibly moist and juicy (thank you, Tommy), and that I was invited anytime to make them for him and Angie (and for Cheyanne, once she has enough teeth to gobble one down!).

Serves 6

16 ounces ground 90% lean
   turkey or beef
6 tablespoons (1½ ounces) dried
   fine bread crumbs
1 teaspoon dried parsley flakes

⅓ cup Kraft fat-free mayonnaise
3 (¾-ounce) slices Kraft reduced-
   fat American cheese
6 reduced-calorie hamburger
   buns

In a large bowl, combine meat, bread crumbs, parsley flakes, and mayonnaise. Mix well to combine. Using a ⅓-cup measuring cup as a guide, form into 6 patties. Evenly arrange patties in a large skillet sprayed with butter-flavored cooking spray. Brown patties for 3 to 4 minutes on each side. Cut cheese slices in half diagonally. Arrange a slice of cheese on top of each patty. Lower heat, cover, and continue cooking for 1 to 2 minutes or until cheese melts. Evenly arrange patties in hamburger buns.

Each serving equals:

HE: 2½ Protein, 1⅓ Bread, 9 Optional Calories

241 Calories, 9 gm Fat, 19 gm Protein, 21 gm Carbohydrate, 474 mg Sodium, 89 mg Calcium, 1 gm Fiber

DIABETIC: 2½ Meat, 1½ Starch

All-Star Melody Casserole

■ ❋ ■

Do you remember dancing to music from *American Bandstand,* or are you a big-band "baby" like me, who fox-trotted to Glenn Miller? Those are songs we'll never forget—just as this fun and flavorful supper dish is the kind of down-home cooking that defined comfort food then and still does now! *Serves 6*

8 ounces ground 90% lean turkey
   or beef
½ cup chopped green bell pepper
½ cup chopped onion
1 (10¾-ounce) can Healthy
   Request Tomato Soup
1¾ cups (one 15-ounce can)
   Hunt's Tomato Sauce

1 teaspoon dried parsley flakes
1½ cups hot cooked elbow macaroni, rinsed and drained
1½ cups frozen whole-kernel
   corn, thawed
4 (¾-ounce) slices Kraft reduced-
   fat American cheese

Preheat oven to 350 degrees. Spray an 8-by-8-inch baking dish with butter-flavored cooking spray. In a large skillet sprayed with butter-flavored cooking spray, brown meat, green pepper, and onion. Stir in tomato soup, tomato sauce, and parsley flakes. Add macaroni and corn. Mix well to combine. Pour mixture into prepared baking dish. Bake for 20 minutes. Evenly arrange cheese slices over top. Continue baking for 10 minutes. Place baking dish on a wire rack and let set for 5 minutes. Divide into 6 servings.

HINT: 1. 1 cup uncooked elbow macaroni usually cooks to about 1½ cups.
      2. Thaw corn by placing in a colander and rinsing under hot water for one minute.

Each serving equals:
HE: 1⅔ Protein, 1½ Vegetable, 1 Bread, ¼ Slider, 10 Optional Calories
218 Calories, 6 gm Fat, 13 gm Protein, 28 gm Carbohydrate, 781 mg Sodium, 98 mg Calcium, 3 gm Fiber
DIABETIC: 1½ Meat, 1½ Vegetable, 1 Starch/Carbohydrate

Mainstay Meatloaf

■ ❋ ■

It's a truck-stop tradition that reaches from Maine to Malibu, Cliff tells me—meatloaf is a menu must! It makes sense to me. Since truckers spend so much time away from home, they want the foods they eat while on the road to make them feel, even for a just a little while, that they're close to the people who love them. Meatloaf has that special power, especially this wonderfully old-fashioned-style recipe!

Serves 6

16 ounces ground 90% lean
  turkey or beef
½ cup (1½ ounces) quick oats
¾ cup finely chopped onion
½ cup Heinz Light Harvest
  Ketchup or any reduced-
  sodium ketchup ☆

2 tablespoons water
1 teaspoon dried parsley flakes
⅛ teaspoon black pepper

Preheat oven to 350 degrees. Spray a 9-by-5-inch loaf pan with butter-flavored cooking spray. In a large bowl, combine meat, oats, onion, ¼ cup ketchup, water, parsley flakes, and black pepper. Mix well. Pat mixture into prepared loaf pan. Bake for 30 minutes. Spread remaining ¼ cup ketchup evenly over partially baked meatloaf. Continue baking for 20 to 25 minutes. Place loaf pan on a wire rack and let set for 5 minutes. Cut into 6 servings.

Each serving equals:
HE: 2 Protein, ⅓ Bread, ¼ Vegetable, ¼ Slider

171 Calories, 7 gm Fat, 15 gm Protein, 12 gm Carbohydrate, 76 mg Sodium, 23 mg Calcium, 1 gm Fiber

DIABETIC: 2 Meat, 1 Starch/Carbohydrate

All-American Spaghetti with Meat Sauce

■ ❄ ■

It may have had its origins in Italy, but I like to think that we've taken this tasty ethnic entree into our American hearts! It certainly fits my definition of comfort food, but it also suits our American way of life because it's a speedy meal to prepare. When they were growing up, my kids looked forward to Spaghetti Night—and so did their mom, because I didn't have to spend ages in the kitchen preparing dinner.

Serves 4

8 ounces ground 90% lean turkey
    or beef
½ cup finely chopped onion
1¾ cups (one 15-ounce can)
    Hunt's Tomato Sauce
¾ cup water
½ cup (one 2.5-ounce jar) sliced
    mushrooms, undrained

2 teaspoons pourable Sugar Twin
    or Sprinkle Sweet
1½ teaspoons Italian seasoning
2 cups hot cooked spaghetti,
    rinsed and drained
¼ cup (¾ ounce) grated Kraft
    fat-free Parmesan cheese

In a large skillet sprayed with olive oil–flavored cooking spray, brown meat and onion. Stir in tomato sauce, water, and undrained mushrooms. Add Sugar Twin and Italian seasoning. Mix well to combine. Lower heat and simmer for 10 minutes, stirring occasionally. For each serving, place ½ cup spaghetti on a plate, spoon a full ¾ cup meat sauce over spaghetti, and sprinkle 1 tablespoon Parmesan cheese over top.

HINT: 1½ cups broken uncooked spaghetti usually cooks to about 2 cups.

Each serving equals:
HE: 2¼ Vegetable, 1¾ Protein , 1 Bread, 1 Optional Calorie

241 Calories, 5 gm Fat, 16 gm Protein, 33 gm Carbohydrate, 782 mg Sodium, 33 mg Calcium, 5 gm Fiber

DIABETIC: 2 Vegetable, 2 Meat, 1 Starch

Sloppy Joes

■ ❋ ■

When I was a child, I used to wonder who Joe was, and if he was really so messy that people called him Sloppy Joe! (Maybe I also wondered because my name, JoAnna, is easily shortened to Jo, too!) But whoever invented this irresistibly saucy and spicy blend of ground meat and tomato sauce is definitely "neat" in my opinion. I think you'll find that this recipe is just as easy as opening a can of commercial sloppy joe sauce—and tastes deliciously homemade!   *Serves 6*

16 ounces ground 90% lean
  turkey or beef
¾ cup finely chopped onion
¾ cup finely chopped green bell
  pepper
½ cup Heinz Light Harvest
  Ketchup or any reduced-
  sodium ketchup
½ cup water

1 tablespoon white vinegar
1 tablespoon Worcestershire
  sauce
1 tablespoon yellow mustard
1 tablespoon pourable Sugar
  Twin or Sprinkle Sweet
6 reduced-calorie hamburger
  buns

In a large skillet sprayed with butter-flavored cooking spray, brown meat, onion, and green pepper. Stir in ketchup and water. Bring mixture to a boil. Add vinegar, Worcestershire sauce, mustard, and Sugar Twin. Mix well to combine. Lower heat and simmer for 6 to 8 minutes, stirring occasionally. For each sandwich, spoon about ½ cup filling between two halves of a hamburger bun.

Each serving equals:

HE: 2 Protein, 1 Bread, ½ Vegetable, ¼ Slider, 1 Optional Calorie

227 Calories, 7 gm Fat, 16 gm Protein, 25 gm Carbohydrate, 298 mg Sodium, 28 mg Calcium, 2 gm Fiber

DIABETIC: 2 Meat, 1 Starch, ½ Vegetable

Broccoli-Ham Casserole

■ ❅ ■

Okay, so former President Bush and my husband, Cliff, won't be digging in (nor will any other members of the Broccoli Haters' Club), but for the rest of us, here's a wonderfully cheesy, crusty-topped dish that deserves to be on every cook's Top Ten List! I think casseroles like this one are truly all-American classics!   *Serves 6*

1 (10¾-ounce) can Healthy
   Request Cream of Mushroom
   Soup
1 cup Kraft fat-free mayonnaise
1 egg, beaten, or equivalent in
   egg substitute
¾ cup (3 ounces) shredded Kraft
   reduced-fat Cheddar cheese
½ cup (one 2.5-ounce jar) sliced
   mushrooms, drained
1 teaspoon Italian seasoning

2 teaspoons dried onion flakes
4 cups frozen cut broccoli,
   thawed
1 full cup (6 ounces) diced
   Dubuque 97% fat-free ham or
   any extra-lean ham
¼ cup (¾ ounce) grated Kraft
   fat-free Parmesan cheese
10 Ritz Reduced Fat Crackers,
   made into crumbs

Preheat oven to 325 degrees. Spray an 8-by-12-inch baking dish with butter-flavored cooking spray. In a medium bowl, combine mushroom soup, mayonnaise, egg, Cheddar cheese, mushrooms, Italian seasoning, and onion flakes. Spread half of soup mixture into prepared baking dish. Evenly sprinkle broccoli and ham over top. Spread remaining soup mixture over broccoli and ham. In a small bowl, combine Parmesan cheese and cracker crumbs. Sprinkle mixture evenly over top. Lightly spray top with butter-flavored cooking spray. Bake for 50 to 55 minutes. Place baking dish on a wire rack and let set for 5 minutes. Divide into 6 servings.

HINT: 1. Thaw broccoli by placing in a colander and rinsing under hot water for one minute.
       2. A self-seal sandwich bag works great for crushing crackers.

Each serving equals:
HE: 1⅔ Protein, 1½ Vegetable, ⅓ Bread, ½ Slider, 14 Optional Calories
186 Calories, 6 gm Fat, 12 gm Protein, 21 gm Carbohydrate, 1085 mg Sodium, 167 mg Calcium, 2 gm Fiber
DIABETIC: 1½ Meat, 1½ Vegetable, 1 Starch/Carbohydrate

No-Fuss Scalloped Potatoes and Ham

■ ❄ ■

Since we're a nation of pioneers and immigrants, many of our best-loved food traditions came from that old saying "Necessity is the mother of invention." Well, I'm the daughter of a mother who was very inventive when it came to feeding her family. This recipe of scalloped potatoes and ham tastes luxuriously creamy and rich but contains only a modest amount of meat. Whether you're a Yankee or a Midwestern farm wife, it's smart to be thrifty—and important to eat well!

Serves 4

4½ cups (15 ounces) shredded
    loose-packed frozen
    potatoes
½ cup finely chopped onion
1 (10¾-ounce) can Healthy
    Request Cream of Mushroom
    Soup

¼ cup Land O Lakes no-fat sour
    cream
2 teaspoons dried parsley flakes
⅛ teaspoon black pepper
1½ cups (9 ounces) diced
    Dubuque 97% fat-free ham or
    any extra-lean ham

Preheat oven to 350 degrees. Spray an 8-by-8-inch baking dish with butter-flavored cooking spray. In a large bowl, combine potatoes and onion. Stir in mushroom soup, sour cream, parsley flakes, and black pepper. Add ham. Mix well to combine. Spread mixture into prepared baking dish. Cover and bake for 1 hour. Uncover and continue baking for 15 minutes. Place baking dish on a wire rack and let set for 5 minutes. Divide into 4 servings.

Each serving equals:
HE: 1½ Protein, ¾ Bread, ¼ Vegetable, ½ Slider, 16 Optional Calories
204 Calories, 4 gm Fat, 13 gm Protein, 29 gm Carbohydrate, 737 mg Sodium, 108 mg Calcium, 2 gm Fiber
DIABETIC: 1½ Meat, 1 Starch

Superb Ham Loaf

■ ❋ ■

So many inventive and enduring recipes emerged from 1950s kitchens, I figure maybe the women who'd done their part for the war effort in the previous decade had to find a new outlet for all that energy and creativity! This is one of those dishes, a thrifty blend of handy ingredients that can feed an entire family inexpensively and well.

Serves 6

3 cups (24 ounces) finely ground
    Dubuque 97% fat-free ham or
    any extra-lean ham
¾ cup (2¼ ounces) quick oats
¾ cup finely chopped onion
¼ cup reduced-sodium tomato
    juice

2 tablespoons Land O Lakes no-
    fat sour cream
1 teaspoon dried parsley flakes
⅛ teaspoon black pepper
2 (¾-ounce) slices Kraft reduced-
    fat Swiss cheese

Preheat oven to 350 degrees. Spray a 9-by-5-inch loaf pan with butter-flavored cooking spray. In a large bowl, combine ham, oats, onion, tomato juice, sour cream, parsley flakes, and black pepper. Mix well to combine. Pat mixture into prepared loaf pan. Bake for 30 minutes. Cut cheese slices in half diagonally. Evenly arrange cheese pieces over top. Continue baking for 25 to 30 minutes. Place loaf pan on a wire rack and let set for 5 minutes. Cut into 6 servings.

Each serving equals:

HE: 3 Protein, ½ Bread, ⅓ Vegetable, 7 Optional Calories

166 Calories, 6 gm Fat, 16 gm Protein, 12 gm Carbohydrate, 824 mg Sodium, 17 mg Calcium, 1 gm Fiber

DIABETIC: 3 Meat, 1 Starch/Carbohydrate

Chocolate Chip Munch Cookies

■ ❋ ■

Baking healthy cookies is a real challenge, because you know I won't settle for less than pleasing when it comes to creating yummy treats! The United States is a country of cookie lovers unmatched around the world, so I wanted this section to include something you could prepare for cookie exchanges, kids' parties, and just about anytime at all. My son-in-law, John, gave this one a perfect ten!

Serves 12 (3 each)

⅓ cup reduced-calorie margarine

¼ cup Land O Lakes no-fat sour cream

1 egg or equivalent in egg substitute

½ cup pourable Sugar Twin or Sprinkle Sweet

1 teaspoon vanilla extract

1 cup + 2 tablespoons all-purpose flour

½ teaspoon baking soda

⅓ cup (1½ ounces) mini chocolate chips

Preheat oven to 375 degrees. Spray 3 medium-sized cookie sheets with butter-flavored cooking spray. In a large bowl, combine margarine, sour cream, and egg. Stir in Sugar Twin and vanilla extract. Add flour and baking soda. Mix gently just to combine. Fold in chocolate chips. Drop batter by teaspoonfuls to form 36 cookies. Lightly flatten cookies with the bottom of a glass sprayed with butter-flavored cooking spray. Bake for 7 to 9 minutes. Don't overbake. Remove cookies from sheets and place on wire racks to cool.

Each serving equals:

HE: ⅔ Fat, ½ Bread, ¼ Slider, 12 Optional Calories

92 Calories, 4 gm Fat, 2 gm Protein, 12 gm Carbohydrate, 123 mg Sodium, 15 mg Calcium, 0 gm Fiber

DIABETIC: 1 Fat, 1 Starch/Carbohydrate

Peanut Butter Cookies

■ ❋ ■

I remember reading a biography of George Washington Carver when I was young and being amazed at all the uses he discovered for the peanut crop of his native South. As a peanut lover all my life, I can tell you that one of my favorite ways to enjoy them is in a great cookie recipe. You'll be amazed at how intense the peanut flavor is in each and every bite! *Serves 12 (3 each)*

1½ cups all-purpose flour
¾ cup pourable Sugar Twin or
   Sprinkle Sweet
1 teaspoon baking powder
¾ cup Peter Pan reduced-fat
   peanut butter

2 tablespoons Land O Lakes
   no-fat sour cream
1 egg or equivalent in egg
   substitute
¼ cup skim milk
1 teaspoon vanilla extract

Preheat oven to 350 degrees. In a large bowl, combine flour, Sugar Twin, and baking powder. In a small bowl, combine peanut butter and sour cream. Stir in egg, skim milk, and vanilla extract. Add peanut butter mixture to flour mixture. Mix well to combine. Drop by teaspoonfuls onto ungreased baking sheets to form 36 cookies. Flatten cookies with tines of a fork, crisscross style. Bake for 8 to 12 minutes. Remove cookies from sheets and place on a wire rack to cool.

Each serving equals:
HE: 1 Protein, 1 Fat, ⅔ Bread, 15 Optional Calories

149 Calories, 5 gm Fat, 9 gm Protein, 17 gm Carbohydrate, 150 mg Sodium, 42 mg Calcium, 1 gm Fiber

DIABETIC: 1 Meat, 1 Fat, 1 Starch

Chewy Walnut Brownies

■ ❋ ■

If you're looking for a bake sale winner or the perfect treat to serve your book club members, I recommend these scrumptious, nutty classics! The ingredients may seem unusual and surprising, but I'd love to see the real surprise on your face when you take your first bite. Some people like their brownies fudgy and others like them cake-y, but everyone seems to like these just fine!

Serves 8 (2 each)

¾ cup all-purpose flour
¼ cup unsweetened cocoa
½ cup pourable Sugar Twin or
    Sprinkle Sweet
¼ cup (1 ounce) chopped
    walnuts
⅓ cup Land O Lakes no-fat sour
    cream

⅓ cup unsweetened applesauce
1 egg or equivalent in egg
    substitute
¼ cup water
2 teaspoons vanilla extract

Preheat oven to 350 degrees. Spray a 9-by-9-inch cake pan with butter-flavored cooking spray. In a large bowl, combine flour, cocoa, and Sugar Twin. Stir in walnuts. In a small bowl, combine sour cream, applesauce, egg, water, and vanilla extract. Add liquid mixture to dry mixture. Mix gently just to combine. Spread batter into prepared cake pan. Bake for 20 to 24 minutes or just until the edges are firm and center is almost set. Place cake pan on a wire rack and let set for at least 10 minutes. Cut into 16 bars.

Each serving equals:
HE: ½ Bread, ¼ Protein, ¼ Fat, ¼ Slider, 8 Optional Calories

99 Calories, 3 gm Fat, 4 gm Protein, 14 gm Carbohydrate, 19 mg Sodium, 30 mg Calcium, 1 gm Fiber

DIABETIC: 1 Starch/Carbohydrate, ½ Fat

Banana Nut Bread

■ ❄ ■

I used to wonder what people thought of bananas when they saw this tropical fruit for the first time! They look like nothing else, they have all the sweetness of the sun that helps them grow, and they're at their best when they're almost too ripe to enjoy! This is a perfect recipe to have on hand when you're faced with a couple of nearly black-skinned bananas, because they're incredibly sweet at that point. Mash them well and make this tasty bread, which is even better the next day!

Serves 8 (1 thick or 2 thin)

1½ cups all-purpose flour
1 (4-serving) package JELL-O sugar-free instant banana cream pudding mix
1 teaspoon baking powder
1 teaspoon baking soda
¼ cup (1 ounce) chopped walnuts

⅔ cup (2 medium) mashed bananas
1 egg, beaten, or equivalent in egg substitute
⅓ cup Land O Lakes no-fat sour cream
⅓ cup skim milk

Preheat oven to 350 degrees. Spray a 9-by-5-inch loaf pan with butter-flavored cooking spray. In a large bowl, combine flour, dry pudding mix, baking powder, baking soda, and walnuts. In a small bowl, combine mashed bananas, egg, sour cream, and skim milk. Add liquid mixture to dry mixture. Mix gently just to combine. Spread batter into prepared loaf pan. Bake for 50 to 60 minutes or until a toothpick inserted near center comes out clean. Place loaf pan on a wire rack and let set for 5 minutes. Remove bread from pan and continue cooling on wire rack. Cut into 8 thick or 16 thin slices.

Each serving equals:

HE: 1 Bread, ½ Fruit, ¼ Protein, ¼ Fat, ¼ Slider, 6 Optional Calories

159 Calories, 3 gm Fat, 5 gm Protein, 28 gm Carbohydrate, 412 mg Sodium, 75 mg Calcium, 1 gm Fiber

DIABETIC: 1½ Starch/Carbohydrate, ½ Fruit, ½ Fat

The Ultimate Banana Split Dessert

■ ■ ■

People keep worrying that I'll run out of banana split dessert ideas, but really, how could that happen when my inspiration is so "out of this world"? I wasn't sure what to call this one until Cliff told me, "JoAnna, this just might be the ultimate!" I'll admit that stirring up something that special takes a bit more time than many of my recipes, but I bet you'll agree that this one is worth the extra effort!

Serves 8

12 (2½-inch) graham cracker squares ☆

1 (4-serving) package JELL-O sugar-free vanilla cook-and-serve pudding mix

1 (4-serving) package JELL-O sugar-free strawberry gelatin

4 cups water ☆

1 cup (1 medium) sliced banana

2 cups sliced fresh strawberries

1 (4-serving) package JELL-O sugar-free instant chocolate pudding mix

1⅓ cups Carnation Nonfat Dry Milk Powder ☆

1 (4-serving) package JELL-O sugar-free instant vanilla pudding mix

1 cup (one 8-ounce can) crushed pineapple, packed in fruit juice, undrained

1 cup Cool Whip Lite ☆

4 maraschino cherries, halved

Evenly arrange 9 graham cracker squares in a 9-by-9-inch cake pan. In a medium saucepan, combine dry cook-and-serve pudding mix, dry gelatin, and 1½ cups water. Cook over medium heat until mixture thickens and starts to boil, stirring often. Remove from heat. Gently stir in banana and strawberries. Place saucepan on a wire rack to cool. Meanwhile, in a medium bowl, combine dry instant chocolate pudding, ⅔ cup dry milk powder, and 1½ cups water. Mix well using a wire whisk. Carefully spoon pudding mixture over graham cracker "crust." Refrigerate for 5 minutes. Evenly spoon partially cooled fruit mixture over set chocolate layer. Refrigerate for 30 minutes. In another medium bowl, combine dry instant vanilla pudding mix, remaining ⅔ cup dry milk powder, undrained pineapple, and remaining 1 cup water. Mix well using a wire whisk. Blend in ½ cup Cool Whip Lite. Spread topping mixture evenly over fruit layer. Crush remaining 3 graham crackers. Evenly sprinkle cracker crumbs over topping layer. Drop remaining Cool Whip Lite by tablespoonful to form 8

mounds. Garnish each mound with a cherry half. Refrigerate for at least 1 hour. Cut into 8 servings.

HINT: A self-seal sandwich bag works great for crushing graham crackers.

Each serving equals:
HE: ¾ Fruit, ½ Skim Milk, ½ Bread, ¾ Slider, 8 Optional Calories

174 Calories, 2 gm Fat, 9 gm Protein, 30 gm Carbohydrate, 511 mg Sodium, 150 mg Calcium, 2 gm Fiber

DIABETIC: 1½ Starch/Carbohydrate, 1 Fruit, ½ Skim Milk

As American As Apple Pie

■ ■ ■

It's been a symbol of family and goodness for as long as I can remember, and there is probably no more treasured culinary symbol of who we are as a nation than the humble apple pie. It celebrates the bounty of our orchards, and it recalls a time when parents and children gathered nightly around the dinner table to give thanks for the blessings of the day. As desserts go, there are few greater "blessings" than a slice of apple pie!

Serves 8

1 Pillsbury refrigerated unbaked 9-inch piecrust
1 (4-serving) package JELL-O sugar-free vanilla cook-and-serve pudding mix
½ cup unsweetened apple juice
½ cup water
1½ teaspoons apple pie spice
3½ cups (7 small) cored, peeled, and sliced cooking apples

Let piecrust set at room temperature for 10 minutes. Meanwhile, in a medium saucepan, combine dry pudding mix, apple juice, and water. Stir in apple pie spice. Add apples. Mix well to combine. Cook over medium heat until mixture thickens and apples soften, stirring often. Remove from heat. Place saucepan on a wire rack and let set for at least 5 minutes. Cut the piecrust in half on the folded line. Gently roll each half into a ball. Wipe counter with a wet cloth and place a sheet of waxed paper over damp spot. Place one of the balls on the waxed paper. Cover with another piece of waxed paper and roll out into a 9-inch circle, with rolling pin. Carefully remove waxed paper from one side and place crust into an 8-inch pie plate. Remove other piece of waxed paper. Evenly spoon apple mixture into piecrust. Repeat process of rolling out remaining piecrust half. Place second crust over top of pie and flute edges. Make about 8 slashes with a knife to allow steam to escape. Bake at 425 degrees for 15 minutes. Reduce heat to 350 degrees and continue baking for 30 minutes. Place pie plate on a wire rack and allow to cool completely. Cut into 8 servings.

HINT: Place piece of uncooked elbow macaroni upright in center of pie to keep filling from cooking out of crust.

Each serving equals:
HE: 1 Fruit, ½ Bread, ¾ Slider
167 Calories, 7 gm Fat, 1 gm Protein, 25 gm Carbohydrate, 158 mg Sodium, 5 mg Calcium, 1 gm Fiber
DIABETIC: 1½ Starch/Carbohydrate, 1 Fruit, ½ Fat

Chocolate Cake with Chocolate Frosting

■ ❋ ■

I'm not sure if anyone's done a survey to figure out the most popular choice for birthday cakes, but I'm pretty sure the winner in each of the fifty states would be Chocolate Times Two—an all-chocolate cake like this one! The next time an occasion calls for spectacular sweetness and a dessert that is rich, rich, rich, choose chocolate, chocolate, chocolate!

Serves 8

1½ cups all-purpose flour
¾ cup pourable Sugar Twin or Sprinkle Sweet
¼ cup unsweetened cocoa
1 teaspoon baking powder
1 teaspoon baking soda
⅓ cup Kraft fat-free mayonnaise
¼ cup Land O Lakes no-fat sour cream
1 tablespoon vanilla extract ☆

2 cups water ☆
1 (8-ounce) package Philadelphia fat-free cream cheese
1 (4-serving) package JELL-O sugar-free instant chocolate pudding mix
⅔ cup Carnation Nonfat Dry Milk Powder
¾ cup Cool Whip Free

Preheat oven to 350 degrees. Spray a 9-by-9-inch cake pan with butter-flavored cooking spray. In a large bowl, combine flour, Sugar Twin, cocoa, baking powder, and baking soda. In a small bowl, combine mayonnaise, sour cream, 2 teaspoons vanilla extract, and ¾ cup water. Add liquid mixture to dry mixture. Mix gently just to combine. Spread batter into prepared cake pan. Bake for 25 to 30 minutes or until a toothpick inserted near center comes out clean. Place cake pan on a wire rack and allow to cool completely. In a large bowl, stir cream cheese with a spoon until soft. Add dry pudding mix, dry milk powder, and remaining 1¼ cups water. Mix well using a wire whisk. Blend in remaining 1 teaspoon vanilla extract and Cool Whip Free. Spread frosting mixture evenly over cooled cake. Cut into 8 servings. Refrigerate leftovers.

Each serving equals:
HE: 1 Bread, ½ Protein, ¼ Skim Milk, ½ Slider, 16 Optional Calories

161 Calories, 1 gm Fat, 6 gm Protein, 32 gm Carbohydrate, 434 mg Sodium, 134 mg Calcium, 1 gm Fiber

DIABETIC: 1½ Starch/Carbohydrate, ½ Meat

Potluck Deviled Eggs

■ ■ ■

Here's another beloved kitchen classic that appears on party and picnic tables everywhere! These are delightfully tangy and will appeal to guests young and old. You can vary the flavor by the type and spiciness of the mustard you choose, but keep in mind the varied tastes of your family and opt for the mildest among them.   *Serves 4 (2 halves)*

4 hard-boiled eggs	*1 teaspoon yellow mustard*
¼ cup Kraft fat-free mayonnaise	*Dash paprika*
2 tablespoons sweet pickle relish	

Cut eggs in half lengthwise and remove yolks. Place yolks in a medium bowl and mash well, using a fork. Add mayonnaise, pickle relish, and mustard. Mix well to combine. Refill egg-white halves by evenly spooning yolk mixture into each. Lightly sprinkle paprika over top. Cover and refrigerate for at least 30 minutes.

Each serving equals:

HE: 1 Protein (limited), 18 Optional Calories

97 Calories, 5 gm Fat, 7 gm Protein, 6 gm Carbohydrate, 245 mg Sodium, 27 mg Calcium, 0 gm Fiber

DIABETIC: 1 Meat

Hot Fudge Sundae

■ ■ ■

What dessert is more delectably American than an ice-cream sundae with the "works"? I had fun creating (and taste-testing) this sweet and luscious delight that's sure to please the kids in your house—especially the big ones! I think you'll be surprised at how easy this homemade fudge sauce is to prepare, and I hope you'll make it a fixture for all the birthdays yet to come.   *Serves 6*

1 (4-serving) package JELL-O sugar-free chocolate cook-and-serve pudding mix

⅔ cup Carnation Nonfat Dry Milk Powder

1½ cups water

¼ cup (½ ounce) miniature marshmallows

1 tablespoon reduced-calorie margarine

1 teaspoon vanilla extract

3 cups Wells' Blue Bunny sugar- and fat-free vanilla ice cream or any sugar- and fat-free ice cream

6 tablespoons Cool Whip Lite

3 maraschino cherries, halved

In a medium saucepan, combine dry pudding mix, dry milk powder, and water. Cook over medium heat until mixture thickens and starts to boil, stirring constantly. Remove from heat. Add marshmallows, margarine, and vanilla extract. Mix well to combine. For each sundae, spoon ½ cup ice cream into a sundae or dessert dish, drizzle ⅓ cup hot fudge sauce over ice cream, top with 1 tablespoon Cool Whip Lite, and garnish with a cherry half.

HINT: Also good with 1 teaspoon chopped pecans sprinkled over top.

Each serving equals:
HE: ⅓ Skim Milk, ¼ Fat, 1 Slider, 15 Optional Calories

157 Calories, 1 gm Fat, 7 gm Protein, 30 gm Carbohydrate, 204 mg Sodium, 107 mg Calcium, 0 gm Fiber

DIABETIC: 1½ Starch/Carbohydrate, ½ Fat

Grandma's Cinnamon Rolls

■ ❄ ■

When my grandmother made cinnamon rolls from scratch, I used to sit in her kitchen on a stool and watch the dough rise. It seemed to take forever, but it smelled so good, I was willing to wait. Well, with the wonderful prepared-dough products in the refrigerated case at the market, I don't have to wait any-more—and neither do you! These taste even better than the delicious aroma from the oven.

Serves 8 (2 each)

*1 (11-ounce) can Pillsbury refrig-
erated French loaf*
*½ cup pourable Sugar Twin or
Sprinkle Sweet*

1 teaspoon ground cinnamon
1 cup raisins

Preheat oven to 375 degrees. Spray two baking sheets with butter-flavored cooking spray. Carefully unroll French loaf and lightly spray top with butter-flavored cooking spray. In a small bowl, combine Sugar Twin and cinnamon. Evenly sprinkle mixture over top. Sprinkle raisins evenly over cinnamon mix-ture. Reroll French loaf, jelly-roll style. Cut into 16 slices. Evenly arrange slices on prepared baking sheets. Bake for 8 to 12 minutes or until light golden brown. Lightly spray tops with butter-flavored cooking spray. Place baking sheets on wire racks and allow rolls to cool.

Each serving equals:
HE: 1 Bread, 1 Fruit, 6 Optional Calories
157 Calories, 1 gm Fat, 4 gm Protein, 33 gm Carbohydrate, 246 mg Sodium,
14 mg Calcium, 1 gm Fiber
DIABETIC: 1 Starch, 1 Fruit

Chocolate Milkshake

■ ■ ■

When your tastebuds are clamoring for cool and creamy, luscious and thick, only one thing will do: the classic drink of teenagers everywhere, and a tradition you never outgrow! To enjoy this at its best, drink it right up, or it will start to lose its wonderful "oomph." *Serves 4 (1 cup)*

1 (4-serving) package JELL-O sugar-free instant chocolate fudge pudding mix
⅔ cup Carnation Nonfat Dry Milk Powder

2 cups water
1⅓ cups Wells' Blue Bunny sugar- and fat-free vanilla ice cream or any sugar- and fat-free ice cream

In a blender container, combine dry pudding mix, dry milk powder, and water. Cover and process on BLEND for 30 seconds. Add ice cream. Re-cover and continue processing on BLEND for 30 seconds or until mixture is smooth. Serve at once.

Each serving equals:

HE: ½ Skim Milk, ¾ Slider, 10 Optional Calories

128 Calories, 0 gm Fat, 7 gm Protein, 25 gm Carbohydrate, 435 mg Sodium, 209 mg Calcium, 0 gm Fiber

DIABETIC: 1 Starch/Carbohydrate, ½ Skim Milk

COAST-TO-COAST
COOKING HEALTHY
MENUS

■ ■ ■

NEW ENGLAND

First Snowfall of the Season Brunch

■ ■ ■

New England Clam Chowder
Baked Maple-Glazed Carrots
"Almost" Boston Baked Beans
Creamed Turkey over Savory Cornbread
Plymouth Rock Cranberry Pie

THE EASTERN SEABOARD

Chesapeake Bay Seafood Supper

■ ■ ■

Manhattan Clam Chowder
Maryland Crab Cakes
Schnitzel Beans
City Lights Carrot Salad
Lady Baltimore Cake

THE SOUTH

Kentucky Derby "Tailgate" Luncheon

■ ■ ■

Southern Buttermilk Spoon Bread
Dixie Grits Casserole
Pulled-Pork Sandwiches
Down-Home Green Beans
Raisin Bread Pudding with Rum Sauce

THE SOUTHWEST

Spicy Summer Siesta-Fest

■ ■ ■

Blended Magical Margaritas
Gringo Nachos
Rio Grande Pork Tenders
Ranch Hand Green Bean Bake
San Antonio Pecan Chocolate Cream Pie

THE WEST
Dusk over Diamond Head Luau

■ ■ ■

Lanai Sunset Punch
Pineapple-Kiwi Fruit Salad
Orange Romaine Salad
California Harvest Pizza
Waikiki Lemon Coconut Cream Pie

THE NORTHWEST
Cozy Buffet for a Rainy Day

■ ■ ■

Idaho Potato Chowder
Northwest Territory Crab au Gratin
Puget Sound Salmon Loaf
Walla Walla Creamed Onion Bake
Oregon Trail Berry Crumb Pie

THE HEARTLAND
State Fair Supper

■ ■ ■

Sweet-and-Sour Slaw
Middle America German Potato Salad
Iowa Corn Relish
Braised Pork and Cabbage
Covered Wagon Rhubarb Pie

ALL-AMERICAN CLASSICS
Comfort Food Potluck Party

■ ■ ■

Cream of Tomato Soup
Mom's Baked Macaroni and Cheese
Time-Honored Tuna-Noodle Casserole
Mom's Jelled Fruit Salad
As American As Apple Pie

MAKING HEALTHY EXCHANGES WORK FOR YOU

■ ■ ■

You're ready now to begin a wonderful journey to better health. In the preceding pages, you've discovered the remarkable variety of good food available to you when you begin eating the Healthy Exchanges way. You've stocked your pantry and learned many of my food preparation "secrets" that will point you on the way to delicious success.

But before I let you go, I'd like to share a few tips that I've learned while traveling toward healthier eating habits. It took me a long time to learn how to eat *smarter*. In fact, I'm still working on it. But I am getting better. For years, I could *inhale* a five-course meal in five minutes flat—and still make room for a second helping of dessert!

Now I follow certain signposts on the road that help me stay on the right path. I hope these ideas will help point you in the right direction as well.

1. **Eat slowly** so your brain has time to catch up with your tummy. Cut and chew each bite slowly. Try putting your fork down between bites. Stop eating as soon as you feel full. Crumple your napkin and throw it on top of your plate so you don't continue to eat when you are no longer hungry.

2. **Smaller plates** may help you feel more satisfied by your food portions *and* limit the amount you can put on the plate.

3. **Watch portion size.** If you are *truly* hungry, you can always add more food to your plate once you've finished your initial serving. But remember to count the additional food accordingly.

4. **Always eat at your dining-room or kitchen table.** You deserve better than nibbling from an open refrigerator or over the sink. Make an attractive place setting, even if you're eating alone. Feed your eyes as well as your stomach. By always eating at a table, you will become much more aware of your true food intake. For some reason, many of us conveniently "forget" the food we swallow while standing over the stove or munching in the car or on the run.

5. **Avoid doing anything else while you are eating.** If you read the paper or watch television while you eat, it's easy to consume too much food without realizing it, because you are concentrating on something else besides what you're eating. Then, when you look down at your plate and see that it's empty, you wonder where all the food went and why you still feel hungry.

Day by day, as you travel the path to good health, it will become easier to make the right choices, to eat *smarter.* But don't ever fool yourself into thinking that you'll be able to put your eating habits on cruise control and forget about them. Making a commitment to eat good healthy food and sticking to it takes some effort. But with all the good-tasting recipes in this Healthy Exchanges cookbook, just think how well you're going to eat—and enjoy it—from now on!

Healthy Lean Bon Appetit!

INDEX

ABOUT THE AUTHORS

■ ■ ■

JOANNA M. LUND is the author of the bestselling *Healthy Exchanges Cookbook, HELP: Healthy Exchanges Lifetime Plan,* and other books. She has been profiled in national and local publications including *People,* the *New York Times,* and *Forbes,* and been featured on hundreds of radio and television shows. She appears regularly on QVC. A popular speaker with weight-loss, cardiac, diabetic, and other health-support groups, she lives in DeWitt, Iowa.

BARBARA ALPERT is the author of *Child of My Heart, The Love of Friends,* and *No Friend Like a Sister,* and the co-author of many other books, including *Make a Joyful Table, Dessert Every Night!,* and *HELP: Healthy Exchanges Lifetime Plan,* with JoAnna M. Lund. A former executive editor for Bantam Books, she has published articles in *Cosmopolitan, Hemispheres, New York Runner,* and *ParentSource* magazines. She teaches book editing as an Adjunct Associate Professor at Hofstra University in New York.